Globalizing
Critical Theory

New Critical Theory
General Editors:
Patricia Huntington and Martin J. Beck Matuštík

The aim of *New Critical Theory* is to broaden the scope of critical theory beyond its two predominant strains, one generated by the research
program of Jürgen Habermas and his students, the other by postmodern cultural studies.
The series reinvigorates early critical theory—as developed by Theodor Adorno, Herbert
Marcuse, Walter Benjamin, and others—but from more decisive post-colonial and post-
patriarchal vantage points. *New Critical Theory* represents theoretical and activist concerns about class, gender, and race, seeking to learn from as well as nourish social liberation movements.

Globalizing Critical Theory

Edited by Max Pensky

ROWMAN & LITTLEFIELD PUBLISHERS, INC.
Lanham • *Boulder* • *New York* • *Toronto* • *Oxford*

ROWMAN & LITTLEFIELD PUBLISHERS, INC.

Published in the United States of America
by Rowman & Littlefield Publishers, Inc.
A wholly owned subsidiary of The Rowman & Littlefield Publishing Group, Inc.
4501 Forbes Boulevard, Suite 200, Lanham, Maryland 20706
www.rowmanlittlefield.com

PO Box 317
Oxford
OX2 9RU, UK

British Library Cataloguing in Publication Information Available

Library of Congress Cataloging-in-Publication Data

Globalizing critical theory / edited by Max Pensky.
   p. cm. — (New critical theory)
   Includes bibliographical references and index.
   ISBN 0-7425-3449-9 (hardcover : alk. paper) — ISBN 0-7425-3450-2
(pbk. : alk. paper)
   1. Critical theory. 2. Frankfurt school of sociology. 3. Globalization.
   I. Pensky, Max, 1961– II. Series.
   HM467.G58 2005
   301'.01—dc22

                                                                        2004013905

Printed in the United States of America

♾™ The paper used in this publication meets the minimum requirements of American
National Standard for Information Sciences—Permanence of Paper for Printed Library
Materials, ANSI/NISO Z39.48-1992.

Contents

Part III: Race, Memory, Forgetting

Part IV: Globalizing Visions: Science, Technology, Aesthetics

Globalizing Theory,
Theorizing Globalization: Introduction

Max Pensky

In the theory business, globalization is booming. Across a remarkable range of disciplines in contemporary American humanities and social sciences, the work dedicated to globalization over the past decade or so has generated a huge literature. However, work on globalization has for the most part further entrenched rather than unified academic distinctions. In economics, globalization has with few exceptions become a euphemism for the supremacy of neoclassical theory and the defense of free markets. In political science and quantitative sociology, the deadlock between realists and internationalists continues to assume that institutional performance is the best indicator of political stability or change. Nonquantitative or normative political theorists, on the other hand, have introduced a range of new theoretical questions, such as the globalization of public spheres and the emergence of postnational civil societies, crises of sovereignty, new theories of citizenship and cross-border commitments, or supernational political imaginaries, schemes for cosmopolitan democracy, and so forth. Within humanities departments, globalization has for the most part been understood from the particular perspective of European literary theory, Marxism, or even psychoanalysis and their often ambiguous application to political realities. In departments of English or comparative literature or area studies departments or programs, a great deal of work has appeared on the cultural aspects of globalization, such as the production of cultural hybridity or diasporic public spheres as sites of resistance against an otherwise hegemonic Americanization of global culture or Foucault-inspired theories of micropolitics arising from the increasing dedifferentiation of the global and the local under current conditions.

Theories of globalization, in other words, are multiple and discordant, reflecting not only the mutual indifference of various disciplinary projects

1

within the contemporary academy but often incommensurate theoretical axioms and methodological assumptions as well. In itself, this situation need not
be taken as a problem to be solved. Indeed, the messy pluralism of current
theories of globalization can be taken as part of a very desirable development:
the abandonment of the last remnant of an outdated ideology of absolute theoretical mastery, the idea that a single, unified theory is intrinsically preferable to a lot of disunited ones. The very notion of parsimony of explanation
has always been very difficult to square with the particular challenges of the
human sciences. In this case, we could even say that "globalization" signifies
a declaration of theoretical pluralism, just as, at the same time, it names a single object for social and political theory. Like a Kantian regulative ideal, it
names a project wherein theoretical unanimity, like the final explanation, is to
be postponed indefinitely on methodological grounds. Or to put the matter in
Derridean terms, "globalization" is such an eminently deconstructible concept because it posits the very idea of a final member in a series of things to
be explained—a wholly intelligible totality, a globe as the set of all points
equidistant from an unnameable center, a final fit between *explanandum* and
explanans—while simultaneously permanently deferring just that totality by
understanding the distinctive break of the global era in terms of hypercom-
plexity: of multiple and complex interactive flows of energy, capital, and people; shifting and unstable sites for the productions of truths and identities; and
dizzying transformations of hidebound social structures—in short, the impossibility of anything fixed, total, comprehensible, or global. Constantly
self-accelerating processes of capital and data flows cause all that is solid to
melt into air.

As we attempt to find the unifying thread in current theories of globalization,
then, we should keep this basic tension in the foreground since it is not only a
tension between explanation and its deferral or between totality and multiplicity but also a normative indeterminacy or, better, a normative antinomy.[1]

I

Theories of globalization are theories about dramatic or qualitative changes
that result from the increase in volume and complexity in the flows of capital, information, and people. This increase provokes a thickening and intensification of networks of causality, such that geographical place or the distinction between the global and the local is resignified. Moreover, in a
qualitative sense, the new complexity of global causality visibly exceeds the
capacities of political bodies—in particular, sovereign nation-states—to
maintain effective control. This results in a structural challenge to national-

state sovereignty as states struggle to guide increasingly unregulated financial and labor markets, control the movement of people across national borders, address the horrific consequences of radically uneven capital accumulation between global regions, and cope with increasingly regional or global ecological risks. The same process that emancipates markets to produce spectacular wealth also generates new modes of global poverty and immiseration that seem less remediable than ever. The same process that generates increasing instability and risk also produces thicker and deeper communicative networks and, along with them, the objective possibility of a global public sphere or even elements of a global civil society in which political will and efficacy might for the first time develop commensurate with the challenges they face. The same process that produces ever more savage inequalities and ever more laming forms of political and social exclusion also generates a "globalization from below" or even a "counterglobalization" forming new cultural hybridities, new forms of citizenship and belonging, new modes of political agency, and even new languages of political resistance. The same process that sponsors new political imaginaries and new institutional fantasies both on the super- and the subnational levels also seems to provoke reactionary reactivations, whether in the form of nineteenth-century national-state ambitions or premodern theocracies. To deploy the concept of "globalization," in short, always entails generating an antinomial or internally conflicting array, a set of mutually antagonistic valences that seem to both lack and presuppose a third or higher perspective from which they can be seen, in the Hegelian sense, as moments.[2]

This aspect of globalization (dialectics, that is) can be definitively located neither in the congeries of phenomena that a theorist might look at nor in the concept of globalization with which the theorist attempts to group otherwise dissimilar phenomena together. Rather, what Adorno called the "force field," the space between the basic concept and the phenomena it names, is the space where the dialectical aspect of globalization is most relevant for theory. Indeed, one immediate and welcome inheritance from first-generation critical theory is the idea that the analysis of social formations cannot be pursued in isolation from a social epistemology in which the practice of concept formation becomes the chief object of study. Concepts do not come from nowhere, and they certainly do not emerge intact from a pure act of observation. Concepts, as Horkheimer always stressed, are themselves complex social performances that contain within them, in microcosm, the social totality that generates them. For this reason, an imminent critique of the structure and deployment of theoretical concepts is not a propaedeutic to critical social theory but rather is social theory.[3] The concept of "globalization" is itself the product of the same set of phenomena organized by the concept itself. Conversely, from the point of view of theory, the concept is a necessary but not sufficient condition for the possibility of the phenomena organized by it.

The purpose of this volume, *Globalizing Critical Theory*, is in this sense clear: it is to ask theorists who have been influenced by the theoretical tradition of critical theory—both in its "first generation" of Horkheimer and Adorno, Benjamin, or Marcuse and its "second generation of Habermas—to work in aspects of globalization and to show how globalization theory is critical theory and, conversely, how critical theory is a theory of globalization. In doing so, I hope that it will become clear that the collection as a whole takes some important preliminary steps toward fulfilling what I myself take to be three essential challenges for this "chiasm," to use Adorno's term of choice— globalizing critical theory and critical theories of globalization. In the remainder of this introduction, I offer some preliminary thoughts on these three challenges: theoretical self-reflexivity, a transformed and invigorated form of interdisciplinarity, and the adoption of a weak foundationalism.

II

In order for any social theory "of" globalization—and here there is the same ambiguity between dative and genitive that Kant had built into his notion of a critique "of" reason—to accommodate this dialectical structure of the concept of globalization itself, the theory would have to assume this very structure as a basic methodological postulate, to incorporate it into its own production, rather than solve it as a problem or bracket it as a limit-condition. But I would argue that the incorporation of the dialectical indeterminacy of the object in a theory of globalization could succeed only by the theory also becoming self-reflexive to a degree that is rarely achieved by social theory. By "self-reflexive," I mean that theory has to include the social, political, economic, and cultural conditions and contexts for its own production within the purview of things that theory needs to explain. As the members of the Institute for Social Research were keenly aware, theory, which attempts to explain social practices, is itself a social practice and is itself dependent on specifically modern conditions. If social theory proceeds in ignorance of its own social and material context, it cannot register the dialectics of its object since it cannot register how it and its object (whether "society" or "globalization") mutually constitute one another. A self-reflective theory would have to aggressively generate accounts of its theoretical object while simultaneously, in a different register, maintaining a running account of the interplay between the constitution of its object and its own possibility. Theory and metatheory, to put the matter differently, would have to be choreographed into an ongoing and dynamic entwining in which each, from its own perspective, illuminates and deepens the work of the other.

There seems to me to be no set formula for how a social theory is to succeed in introducing self-reflexivity as a methodological postulate. At the minimum, it calls for a sort of stubborn mindfulness concerning the contingent location of general claims; this demand alone would be extraordinarily welcome in contemporary theories of globalization, many of which uncritically accept the purity of their own conditions for production without raising even the hint of a worry about the social, institutional, historical conditions for theory production. Maximally, a consistently self-reflexive social theory would become a properly dialectical theory. In fact, I would argue that "self-reflective" here can serve as a rough equivalent for "critical": a critical theory of globalization is a theory that has become highly self-reflective concerning the relation between the possibility of theoretical production and the object of theoretical explanation.

Such self-reflexivity, of course, can often appear as a prim and tiresome exercise, a sort of interminable and ultimately disingenuous disavowal. And yet differently pictured—and at their best the first-generation critical theorists did just this—theoretical self-reflexivity is to be understood not as a hygienic supplement to the real work of theory but rather as dialectics itself: dialectics not as a metaphysical claim or as a justification for historical narrative but rather as a methodological commitment commensurate to the shifting ground of its own possibility and responsibility. Adorno often searched for ways of expressing this conception of dialectics as a methodological rather than a metaphysical commitment. He mentions, for example, dialectics as a kind of stringency or obstinacy in thinking, the principle that a theorist has to *keep thought going*, according to which a theorist would continue to interrogate her own enabling conditions and limits and would therefore confront pitfalls of self-referentiality, circularity, or infinite regress without assuming in advance what the outcome of that confrontation will be. In this sense, a dialectical theory is simply one that incorporates a durable methodological commitment never to take the relation between its own activity and its object as fixed or unproblematic. It harbors no firm commitments to any matters of fact regarding what theories should do and how they should look. It is unwilling to accept prepackaged notions concerning the relative value of empirical data while nevertheless insisting on a constitutive (if prickly) relationship with empirical research. It is prepared to shift back and forth nimbly between various rhetorical strategies.[4]

In addition to a mode of self-reflexivity, a new kind of critical globalization theory would require a new form of interdisciplinarity. Putting it this way is misleading, though, since the form of interdisciplinarity I have in mind is actually quite a bit older than the one I think it should replace. Specifically in humanities departments, the value of interdisciplinarity in the contemporary American academy has always been something of a mirage. For all the lip service paid to the ideal of interdisciplinarity in the form of grant proposals and funding guidelines, curricular revisions, curriculum vitae and cover letters, book reviews, promotion protocols, and the like, it remains the case that interdisciplinarity is rarely if ever defined in more than the most vague and noncommittal language. In humanities departments such as English or area studies, it is often a euphemistic formulation for the practice of cultural studies in which scholars with preparations in literary theory follow their mentors in the analysis of cultural formations as texts. But interdisciplinarity only very rarely entails the adoption of axiomatic assumptions and methodologies foreign to one's own discipline: for example, while English PhDs may find themselves writing about global human rights regimes, they almost never do so by learning (or even becoming aware of) quantitative or policy analysis. Finally, contemporary academic notions of interdisciplinarity typically—and oddly, to my mind—assume that the single individual researcher is the appropriate unit of analysis; in other words, according to the interdisciplinary ideal, each one of us is to become a sort of interdisciplinary "institution in a single case," to paraphrase Gehlen, in the interest of pursuing our own individual research project for which we will receive undivided credit.

Nothing could be farther from this than the vision of interdisciplinarity that the early Institute for Social Research had in mind, in which each member of a research team represented a different but not incommensurable set of disciplinary postulates and methods, guided by the idea that large and inherently complex social phenomena would have to be investigated through and beyond current disciplinary frontiers. The set of disciplines represented in a given research project, that is, would be determined by the project itself and not by institutional parameters for academic success. No insurmountable disagreement concerning axioms or methods should be predicted in advance; in fact, it is just those arguments over supposed incommensurables that desperately needs to take place if theories are to be valuable.[5]

This seventy-year-old dream of interdisciplinary teams has, of course, not triumphed as a model for humanities and social science faculties in the twentieth-century academy, nor did it prove especially viable for the Institute for Social Research itself: Horkheimer himself proved to be a master of the concealed blade in academic battles; his researchers were often as not paralyzed by bitter disagreements over every imaginable theoretical and political issue, and, arguably, the Institute's members never really mastered the methodological sophistication regarding the generation and analysis of empirical data that Horkheimer claimed they needed. Nevertheless, Horkheimer's quasi-academic research institute remains, in my view, a far more plausible institutional site for globalization theory production than the work of isolated polymaths laboring under their own disciplinary stars. Moreover, adopting a variant of Horkheimer's version of institutional rather than individualistic interdisciplinarity allows us to raise one of the many questions implicit in my plea for theoretical self-reflexivity: what sort of institutional arrangements and competencies would a critical theory of globalization require? Arjun Appadurai, for example, observes the irony of theories of cultural globalization arising from area studies programs whose very justification is severely challenged by globalization itself. Appadurai condemns what he calls the "double apartheid" in contemporary globalization theories: within the American academy, humanities departments convert "globalization" into a mere trope for processing familiar concerns about postmodernity, subjectivity, agency, representation, and the like, problems that are deeply parochial outside the academy, where debates on globalization are either economic and hence dominated by neoclassical economics or cultural and preoccupied with the possibility of cultural survival. In a second apartheid, the poor remain entirely excluded from participation in both political and theoretical discourse both within and outside the academy. Appadurai calls for a fundamental rethinking of the institutional and social bases for theory production—just the sort of self-reflexivity I had in mind—via a new interdisciplinarity not just between academic disciplines within the academy but also inside and outside the academy, in shifting geographical locations, in the service of a "grassroots" theory production in which the uneven capital accumulation that is an enabling condition for theory production within the First World is consciously contested through efforts at a broader and less parochial conception of what theory is in the first place, what its limit-conditions and rewards are, who is authorized to produce it, how it is and is not tied to particular local or national imaginaries, and so on. Durable interdisciplinarity requires not just institutional innovation, then, but also that globalization theory rethink its own parochialism and therefore globalize itself by dispersing itself far more radically through rather than over those persons covered under its concept.[6]

The third and probably most contentious challenge for a critical theory of globalization is the need to clarify socially embedded forms of rationality as a normative ground of criticism, which I will defend as a form of weak foundationalism.

Thinking back to their signature essays from the 1930s, Horkheimer and Adorno analyzed the dominant models of philosophical theory of their time—logical positivism and Heideggerian fundamental ontology—as mutually opposed and therefore intimately linked expressions of the imperatives of industrial capital, that is, as ideological performances. Positivism's insistence on the availability of preinterpretive or presocial facts masked the socioeconomic prerequisites for the explanation of a socially constructed and administered world; on the other hand, Heidegger's fundamental ontology degenerated into the hollow invocation of authority as a formal principle of thinking. Both relinquished the possibility of seeing the social as both a product and a cause of ongoing human practices and choices; both abandoned the ambition of theorizing the social from a normative point of view, grounded in a conception of reason tied to a conception of human flourishing.

With a great deal of caution, I would suggest that we see some parallels between what Horkheimer and Adorno diagnosed as the loss of the normativity of reason in the dominant traditions of positivism and Heidegger and what we see today as the two dominant theoretical strains in formulating theories of globalization. On the one side, neoclassical economic theory can defend market deregulation as the cure-all to social ills only insofar as it attributes a sort of superhuman rational agency to free markets and their genius. This conception of rational agency is that of the rational agent as utility maximizer familiar from microeconomics. The normative evacuation of this conception of rational choice is of course taken as a precondition for a value neutrality that will be applicable universally across each and every social and cultural context. Yet Weber's familiar analysis of the costs of insubstantial or purely formal conceptions of rationality, in which the choice of ends cannot be evaluated according to reasons, seems as apt as ever.

On the other side, theories focusing on the "other side" of globalization—for example, the production of new or hybrid identities, diasporic public spheres, and new modes of political or cultural resistance—are often derived from Foucauldian social philosophy, from British Marxist cultural studies, from Derridean deconstruction, or other modes of contemporary literary analysis, many of them grandchildren of Heideggerian philosophy itself. It is a shopworn but nevertheless still relevant worry that this range of theories, unlike rational choice versions of economic theory, deals with very potent normative ambitions: they are all essentially unmasking theories and are critical insofar as they zero in on the gap or disjuncture between the public face of a particular social formation or practice and its actual function. These theories, however, are all cousins, related by the common challenge of explaining, in terms that their own vocabularies allow, the conceptions of subjective agency and positive freedom from delusion and oppression, in whose service social practices need to be unmasked in the first place. Horkheimer and Adorno, as is well known, encountered the same problem, although for rather different reasons and with a quite different resolution. They attempted to indicate socially embodied reason as a necessary condition for emancipation from oppression but were also convinced of the impossibility of doing this by traditional theoretical means in the context of a society where such reason has become fugitive and is available only in traces and as negative spaces. They responded to this challenge not by abandoning the idea of a foundational account of social rationality but rather by shifting rhetorical strategies and, increasingly, in radical methodological experimentation. As often happens, the radicalism acquired a life of its own, and by the 1960s, works such as Adorno's *Negative Dialectics* or *Aesthetic Theory* had become quite distant in both tone and intent from the empirically informed work of the Institute for Social Research as well as Adorno's equally important popular political writings from the postwar years. At the time of his death, Adorno still could not close the antinomy he had opened between theory and nontheory. But the view that he abandoned the notion of a foundational commitment to social rationality itself is simply not true. It is true, on the other hand, that he failed to make this very antinomy properly dialectical, that he allowed the normative poles of his work to freeze so that the negative polarity remained theoretical, while the positive (if I can put it this way) was exiled to his interventions in the nascent political culture of postwar Germany.

My sense is that theorists of globalization who inherit the range of unmasking traditions I discussed previously are faced with a similar dilemma. Their own theoretical legacies do not endow them with the cognitive resources necessary to address the problem of foundationalism, that is, the problem of how to nominate a conception of socially embodied reason as the normative orientation for critical interventions. For this reason, they misconstrue their options as a stark choice between strong foundationalism and no foundationalism at all. On the contrary, it seems that globalization theorists who wish to emancipate their theories from parochialism, as Appadurai urges, but who also want to present a normative conception of globalization and its resistances are all compelled to choose from a spectrum of weak foundationalisms: claims to rationality that are strong enough to make normative claims plausible but weak enough to pass the test of what Habermas calls postmetaphysical thinking: that is, conceptions of reason entailing formal and procedural, "thin" accounts of intersubjective agreement. On this I agree with Habermas—and Rawls—that the weakest possible rational foundationalism is also the best and that such a weak version will consist of a set of justificatory performances rather than a precise taxonomy of moral truths.

At the same time, I would also like to contend that a theory of globalization cannot be content with just a thin account of social reason. Such an account, on its own, is not only vulnerable to too many suspicions regarding an ethnocentric fallacy. In addition, it seems clear that a thin account of reason, while desirable in many ways, still would never be able to provide a globalization theorist with the semantic resources necessary to make effective use of the category of reason itself. In other words, the very variety of socially embodied rational practices across a spectrum of sites and through a multiplicity of conditions requires a phenomenological language in which rational practices can be called the same and nonrational practices can be called not the same. Along with a thin account of reason as a set of justificatory discursive practices, then, philosophical anthropology or theories of embodiment would have to be involved in a normative foundation for a critical theory of globalization. It is not clear to me how such theories on their own could generate enough normative momentum to meet the need of a social theory offering a normative account of the dynamics of globalization. Nor is it clear how foundational but nonrational accounts of agency, such as a philosophical anthropology, would satisfy the condition of theoretical self-reflexivity, which would require that the social theorist have access to the same rationality, from the observer perspective, that she would have in the participant perspective of a social actor. This makes it tempting to suppose that the best form of weak foundationalism would be one that somehow combined a thin conception of rationality and a substantive philosophical anthropology regarding how humans respond to sudden and epochal cultural transformations, how they seek to reconstitute their cultures as meaningful and whole, and how they accommodate difference and newness in the form of cultural hybridization. The critical globalization theorist should ask how discursive practices of justification, across cultural differences, come into relation with anthropological needs: the need to escape suffering and fear, the need for social solidarity and inclusion, and the need to flourish, however understood. And this synthesis of reason and body means that the globalization theorist will attempt to register and analyze how different discursive practices articulate and defend these needs as responses to globalization processes—how people, very differently situated, extend justified claims that their needs need to count.

III

Horkheimer and Adorno were Eurocentrists. While taking Marx seriously on the globalizing effects of capital flows, they never seemed to grasp the significance of Marx's argument that the dynamics of capital formation originates from the European periphery and then promptly renders the very distinction between center and periphery indeterminable. They remained profoundly incurious about the political and cultural significance of what is arguably the most significant of capital's border-blurring effects: its capacity to undo previously fixed boundaries between West and its Other or between traditional and modern cultures and epistemologies. They devoted virtually no attention to the problems that dominate the current research agenda for contemporary cultural studies: the social conditions for the construction of identities and the forma-tion of polities and the sense in which those conditions can come under the will of those affected by them. The Frankfurt School cannot be accused of a run-of-the-mill Eurocentrism. It was highly deliberate and quite reflective in its way. Attempting to explain a Western phenomenon constituting the precondi-tions for globalization—that is, the advent of modernity—the critical theorists nevertheless resisted the logic of their own subject matter in the mistaken be-lief that an adequate theory of capital expansion had to remain tied to the small set of cognitive commitments underlying the European experience of Enlight-enment. But in doing so, by placing that European historical experience as the unquestioned center of their own self-understanding, they accepted at face value and hence inadvertently reproduced the very distinction that they should have contested most strongly: that between center and periphery in the context of globalization. This is a legacy that even Habermas, for all his energetic dis-avowals of the legacy of first-generation critical theory, has not yet adequately resolved. In effect, critical theory transformed itself into a form of area stud-ies that had its own locality and its own parochial interests backed up by pu-tative claims about the dynamics of capitalization. And it is no accident that critical theory remains, to this day, linked both cognitively and institutionally to area studies within the academy, even as this linkage is contested from within. From Marx and Weber—in fact from Hegel—critical theory inherited the paradoxical legacy of a parochial theory of the West that defended its own parochialism with global claims about the agency of its object.

I think we can recover the Frankfurt School's synthesis of reason and body—that is, its vision of a subversive collective imagination—without fol-lowing its Eurocentric missteps. As Appadurai has suggested in his 1996 work *Modernity at Large*, we ought to take seriously the claim that global-ization is, among many other things, also the setting in motion of a kaleido-scopic play of new forms of collective imagination whose mental borders have become as porous as their physical frontiers. Appadurai, a cultural an-thropologist, wants to identify the emergence of new modes of collective imagination as a set of new social facts. For him, the chief cultural relevance of globalization is the new imaginative forces set loose by the linked phe-nomena of migration and media and typified by the hybridity produced in di-asporic cultures. No fan of critical theory, Appadurai rejects both the Frank-furt School's Weberian reading of instrumental rationality and its elitist diagnosis of popular culture as mass culture. Rather than seeing imagination relentlessly purged from daily life by the effects of instrumental reason, Ap-padurai wants to mark the different ways that imagination in fact reenters daily life through transformations of human migration and mass media, how diasporic public spheres embody collective imaginations in unpredictable and unstable ways, and how these imagined alternatives, unlike simple fantasy, provide the world-disclosing semantic resources for new social projects, how they "move the glacial force of the *habitus* into the quickened beat of improvisation for large groups of people."[7]

Let me conclude with the suggestion that a sort of critical imagination that we can tease out of Appadurai's work, mutatis mutandis, might initially serve as an approximation of the version of weak foundationalism that I had wished for earlier. In this sense, critical globalization theory would bring to its object a normative commitment to investigating just those discursively structured justificatory practices in which collectives ask, from a variety of different cultural locations, to have a say in the way that globalization will affect their own interests; in which they reinterpret and resignify their own cultural commitments under the enhanced causality of globalization; in which they think, feel, and dream beyond the cognitive box of national-state citizenship and durable national belonging; in which they engage in institutional imaginings of alternative polities and alternative ways of understanding how democracies work; and in which they articulate demands for justice, or for plenty, or for release from suffering, or for recognition and acknowledgment through discourses that will be discordant and unnerving. Critical globalization theory would need to learn to travel, certainly, to rediscover the unquenchable curiosity in the inexhaustible symbolic creativity of human collectivities, a curiosity that contemporary political theory often seems to lack. It would, for this same reason, also have to remember the kind of tough-minded utopianism that the early Frankfurt School had first insisted on.[8]

IV

Since the chapters in *Globalizing Critical Theory* speak quite well for themselves, I will refrain from offering digests of their contents here, as is often the custom in anthologies. But a word on organization is in order: in issuing invitations to the authors, I did not give specific instructions of any kind. The contributions, nevertheless, aggregated nicely into the divisions reflected in the table of contents. The first section reproduces two short interventions by dating from the first half of 2003 in the context of the American invasion of Iraq. In the first of these chapters, Jürgen Habermas condemns the emergent imperial traits of an America that appears bent on the adoption of a new kind of hegemonic status. In the second chapter, Habermas and longtime intellectual adversary Jacques Derrida join forces to plead for a new, more assertive European foreign policy as a definitive response to America's global unilateralism. While Derrida merely cosigned this manifesto (illness prevented him from coauthoring it with Habermas as they had originally planned), the joint declaration, originally published in German and French national newspapers, is a powerful intervention in an emergent European public sphere. It argues, controversially, that a "core Europe"—principally France and Germany— must take the lead in pressing for a unified European foreign policy and must do this by appealing to a European political collective identity grounded in the European alternative to a distinctively American version of political modernity.[9]

The second section focuses on the conditions for articulation of this kind of political intervention: the changing nature and structure of a public sphere—or spectrum of public spheres—increasingly emancipated from their institutional and existential rootedness in national cultures. The prospect of a global public sphere has yet to be realized, for better and worse. But the transformation of the public sphere in the last decades of the twentieth century through revolutions in information technology and the accelerated flow of information and images is undeniable. Nancy Fraser, James Bohman, María Pía Lara, and Peter Hohendahl take up various aspects of the promises and risks of a nascent postnational political public sphere.

The third section contains three chapters dealing with the transformation of the past—or the transformation of modes of appropriation, dissemination, and critical examination of it. Clay Steinman demonstrates that the work of the Institute for Social Research from the 1930s still bears crucial importance for the work of critical race theory in the present; Thomas McCarthy argues for a reappropriation, under new conditions, of Adorno's arguments for "coming to terms with the past" in the context of the American memory of slavery. Andreas Huyssen, in sharp contrast to McCarthy, wants to recover from the tradition of critical theory a politically vital power of release from forms of memory, that is, a mode of critical forgetting.

The final section includes Eduardo Mendieta's extended reflection on the bases in critical theory for a new theory of globalized science and technology as well as three works on globalization and aesthetics: following Mendieta's lead, F. Scott Scribner presents a Benjamin-inspired account of new forces of a global imaginary within the structures of media technology. Carsten Strathausen reflects on the contemporary relevance of Adorno's *Aesthetic Theory* both within and beyond the context of contemporary art, and Silvia L. López extends this reflection to conditions for the appropriation of Adorno's aesthetics in Latin America.

The original inspiration for putting together this collection of chapters was a D.A.A.D. summer seminar, "Critical Theory Revisited," organized and directed by Peter Uwe Hohendahl at Cornell University in the summer of 2001. I was happy to accept Professor Hohendahl's invitation to invite members of that seminar, together with several other writers, to contribute chapters to the present volume. I would like to offer special thanks to Professor Hohendahl for his invitation and enormously generous and helpful role in guiding this project to completion. In addition, thanks to series editors Martin Beck Matustik and Patricia Huntington for including this collection in their New Critical Theory series at Rowman & Littlefield.

Chapter 8 originally appeared as "*Vergangenheitsbewältigung* in the United States: On the Politics of the Memory of Slavery," *Political Theory* 30, no. 5 (2000): 623–48. Copyright by Thomas McCarthy. Reprinted by permission of Sage Publications Inc.

NOTES

1. Cf. Fredric Jameson and Masao Miyoshi's conception of globalization as "a communicational concept which alternately masks and transmits cultural or economic meanings"; it "has secretly been transformed into a vision of the world market and its newfound interdependence." Fredric Jameson and Masao Miyoshi, "Introduction," in *The Cultures of Globalization*, ed. Fredric Jameson and Masao Miyoshi (Durham, N.C.: Duke University Press, 1998), 4.

2. "New research on globalization often uncritically assimilates the topic into ongoing projects. No inquiry is made as to whether existing methods, aims and assumptions need to be reconfigured accordingly. The result is a proliferation of not only highly differentiated discourses of globalization, but also a range of definitions of globalization itself." Jeffrey R. DiLeo, "Whose Theory, Which Globalization? Notes on the Double Question of Theorizing Globalism and Globalizing Theory," *Symploke* 9 (2001): 1–2.

3. See Max Horkheimer, "Notes on Institute Activities," in *Critical Theory and Society: A Reader*, ed. Stephen Eric Bronner and Douglas MacKay Kellner (New York: Routledge, 1989), 264.

4. I think this idea corresponds, roughly, with Douglas Kellner's sweeping description of a critical theory of globalization: "a critical theory of globalization attempts to specify the interconnections and interdependencies between different levels such as the economic, political, cultural and psychological, as well as between different flows of products, ideas and information, people and technology. Critical theory describes the mediations between different phenomena, the systemic structure which organizes phenomena and processes into a social system, and the relative autonomy of the parts, such that there are both connections and disjunctions between, say, the economy and culture. Concerned to relate theory to practice, critical theory also attempts to delineate the positive potentials for greater freedom and democratization, as well as the dangers of greater domination, oppression, and destruction. Grounded in historical vision, critical theory stresses the continuities and discontinuities between past, present, and future, and the possibility of constructive political action and individual and group practice, grounded in positive potentials in the current constellation

of forces and possibilities." Douglas Kellner, "Globalization and the Postmodern Turn," at http://www.gseis.ucla.edu/courses/ed253a/dk/GLOBPM.htm.

5. In Horkheimer's words, "Today . . . all depends on organizing research around current philosophical problematics, which, in turn, philosophers, sociologists, political economists, historians and psychologists engage by joining enduring research groups in order to do together what in other areas one is able to do alone in the laboratory and what all true scientists have always done: namely, to pursue their philosophical questions directed at the big picture with the finest scientific methods, to transform and to make more precise these questions as the work progresses, to find new methods, and yet never lose sight of the whole. In this way, no positive or negative answers to philosophical questions can be given. Instead, the philosophical questions themselves are dialectically integrated into the empirical scientific process; that is to say, their answers are to be found in the progress of substantive knowledge that also affects their form. This approach to the science of society cannot be mastered by one person alone: given the vast subject matter as well as the variety of indispensable scientific methods whose assistance is called for." Bronner and Kellner, *Critical Theory and Society*, 265.

6. Arjun Appadurai, "Grassroots Globalization and the Research Imagination," in *Globalization*, ed. Arjun Appadurai, 1–21 (Durham, N.C.: Duke University Press, 2001).

7. Arjun Appadurai, *Modernity at Large: Cultural Dimensions of Globalization* (Minneapolis: University of Minnesota Press, 1996), 6.

8. It seems appropriate to let Herbert Marcuse have the last word on this: "At the given stage of development, the constructive character of critical theory emerges anew. From the beginning, it did more than simply register and systematize facts. Its impulse came from the force with which it spoke against the facts and confronted a bad facticity with its better potentialities. Like philosophy, it opposes making reality into a criterion in the manner of complacent positivism [or now, neoliberalism]. But unlike philosophy, it always derives its goals only from present tendencies of the social process. Therefore, it has no fear of the utopia that the new order is denounced as being. When truth cannot be realized within the established social order, it always appears to the latter as mere utopia. This transcendence speaks not against, but for its truth. The utopian element was long the only progressive element in philosophy, as in the construction of the best state and the highest pleasure, of perfect happiness and perpetual peace. The obstinacy that comes from adhering to truth against all appearances has given way in contemporary philosophy to whimsy and uninhibited opportunism. Critical theory preserves obstinacy as a genuine quality of philosophical thought." Herbert Marcuse, "Philosophy and Critical Theory," in Bronner and Kellner, *Critical Theory and Society*, 58.

9. This manifesto by Habermas and Derrida, together with other simultaneous essays (which Habermas had coordinated) by such leading European intellectuals as Umberto Eco and Gianni Vattimo, provoked an intense response in the European press when published in May 2003. These essays, and representative samples of the critical response to them, have been collected in Daniel Levy, Max Pensky, and John Torpey, eds., *Old Europe, New Europe, Core Europe: Transatlantic Relations after the Iraq War* (London: Verso, 2005).

I

GLOBALIZATION AND HEGEMONY: TWO INTERVENTIONS

1

Interpreting the Fall of a Monument

Jürgen Habermas

On April 9, the entire world watched as American troops threw a noose round the neck of the dictator and, surrounded by jubilant throngs of Iraqis, pulled him off his pedestal. The apparently unshakeable monument tottered and then finally fell. But before it crashed satisfyingly to the ground, there was a momentary pause before the force of gravity could overcome the statue's grotesquely unnatural, horizontal posture. Bobbing gently up and down, the massive figure clung, for one last moment, to its horror.

Just as an optical illusion, looked at long enough, will "flip" into a new form, so the public perception of the war in Iraq seemed to perform an about-face at this one scene. The morally obscene—the "shock and awe" inflicted on a helpless and mercilessly bombed population—morphed into the image of joyful citizens freed from terror and oppression in the Shiite district of Baghdad. Both images contain an element of truth, even as they evoke contradictory moral feelings and attitudes. Must ambivalent feelings lead to contradictory judgments?

The matter is simple enough at first glance. A war in violation of international law remains illegal, even if it leads to normatively desirable outcomes. But is this the whole story? Bad consequences can discredit good intentions. Can't good consequences generate their own justifying force after the fact? The mass graves, the underground dungeons, and the testimony of the tortured all leave no doubt about the criminal nature of the regime. The liberation of a brutalized population from a barbaric regime is a great good; among political goods it is the greatest of all. In this regard, the Iraqis themselves, whether they are currently celebrating, looting, demonstrating against their occupiers, or simply apathetic, contribute to the judgment on the moral nature of the war. But for us in Germany, two reactions stand out in the political public sphere.

On one side, pragmatic minds affirm the normative force of the factual. They rely on the powers of practical judgment and a healthy sense of the political limits of morality, which let them appreciate the consequences of victory. In their eyes, drawn-out arguments over the justification for war are simply fruitless. The war is now a historical fact. Others simply capitulate to the force of the factual, whether from conviction or opportunism. They brush aside what they now see as the dogmatism of international law, reasoning that just this dogmatism, held captive by a sort of postheroic squeamishness over the risks and costs of military force, has become blind to the true value of political freedom.

Both of these responses are inadequate. Both succumb to an emotional response to the supposed abstractions of a "bloodless moralism" without having grasped just what the neoconservatives in Washington have actually offered up as their alternative to the domestication of state power through international law. Their alternative is neither political realism nor the pathos of freedom. Instead, the neoconservatives make a revolutionary claim: if the regime of international law fails, then the hegemonic imposition of a global liberal order is justified, even by means that are hostile to international law.

Wolfowitz is not Kissinger. He is a revolutionary, not a cynical technician of political power. To be sure, the American superpower reserves the right to take unilateral action, preemptive if necessary, and to employ all available military means to secure its hegemonic status against all possible rivals. But global power is not an end in itself for the new ideologues. What distinguishes the neoconservatives from the "realist" school of international relations is the vision of an American global political order that has definitively broken with the reformist program of UN human rights policies. While not betraying liberal goals, this vision is shattering the civil limits that the UN Charter—with good reason—had placed on their realization.

At present, the United Nations is certainly not yet in any position to compel a noncompliant member state to guarantee democracy and the rule of law to its own citizens. And the highly selective enforcement of the human rights policy of the United Nations is itself the product of political realities: equipped with veto power, Russia need not fear any armed intervention in Chechnya. Saddam Hussein's use of nerve gas against his own Kurdish population is only one of many chapters in the disgraceful chronicle of failures of a world organization that has averted its gaze even from genocide. In the aftermath of World War II, the core mission of the United Nations—enforcing the prohibition against wars of aggression—eliminated the *jus ad bellum* and placed the sovereignty of individual states under new limits, thus taking a first decisive step on the path toward a cosmopolitan legal order. That core mission is now more crucial than ever before.

For half a century, the United States could count as the pacemaker for progress on this cosmopolitan path. With the war in Iraq, it has not only abandoned this role; it has also given up its role as guarantor of international rights. And its violation of international law sets a disastrous precedent for the superpowers of the future. Let us have no illusions: the normative authority of the United States of America lies in ruins. Neither of the two conditions for a legally permissible use of military force were fulfilled: the war was neither a case of self-defense against an actual attack or the immediate threat of one, nor was it authorized by a decision of the Security Council according to Chapter VII of the UN Charter. Neither Resolution 1441 nor any of the seventeen previous (and "spent") resolutions on Iraq can count as a sufficient authorization. The "coalition of the willing" confirmed this failure performatively as it initially sought a "second" resolution but in the end refused to bring the motion to a vote because it could not even count on the "moral" majority of the Security Council not to veto. The whole procedure turned to farce as the president of the United States repeatedly declared his intention of acting without the mandate of the United Nations if necessary. From the very beginning, the Bush doctrine made it impossible to understand the military deployment in the Gulf region as a mere threat, for this would presuppose that somehow the threatened sanctions could have been averted.

Nor does a comparison with the intervention in Kosovo offer an excuse. Of course, in the case of Kosovo too, there was no authorization by the Security Council. But three circumstances of the intervention there offered legitimation after the fact: First, the intervention aimed at the prevention of ethnic cleansing, which was known at the time of the intervention to be taking place. Second, it was tasked with fulfilling the provision of international law for emergency aid, addressed to all nations. And finally, we can refer to the undisputed democratic and rule-of-law character of all the members of the acting military coalition. Today, normative dissent has divided the West itself.

Already at that time, in April 1999, a remarkable difference had become visible between the continental European and the Anglo-American powers over strategies for justifying military action. The Europeans had drawn the lesson from the disaster at Srebrenica: they understood armed intervention as a way of closing the gap between efficiency and legitimacy that had been opened by earlier peacekeeping operations and thus saw it as a means for making progress toward fully institutionalized civil rights. England and America, conversely, satisfied themselves with the normative goal of promulgating their own liberal order internationally, through violence if necessary. At the time of the intervention in Kosovo, I had attributed this difference to contrasting traditions of legal thought—Kant's cosmopolitanism on the one side and John Stuart Mill's liberal nationalism on the other. But in light of the hegemonic unilateralism that the leading thinkers of the Bush doctrine have pursued since 1991 (see the documentation by Stefan Frölich in the FAZ from April 10th, 2003), one suspects in hindsight that the American delegation had already led the negotiations at Rambouillet from just this peculiar viewpoint. Be that as it may, George W. Bush's decision to consult the Security Council certainly didn't arise from any wish for legitimation through international law, which had long since been regarded, at least internally, as superfluous. Rather, this rear-guard action was desired only insofar as it broadened the basis for a "coalition of the willing" and soothed a worried population.

All this notwithstanding, we should not interpret the neoconservative doctrine as the expression of a normative cynicism. Geostrategic objectives such as securing spheres of influence or access to essential resources, which the doctrine must also meet, may well invite analysis in terms of a critique of ideology. But such conventional explanations trivialize what, until eighteen months ago, was still an unimaginable break with norms that the United States had been committed to. We would do well, in other words, not to guess at motives but to take the doctrine at its word. For otherwise we fail to recognize the truly revolutionary character of a political reorientation, a transformation that finds its sources in the historical experiences of the previous century.

Hobsbawm rightly named the twentieth century the "American century." Neoconservatives can see themselves as "victors" and can take undisputed successes—the reordering of Europe and the Pacific after the surrender of Germany and Japan as well as the reformulation of eastern and central Europe after the collapse of the Soviet Union—as the model for a new world order, all carried out under the leadership of the United States. From the liberal perspective of a *post-histoire*, à la Fukuyama, this model has the advantage of making laborious and awkward discussions of normative goals pointless: what could possibly be better for people than the worldwide spread of liberal states and the globalization of free markets? Moreover, the road there is clearly marked: Germany, Japan, and Russia were forced to their knees by war and the arms race. In today's era of asymmetric warfare, military might is now more attractive than ever since the victor is determined a priori and can purchase victory with relatively few victims. Wars that make the world better need no further justification. From this point of view, at the minor cost of some collateral damage, they remove undisputed evils that would survive under the aegis of a powerless community of nations. Saddam pulled from his pedestal is indeed a sufficient argument for justification.

This doctrine was developed long before the terror attack on the twin towers. The cleverly manipulated mass psychology of the all-too-understandable shock of September 11 certainly helped create the initial climate in which the new doctrine could find widespread support—now in a rather different, more potent version, intensified by the addition of a "war against terrorism." This intensification of the Bush doctrine depends on defining an essentially new phenomenon in the terms of conventional warfare. In the case of the Taliban regime, there was a causal connection between an elusive terrorism and a "rogue state"—an enemy that could be attacked and seized. This provided a model for understanding interstate warfare as a weapon against an insidious threat emerging from highly diffuse and globalized networks.

As opposed to the doctrine's original version, this connection between hegemonic unilateralism and doing battle against a creeping threat introduces the argument for self-defense. But this also imposes new burdens of proof. The American government had to try to convince a global public sphere of contacts between Saddam Hussein and al Qaeda. At least at home, the disinformation campaign was so successful that according to the most recent polls, 60 percent of Americans welcomed the defeat of Saddam as "payback" for the terror attacks of September 11. Apart from the difficulty of the lack of evidence, the Bush doctrine doesn't offer a plausible explanation for even the preventive use of military force. The violence of the new kind of global terrorism—"war in peacetime"—escapes the categories of state warfare. It cannot justify the necessity of revising and loosening the strict clause that regulates states' self-defense in international law and by no means in favor of permitting an anticipated military self-defense.

In the face of enemies who are globally networked, decentralized, and invisible, the only effective kinds of prevention will be on other operative levels. Neither bombs nor rockets, neither fighter jets nor tanks, will be of any help. What will help is the international networking of flows of information among intelligence services and prosecutorial authorities, the control of flows of money, and the rooting out of logistical supplies. The corresponding "security programs" in pursuit of these goals are relevant for civil rights within a state, not international law. Other dangers that arise from failures of negligence in nonproliferation policies (concerning nuclear, chemical, and biological weapons) are at any rate better handled through stubborn negotiation and inspection than with wars of disarmament, as the subdued reaction to North Korea illustrates.

The addition of a war on terrorism to the original doctrine therefore offers no new legitimacy for the pursuit of a hegemonic world order. Saddam pulled from his pedestal remains the argument: a symbol for a new liberal order for an entire region. The war in Iraq is a link in the chain bringing about new world order, justifying itself with the claim that it replaces the futile human rights politics of an exhausted world organization. What's speaking against it?

Moral feelings lead us astray because they attach to individual scenes and particular images. There is no way to avoid the question of how to justify the war as a whole. The crucial issue of dissent is whether justification through international law can and should be replaced by the unilateral, world-ordering politics of a self-appointed hegemon.

Empirical objections to the possibility of realizing the American vision converge in the thesis that global society has become far too complex; the world is no longer accessible to a centralized control, through politics backed up by military power. In the technologically supreme and heavily armed superpower's fear of terrorism, one can sense a "Cartesian anxiety"—the fear of a subject trying to objectify both itself and the world around it, trying to bring everything under control. Politics loses its primacy over the horizontally networked media of both markets and of communication once it attempts to regress to the original, Hobbesian form of a hierarchical security system. A state that sees all its options reduced to the stupid alternatives of war or peace quickly runs up against the limits of its own organizational capacities and resources. It also steers the process of political and cultural negotiation down a false track and drives the costs of coordination to dizzying heights.

But even if the design for a politics of hegemonic unilateralism could be implemented, it would generate side effects that are undesirable according to its own normative criteria. The more that political power (understood in its role as a global civilizing force) is exercised in the dimensions of the military, secret security services, and the police, the more it comes into conflict with its own purposes, endangering the mission of improving the world according to the liberal vision. In the United States itself, the administration of a perpetual "wartime president" is already undermining the foundations of the rule of law. Quite apart from methods of torture that are practiced or tolerated outside the nation's borders, the wartime regime has not only robbed the prisoners in Guantanamo of the rights they are entitled to according to the Geneva Convention but has also expanded the powers of law enforcement and security officials to the point of infringing the constitutional rights of America's own citizens. And wouldn't the Bush doctrine demand normatively counterproductive measures in the (not improbable) scenario that the citizens of Iraq, Syria, Jordan, Kuwait, and so on made a less-than-friendly use of the very democratic freedoms that the American government wants to give them? The Americans liberated Kuwait in 1991; they didn't democratize it.

Above all, however, the American superpower's self-proclaimed role of trustee runs up against the objections of its own allies, who remain unconvinced on good normative grounds of its paternalistic claim to unilateral leadership. There was a time when liberal nationalism saw itself justified in promulgating the universal values of its own liberal order, with military force if necessary, throughout the entire world. This arrogance doesn't become any more tolerable when it is transferred from nation-states to a single hegemonic state. It is precisely the universalistic core of democracy and human rights that forbids their unilateral realization at gunpoint. The universal validity claim that commits the West to its "basic political values," that is, to the procedure of democratic self-determination and the vocabulary of human rights, must not be confused with the imperialist claim that the political form of life and the culture of a particular democracy—even the oldest one—is exemplary for all societies.

The "universalism" of the old empires was of this sort, perceiving the world beyond the distant horizon of its borders only from the centralizing perspective of its own worldview. Modern self-understanding, by contrast, has been shaped by an egalitarian universalism that requires a decentralization of one's own perspective. It demands that one relativize one's own views to the interpretive perspectives of equally situated and equally entitled others. It was precisely the insight of American pragmatism that reciprocal perspective taking paves the way for grasping what is in each case equally good for all parties. The "reason" of modern rational law does not consist of universal "values" that one can own like goods and distribute and export throughout the world. "Values"—including those that have a chance of winning global recognition— don't come from thin air. They win their binding force only within normative orders and practices of particular forms of cultural life. If thousands of Shiites in Nasiriya demonstrate in equal measure against both Saddam and the American occupation, they express the truth that non-Western cultures must appropriate the universalistic content of human rights from their own resources and in their own interpretation, one that will construct a convincing connection to local experiences and interests.

And this is why multilateral will formation in interstate relations is not simply one option among others. From its self-chosen isolation, even the good hegemon, having appointed itself the trustee of general interests, cannot know whether what it maintains is in the interest of others to do is, in fact, equally good for all. There is no sensible alternative to the ongoing development of international law into a cosmopolitan order that offers an equal and reciprocal hearing for the voices of all those affected. The world organization of the United Nations has so far not suffered truly significant damage. Insofar as the "small" member states on the Security Council refused to buckle under pressure from the larger states, it has even gained in regard and influence. The reputation of the world organization can suffer only self-inflicted damage: if it were to try, through compromises, to "heal" what cannot be healed.

NOTE

This chapter originally appeared as "Was bedeutet der Denkmalsturz?" in the *Frankfurter Allgemeine Zeitung*, April, 17, 2003, 33. Translated by Max Pensky. Reprinted by permission of the author.

2

February 15; or, What Binds Europeans Together: A Plea for a Common Foreign Policy, Beginning in Core Europe

Jürgen Habermas and Jacques Derrida

It is the wish of Jacques Derrida and Jürgen Habermas to be cosignatories of what is both an analysis and an appeal. They regard it as necessary and urgent that French and German philosophers lift their voices together, whatever disagreements may have separated them in the past. The following text was composed by Jürgen Habermas, as will be readily apparent. Though he would have liked to very much, because of personal circumstances Jacques Derrida was unable to compose his own text. Nevertheless, he suggested to Jürgen Habermas that he cosign this appeal, and he shares its definitive premises and perspectives: the determination of new European political responsibilities beyond any Eurocentrism; the call for a renewed confirmation and effective transformation of international law and its institutions, in particular the United Nations; and a new conception and a new praxis for the distribution of state authority and so on according to the spirit, if not the precise sense, that refers back to the Kantian tradition. Moreover, many of Jürgen Habermas's points intersect with ones Jacques Derrida has recently developed in his book Voyous. Deux Essais sur la Raison *(2002). Within several days, a book by Jürgen Habermas and Jacques Derrida will appear in the United States, consisting of two conversations that both of them held in New York after September 11, 2002. Despite all the obvious differences in their approaches and arguments, there too their views touch on the future of institutions of international law and the new tasks for Europe.*

We should not forget two dates: not the day the newspapers reported to their astonished readers the Spanish prime minister's invitation to the other European nations willing to support the Iraq war to swear an oath of loyalty to George W. Bush, an invitation issued behind the back of the other countries

27

of the European Union. But we should also remember the fifteenth of February 2003 as mass demonstrations in London and Rome, Madrid and Barcelona, Berlin and Paris reacted to this sneak attack. The simultaneity of these overwhelming demonstrations—the largest since the end of World War II—may well, in hindsight, go down in history as a sign of the birth of a European public sphere.

During the leaden months prior to the outbreak of the war in Iraq, a morally obscene division of labor provoked strong emotions. The large-scale logistical operation of ceaseless military preparation and the frenetic activity of humanitarian aid organizations meshed together as precisely as the teeth of a gear. Moreover, the spectacle took place undisturbed before the eyes of the very population that—robbed of their own initiative—was to be its victim. The precautionary mustering of relief workers, relief services, and relief goods dressed itself in the rash rhetoric of alleviation of suffering yet to be inflicted, the planned reconstruction of cities and administrations yet to be ruined. Like searchlights, they picked out the civilized barbarism of coolly planned death (of how many victims?), of torments long since totted up (of how many injured and mutilated, how many thirsty and hungry?), of the long-planned destruction (of how many residential districts and hospitals, how many houses, museums, and markets?). As the war finally began, the Ernst Jünger aesthetic of the skyline of the nighttime Baghdad, illuminated by countless explosions, seemed almost harmless.

A COMMON EUROPEAN FOREIGN POLICY: WHO FIRST?

There is no doubt that the power of emotions has brought European citizens jointly to their feet. Yet at the same time, the war made Europeans conscious of the failure of their common foreign policy, a failure that has been a long time in the making. As in the rest of the world, the cavalier break with international law has ignited a debate over the future of the international order in Europe as well. But here, the divisive arguments have cut deeper and have caused familiar fault lines to emerge even more sharply. Controversies over the role of the American superpower, on a future world order, and on the relevance of international law and the United Nations all have caused latent contradictions to break into the open. The gap between continental and Anglo-American countries on the one side and "the old Europe" and the central and eastern European candidates for entry into the European Union (EU) on the other side has grown deeper.

In Great Britain, while the special relationship with the United States is by no means uncontested, the priorities of Downing Street are still quite clear.

And the central and eastern European countries, while certainly working hard for their admission into the EU, are nevertheless not yet ready to place limits on the sovereignty that they have so recently regained. The Iraq crisis was only a catalyst. In the Brussels constitutional convention, there is now a visible contrast between the nations that really want a stronger EU and those with an understandable interest in freezing or, at best, cosmetically changing the existing mode of intergovernmental governance. This contradiction can no longer be finessed. The future constitution will grant us a European foreign minister. But what good is a new political office if governments don't unify in a common policy? A Fischer with a changed job description would remain as powerless as Solana.

For the moment, only the core European nations are ready to endow the EU with certain qualities of a state. But what happens if these countries can only find agreement on the definition of "self-interest"? If Europe is not to fall apart, these countries will have to make use of the mechanisms for "strengthened cooperation" created in Nice, as a way of taking a first step toward a common foreign policy, a common security policy, and a common defense policy. Only such a step will succeed in generating the momentum that other member states—initially in the Euro-zone—will not be able to resist in the long run. In the framework of the future European constitution, there can and must be no separatism. Taking a leading role does not mean excluding. The avant-gardist core of Europe must not wall itself off into a new Small Europe. It must—as it has so often—be the locomotive. It is from their own self-interest, to be sure, that the more closely cooperating member states of the EU will hold the door open—and the probability that the invited states will pass through that door will increase the more capable the core of Europe becomes in effective action externally and the sooner it can prove that in a complex global society it's not just divisions that count but also the soft power of negotiating agendas, relations, and economic advantages.

In this world, the reduction of politics to the stupid and costly alternative of war or peace simply doesn't pay. At the international level and in the framework of the United Nations, Europe has to throw its weight on the scale to counterbalance the hegemonic unilateralism of the United States. At global economic summits and in the institutions of the World Trade Organization, the World Bank, and the International Monetary Fund, it should exert its influence in shaping the design for a coming global domestic policy.

Political projects that aim at the further development of the EU are now colliding with the limits of the medium of administrative steering. Until now, the functional imperatives for the construction of a common market and the Euro-zone have driven reforms. These driving forces are now exhausted. A transformative politics, which would demand that member states not just overcome obstacles for competitiveness but also form a common will, must take recourse to the motives and the attitudes of the citizens themselves. Majority decisions on highly consequential foreign policies can only expect acceptance assuming the solidarity of outnumbered minorities. But this presupposes a feeling of common political belonging on both sides. The population must so to speak "build up" their national identities and add to them a European dimension. What is already a fairly abstract form of civic solidarity, still confined largely to members of nation-states, must be extended to include the European citizens of other nations as well.

This raises the question of "European identity." Only the consciousness of a shared political fate and the prospect of a common future can halt outvoted minorities from the obstruction of a majority will. The citizens of one nation must regard the citizens of another nation as fundamentally "one of us." This desideratum leads to the question that so many skeptics have called attention to: are there historical experiences, traditions, and achievements offering European citizens the consciousness of a political fate that has been shared together and that can be shaped together? An attractive, indeed, an infectious "vision" for a future Europe will not emerge from thin air. At present it can arise only from the disquieting perception of perplexity. But it well can emerge from the difficulties of a situation into which we Europeans have been cast. And it must articulate itself from out of the wild cacophony of a multivocal public sphere. If this theme has so far not even gotten on to the agenda, it is we intellectuals who have failed.

THE TREACHERIES OF A EUROPEAN IDENTITY

It's easy to find unity without commitment. The image of a peaceful, cooperative Europe, open toward other cultures and capable of dialogue, floats like a mirage before all of us. We welcome the Europe that found exemplary solutions for two problems during the second half of the twentieth century. The EU already offers itself as a form of "governance beyond the nation-state" that could set a precedent in the postnational constellation. And for decades, European social welfare systems served as a model. Certainly, they have now been thrown on the defensive at the level of the national state. Yet future political efforts at the domestication of global capitalism must not fall below the standards of social justice that they established. If Europe has solved two problems of this magnitude, why shouldn't it issue a further challenge: to defend and promote a cosmopolitan order on the basis of international law, against competing visions?

Such a Europe-wide discourse, of course, would have to match up with existing dispositions that are waiting, so to speak, for the stimulation of a process of self-understanding. Two facts would seem to contradict this bold assumption. Haven't the most significant historical achievements of Europe forfeited their identity-forming power precisely through the fact of their worldwide success? And what could hold together a region characterized more than any other by the ongoing rivalries between self-conscious nations?

Insofar as Christianity and capitalism, natural science and technology, Roman law and the Napoleonic code, the bourgeois-urban form of life, democracy and human rights, and the secularization of state and society have spread across other continents, these legacies no longer constitute a *proprium*. The Western form of spirit, rooted in the Judeo-Christian tradition, certainly has its characteristic features. But the nations of Europe also share this mental habitus, characterized by individualism, rationalism, and activism, with the United States, Canada, and Australia. The "West" encompasses more than just Europe. Moreover, Europe is composed of nation-states that delimit one another polemically. National consciousness, formed by national languages, national literatures, and national histories, has long operated as an explosive force.

However, in reaction to the destructive power of this nationalism, values and habits have also developed that have given contemporary Europe, in its incomparably rich cultural diversity, its own face. This is how Europe at large presents itself to non-Europeans. A culture that for centuries has been beset more than any other culture by conflicts between town and country and sacred and secular authorities, by the competition between faith and knowledge, and by the struggle between states and antagonistic classes has had to painfully learn how differences can be communicated, contradictions institutionalized, and tensions stabilized. The acknowledgment of differences—the reciprocal acknowledgment of the Other in his otherness—can also become a feature of a common identity.

The pacification of class conflicts within the welfare state and the self-limitation of state sovereignty in the framework of the EU are only the most recent examples for this. In the third quarter of the twentieth century, Europe on this side of the Iron Curtain experienced its "golden age," as Eric Hobsbawm has called it. Since then, features of a common political mentality have taken shape, so that others often recognize us as Europeans rather than as Germans or French—and that happens not just in Hong Kong but even in Tel Aviv. And isn't it true? In European societies, secularization is relatively far advanced. Citizens here regard transgressions of the border between politics and religion with suspicion. Europeans have a relatively large amount of trust in the organizational and steering capacities of the state while remaining skeptical toward the achievements of markets. They possess a keen sense of the "dialectic of enlightenment"; they have no naively optimistic expectations about technological progress. They maintain a preference for the welfare state's guarantees of social security and for regulations on the basis of solidarity. The threshold of tolerance for the use of force against persons lies relatively low. The desire for a multilateral and legally regulated international order is connected with the hope for an effective global domestic policy, within the framework of a reformed United Nations.

The fortunate historical constellation in which West Europeans developed this kind of mentality in the shadow of the Cold War has changed since 1989–1990. But February 15 shows that the mentality has survived the context from which it sprang. This also explains why "old Europe" sees itself challenged by the blunt hegemonic politics of its ally and why so many in Europe who welcome the fall of Saddam as an act of liberation also reject the illegality of the unilateral, preemptive, and deceptively justified invasion. But how stable is this mentality? Does it have roots in deeper historical experiences and traditions?

Today we know that many political traditions that command their authority through the illusion of "naturalness" have in fact been "invented." By contrast, a European identity born in the daylight of the public sphere would have something constructed about it from the very beginning. But only what is constructed through an arbitrary choice carries the stigma of randomness. The political-ethical will that drives the hermeneutics of processes of self-understanding is not arbitrary. Distinguishing between the legacy we appropriate and the one we want to refuse demands just as much circumspection as the decision over the interpretation through which we appropriate it for ourselves. Historical experiences are only candidates for a self-conscious appropriation; without such a self-conscious act, they cannot attain the power to shape our identity. To conclude, a few notes on such "candidates," in whose light the European postwar consciousness can win a sharper profile.

HISTORICAL ROOTS OF A POLITICAL PROFILE

In modern Europe, the relation between church and state developed differently on either side of the Pyrenees, differently north and south of the Alps and west and east of the Rhine. In different European countries, the idea of the state's neutrality in relation to different worldviews has assumed different legal forms. Yet within civil society, religion overall assumes a comparably unpolitical position. We may have cause to regret this social privatization of faith in other respects, but it has desirable consequences for our political culture. For us, a president who opens his daily business with open prayer and associates his significant political decisions with a divine mission is hard to imagine.

Civil society's emancipation from the protection of an absolutist regime was not connected with the democratic appropriation and transformation of the modern administrative state everywhere in Europe. But the spread of the ideals of the French Revolution throughout Europe explains, among other things, why politics in both of its forms—as organizing power and as a medium for the institutionalization of political liberty—has been welcomed in Europe. By contrast, the triumph of capitalism was bound up with sharp class conflicts, and this fact has prevented an equally unprejudiced appraisal of the market. That different evaluation of politics and market may back Europeans' trust in the civilizing power of the state and their expectations for its capacity to correct "market failures."

The party system that emerged from the French Revolution has often been copied. But only in Europe does this system also serve as an ideological competition that subjects the sociopathological results of capitalist modernization to an ongoing political evaluation. This fosters the sensibility of citizens for the paradoxes of progress. The contest between conservative, liberal, and socialist agendas comes down to the weighing of two aspects: Do the benefits of a chimerical progress outweigh the losses that come with the disintegration of protective, traditional forms of life? Or do the benefits that today's processes of "creative destruction" promise for tomorrow outweigh the pain of modernization's losers?

In Europe, those who have been affected by class distinctions and their enduring consequences understood these burdens as a fate that can be averted only through collective action. In the context of workers' movements and the Christian socialist traditions, an ethics of solidarity, the struggle for "more social justice," with the goal of equal provision for all, asserted itself against the individualistic ethos of market justice that accepts glaring social inequalities as part of the bargain.

Contemporary Europe has been shaped by the experience of the totalitarian regimes of the twentieth century and through the Holocaust—the persecution and the annihilation of European Jews in which the National Socialist regime made the societies of the conquered countries complicit as well. Self-critical controversies about this past remind us of the moral basis of politics. A heightened sensibility for injuries to personal and bodily integrity reflects itself, among other ways, in the fact that both the Council of Europe and the EU made the ban on capital punishment a condition for entrance.

A bellicose past once entangled all European nations in bloody conflicts. They drew a conclusion from that military and spiritual mobilization against one another: the imperative of developing new, supranational forms of cooperation after World War II. The successful history of the EU may have confirmed Europeans in their belief that the domestication of state power demands a mutual limitation of sovereignty on the global as well as the national-state level.

Each of the great European nations has experienced the bloom of its imperial power. And, what in our context is more important still, each has had to work through the experience of the loss of its empire. In many cases this experience of decline was associated with the loss of colonial territories. With the growing distance of imperial domination and the history of colonialism, the European powers also got the chance to assume a reflexive distance from themselves. They could learn from the perspective of the defeated to perceive themselves in the dubious role of victors who are called to account for the violence of a forcible and uprooting process of modernization. This could support the rejection of Eurocentrism and inspire the Kantian hope for a global domestic policy.

NOTE

This chapter originally appeared in German as "Nach dem Kriege: Das Wiedergeburt Europas," by Jürgen Habermas and Jacques Derrida, in the *Frankfurter Allgemeine Zeitung*, May 31, 2003. Translated by Max Pensky. Reprinted by permission of the authors. Max Pensky's English translation first appeared in *Constellations* (vol. 10, no. 3, 2003) and is reprinted courtesy of Blackwell Publishing.

II

THE GLOBAL PUBLIC SPHERE

3

Transnationalizing the Public Sphere

Nancy Fraser

It is commonplace today to speak of "transnational public spheres." In academic milieus, we increasingly hear references to "diasporic public spheres," "regional public spheres," and even an emerging "global public sphere." And such talk has a clear point. A growing body of media-studies literature is documenting the existence of discursive arenas that overflow the bounds of both nations and states. And numerous scholars in cultural studies are ingeniously mapping the contours of such arenas and the flows of images and signs in and through them. Thus, the idea of a "transnational public sphere" is intuitively plausible, as it seems to have real purchase on social reality.

Nevertheless, this idea raises a theoretical problem. The concept of the public sphere was developed not simply to understand empirical communication flows but also to contribute a normative political theory of democracy. In that theory, a public sphere is conceived as a space for the communicative generation of public opinion, in ways that are supposed to ensure (at least some degree of) moral-political validity. Thus, it matters who participates and on what terms. In addition, a public sphere is supposed to be a vehicle for mobilizing public opinion as a political force. It should empower the citizenry vis-à-vis private powers and permit it to exercise influence over the state. Thus, a public sphere is supposed to correlate with a sovereign power to which its communications are ultimately addressed. Together, these two ideas—the validity of public opinion and citizen empowerment vis-à-vis the state—are essential to the concept of the public sphere in democratic theory. Without them, the concept loses its critical force and its political point.

Yet these two features are not easily associated with the discursive arenas that we today call "transnational public spheres." It is difficult to associate the

notion of valid public opinion with communicative arenas in which the interlocutors do not constitute a political citizenry. And it is hard to associate the
notion of communicative power with discursive spaces that do correlate with
sovereign states. Thus, it is by no means clear what it means today to speak
of "transnational public spheres." From the perspective of democratic theory,
at least, the phrase sounds a bit like an oxymoron.

Nevertheless, we should not rush to jettison the notion of a "transnational
public sphere." Such a notion is indispensable, I think, to those of us who aim
to reconstruct democratic theory in the current "postnational constellation."
But it will not be sufficient merely to refer to such public spheres in a relatively casual commonsense way, as if we already knew what they were.
Rather, it will be necessary to return to square one, to problematize public
sphere theory—and ultimately to reconstruct its conceptions of validity and
communicative power. The trick will be to walk a narrow line between two
equally unsatisfactory approaches. On the one hand, one should avoid an em-
piricist approach that simply adapts the theory to the existing realities, as that
approach sacrifices its normative force. On the other hand, one should also
avoid an excessively externalist approach that invokes ideal theory to con-
demn social reality, as that approach sacrifices critical traction. The alternative, rather, is a critical-theoretical approach that seeks to locate normative
standards and emancipatory political possibilities precisely within the unfolding present constellation.

This project confronts a major difficulty, however. From its inception,
public sphere theory has always been implicitly nationalist; it has always
tacitly assumed a national frame. The same is (largely) true for various
critiques/reconstructions of public sphere theory from the perspectives of
gender, race, and class. Only very recently have the nationalist underpin-
nings of public sphere theory been problematized. The increased salience of
transnational phenomena associated with "globalization," "postcoloniality,"
"multiculturalism," and so on have made it possible—and necessary—to rethink public sphere theory in a transnational frame. These developments
force us to face the hard question: Is the concept of the public sphere so thoroughly nationalist in its deep conceptual structure as to be unsalvageable as
a critical tool for theorizing the present? Or can the concept be reconstructed
within a transnational frame? In the latter case, the task would not simply be
to conceptualize transnational public spheres as actually existing institutions. It would rather be to reformulate the critical theory of the public
sphere in a way that can illuminate the emancipatory possibilities of the
present "postnational constellation."

In this chapter, I want to begin to lay out the parameters for such a discussion. I shall be mapping the terrain and posing the questions rather than of-

fering definitive answers. But I start with the assumption that public sphere theory is in principle an important critical-conceptual resource that should be reconstructed rather than jettisoned, if possible. And my discussion will proceed in three parts. First, I shall sketch the contours of traditional public sphere theory in a way that highlights its implicit national presuppositions, and I shall suggest that those presuppositions have persisted in the major feminist and antiracist critiques and appropriations of the theory. Second, I shall identify several distinct facets of transnationality that problematize both traditional public sphere theory and its feminist and antiracist countertheorizations. Finally, I shall propose some strategies whereby public sphere theorists might begin to respond to these challenges.

My overall aim is to repoliticize public sphere theory, which is currently in danger of being depoliticized. This, we shall see, requires rethinking the problem of scale.

TRADITIONAL PUBLIC SPHERE THEORY AND ITS CRITICAL COUNTERTHEORIZATION: THEMATIZING THE IMPLICIT NATIONAL FRAME

Let me begin by recalling some analytic features of public sphere theory, drawn from the locus classicus of all discussions, Jürgen Habermas's *Structural Transformation of the Public Sphere*. Habermas's inquiry proceeded simultaneously on two levels: 1) the empirical-historical-institutional level and 2) the ideological-critical/ideal-normative level. On both levels, the public sphere was conceptualized as coextensive with a territorial nation-state. Tacitly at least, Habermas's account of the public sphere rested on at least six institutional presuppositions, all of which were implicitly national:

1. Habermas tacitly associated the public sphere with a national state apparatus that exercised sovereign power over a bounded territory and its inhabitants.
2. Habermas tacitly associated the public sphere with a national economy that was territorially based, legally constituted, and subject in principle to state regulation.
3. Habermas tacitly associated the public sphere with a national citizenry that was resident on the national territory and possessed a set of (national) general interests that in turn were largely constituted through and focused on the national economy.
4. Habermas tacitly associated the public sphere with a national language that constituted the medium of public sphere communication.

5. Habermas tacitly associated the public sphere with a national literature that constituted the medium for the formation and reproduction of a (national) subjective orientation to a (national) imagined community and hence of a national identity.

6. Habermas tacitly associated the public sphere with a national infrastructure of communication: a national press and later national broadcast media that report the national news.

These institutional elements are related in public sphere theory in a specific ideal/ideological way, oriented to a specific political project. The point is to generate through (national) processes of public communication (conducted in the national language and through the national press) a body of (national) public opinion. This opinion should reflect the communicatively generated (national) general interest of the (national) citizenry concerning the management and ordering of the common conditions of their (national) life, especially the (national) economy. The further point is to empower the body of (national) public opinion so generated vis-à-vis private powers and the (national) state, to hold the (national) state accountable to the (national) citizenry, and to "rationalize" (national) state domination. So understood, the (national) public sphere is a vital institutional component of (national) democracy.

Empirically, then, public sphere theory highlights historic processes, however incomplete, of democratization of the nation-state. Normatively, it represents a contribution to national democratic theory. On both levels, it serves as a benchmark for identifying and critiquing the democratic deficits of actually existing nation-states. Are all nationals really full members of the public? Can all participate on equal terms? Does private ownership of the national media distort national processes of opinion formation? Does national public opinion attain sufficient effective communicative power to tame private power? Can it succeed in influencing the state to a degree sufficient to rationalize domination?

Insofar as it invited us to explore such questions, classical public sphere theory constituted a critical theory of a specific political project: the project of modern nation-state democratization. The critique of this theory has focused largely on securing the full inclusion of those nationals who were excluded or marginalized within that national frame: propertyless workers, women, racial minorities, and the poor.

My own earlier effort to "rethink the public sphere" represents a case in point. In an article originally published in 1990, I offered four criticisms of what I called, following Habermas, "the liberal model of the bourgeois public sphere."[1] First, I argued, contra that model, that it was not in fact possible for interlocutors in a public sphere to bracket status differentials and to deliberate "as if" they were social equals when they were not; and so I concluded that societal equality is a necessary condition for political democracy. Second, I argued, contra the bourgeois model, that a single comprehensive public sphere is not always preferable to a nexus of multiple publics; and I showed that in stratified societies, the proliferation of subaltern counterpublics could be a step toward greater democracy. Third, I rebutted the bourgeois-liberal view that discourse in public spheres should be restricted to deliberation about the common good and that the appearance of "private interests" and "private issues" is always undesirable. Fourth and finally, I contested the bourgeois view that a functioning democratic public sphere always necessarily requires a sharp separation between civil society and the state. In each case, I demonstrated that the bourgeois model illegitimately truncated the scope of democracy. And I argued instead for a postbourgeois model.

This critique still seems right as far as it went. But I now believe that it did not go far enough. Focused largely on overcoming disparities of participation in national public spheres, my critique represented a radicalization of the national-democratic project. Aiming to overcome the limitations of the bourgeois-liberal model, I sought to ensure full access and real parity of participation to those whom that model excluded or marginalized: women, minorities, and the poor. But I failed to challenge the six national presuppositions of the classical theory of the public sphere.

THE POSTNATIONAL CONSTELLATION: PROBLEMATIZING THE NATIONAL FRAME

Today, however, every one of public sphere theory's six national presuppositions is problematic if not simply patently counterfactual. Let me revisit them one by one, beginning with the following:

1. *National-state sovereignty.* Several developments are problematizing public sphere theory's presupposition of the sovereign, territorially defined national state, which was supposed to constitute the addressee of public sphere communication. No longer unified in a single institutional locus, sovereignty is being disaggregated, broken up into several distinct functions, and assigned to several distinct agencies that function at several distinct levels, some global, some regional, some local and subnational. Military and security functions are being disaggregated, relocated, and rescaled as a result of "humanitarian interventions," "peacekeeping operations," the "war on terrorism," and a host of multilateral

security arrangements. Likewise, criminal law and policing functions are being disaggregated, reaggregated, and rescaled, sometimes upward, as in the case of international war crimes tribunals, the International Criminal Court, "universal jurisdiction," and Interpol, but sometimes downward, as in the case of tribal courts and the privatization of prisons. Meanwhile, responsibility for contract law is being rescaled as a result of the emergence of a private transnational regime for resolving business disputes (a revival of the *lex mercatoria*). Economic steering functions are being rescaled upward to regional trading blocs, such as the European Union, the North American Free Trade Agreement, and Mercosur, and to formal and informal transnational bodies, such as the World Bank, the International Monetary Fund, and the World Economic Forum, but also downward, to municipal and provincial agencies, increasingly responsible for fostering development, regulating wages and taxes, and providing social welfare. In general, then, we are seeing the emergence of a new multileveled structure of sovereignty, a complex edifice in which the country is but one level among others. The result is that states today do not enjoy undivided sovereignty over clearly demarcated territories and bodies of citizens. If public sphere communication is by definition addressed primarily to national states, it cannot today serve the function of rationalizing sovereign domination, as the latter is often exercised elsewhere, by nonstate actors and transstate institutions.

2. *National economy.* Several developments are also problematizing public sphere theory's presupposition of a national economy, which was supposed to constitute the principal object of public sphere concern and the principal focus for generating a national general interest. We need only mention outsourcing, transnational corporations, and offshore business registry to appreciate the extent to which nationally based production is becoming a fiction. Likewise, we need only mention global financial markets, the Euro, and the collapse of the Argentine currency to appreciate the extent to which national currency controls are ephemeral. In these conditions, the very idea of a national economy is suspect, let alone one steered by a national state. If public sphere communication is concerned largely with state management of a national economy, it cannot today serve the function of generating general interest, rationalizing domination, democratizing economic steering, and using "politics to tame markets," as the processes that govern economic relations escape the national frame.

3. *National citizenry.* Several developments are also problematizing public sphere theory's presupposition of a national citizenry, which was

supposed to constitute the subject of public sphere communication. The enhanced salience of such phenomena as migrations, diasporas, dual citizenship arrangements, indigenous community membership, and patterns of multiple residency has made a mockery of the presupposition of a national citizenry, exclusive, sharply demarcated, and resident on a national territory. Every state now has noncitizens on its territory, and every nationality is territorially dispersed. Most states are de facto multicultural and/or multinational, even if they persist in denying that. Thus, nationality and citizenship do not coincide. If the subjects of public sphere communication are fellow nationals and fellow citizens, then such communication can no longer serve its classic function of mobilizing those who constitute a "community of fate" to assert democratic control over the powers that determine the basic conditions of their lives. Not only do such powers reside elsewhere, but those affected by them do not constitute a political community.

4. *National language.* Several developments are also problematizing public sphere theory's presupposition of a single national language, which was supposed to constitute the linguistic medium of public sphere communication. As a result of the population mixing just noted, national languages do not map onto states. The problem is not simply that official state languages were consolidated at the expense of local and regional dialects, although they were. It is also that existing states are de facto multilingual, while language groups are territorially dispersed, and many more speakers are multilingual. Meanwhile, English has been consolidated as the lingua franca of global business and mass entertainment, not to mention academia. Yet language remains a political fault line, threatening to explode countries such as Belgium if no longer Canada while complicating efforts to democratize countries such as South Africa and to erect transnational formations such as the European Union. The upshot is that insofar as state-based public spheres are monolingual, they fail to constitute an inclusive communications community of the whole citizenry. At the same time, however, insofar as public spheres correspond to linguistic communities, they are geographically dispersed and do not correspond to states. In either case, it is difficult to see how public spheres can serve the function of generating a democratic counterpower vis-à-vis a state.

5. *National literature.* These developments also problematize public sphere theory's presupposition of a national literature, which was supposed to constitute a medium for the formation of a solidary national identity. Consider the increased salience of cultural hybridity and hybridization, including the rise of "world literature." Consider also the

rise of global mass entertainment, whether straightforwardly American or merely American-like or Americanizing. Consider finally the spectacular rise of visual culture or, better, of the enhanced salience of the visual within culture and the relative decline of print, the literary, and so on. In all these ways, it is difficult to accord conceptual primacy to the sort of (national) literary cultural formation seen by Habermas (and by Benedict Anderson) as underpinning the subjective stance of public sphere interlocutors. On the contrary, insofar as public spheres require the cultural support of a national identity, rooted in national literary culture, it is hard to see them functioning effectively today absent such solidary bases.

6. *National infrastructure of communication.* Related developments also problematize public sphere theory's presupposition of a national communicative infrastructure, which was supposed to support a set of communicative processes that, however decentered, were sufficiently coherent and politically focused to coalesce in "public opinion." Here we need only consider the profusion of niche media, which may be simultaneously subnational and transnational but which do not in any case function as national media, focused on checking national-state power. We should also note the vastly increased concentration of media ownership by transnational corporations, which despite their tremendous reach are by no means focused on checking transnational power. In addition, many countries have privatized government-operated media outlets, with decidedly mixed results: on the one hand, the prospect of a more independent press and television and more inclusive populist programming, and, on the other, the further spread of market logic, advertisers' power, and dubious amalgams such as talk radio and "infotainment." Finally, we should mention instantaneous electronic, broadband, and satellite information technologies that permit direct transnational communication, bypassing national controls. Together, all these developments signal the denationalization of communicative infrastructure. The effects include some new opportunities for critical/public opinion formation to be sure. But these are accompanied by the disaggregation and complexification of communicative flows. The overall effect is to undermine both the generation of critical public opinion on a large scale and its mobilization as effective communicative power.

In general, then, public spheres are increasingly transnational or postnational with respect to each of the constitutive elements of public opinion. The "who" of communication, previously theorized as a national citizenry, is now a collection of dispersed subjects of communication. The "what" of communication, previously theorized as a national interest rooted in a national economy, now stretches across vast reaches of the globe in a transnational community of fate that is not, however, reflected in concomitantly expansive solidarities and identities. The "where" of communication, once theorized as the national territory, is now deterritorialized cyberspace. The "how" of communication, once theorized as national print media, now encompasses a vast translinguistic nexus of disjoint and overlapping visual cultures. Finally, the addressee of communication, once theorized as state power to be made answerable to public opinion, is now an amorphous mix of public and private transnational powers (suggestively named "the nebuleuse" by Robert Cox) that is neither easily identifiable nor rendered accountable.

RETHINKING THE PUBLIC SPHERE—YET AGAIN

These developments raise the question of whether and how public spheres today could conceivably perform the democratic political functions with which they have been associated historically. For example, could public spheres today conceivably generate public opinion in the strong sense of considered understandings of the general interest that has been filtered through fair, inclusive, and critical argumentation, open to everyone affected? And could public spheres today conceivably bring such public opinion to bear to constrain sovereign powers or their functional equivalents? What sorts of changes (institutional, economic, cultural, and communicative) would be required even to imagine a genuinely democratic (or democratizing) role for transnational public spheres under current conditions? Where are the sovereign powers that public opinion today should constrain? Which publics are relevant to which powers? Who are the relevant members of a given public? In what language(s) and through what media should they communicate? And via what communicative infrastructure?

Answering these questions requires us to identify the critical disjunctures or mismatches of scale that threaten to undermine public sphere theory today—and to figure out how to overcome them. Let me mention just two:

1. One key disjuncture is the mismatch of scale between (national) states on the one hand and (transnational) private powers on the other. Overcoming this mismatch requires institutionalizing new transnational public powers that can constrain transnational private power and be made subject to transnational democratic control.

2. A second key disjuncture is the mismatch of scale between country-based citizenship, (global) communities of fate, and subglobal solidarities.

Overcoming this mismatch requires institutionalizing elements of transnational/quasi-global citizenship; generating concomitantly broad solidarities that cross divisions of language, ethnicity, religion, and nationality; and constructing broadly inclusive public spheres in which common interests can be created and/or discovered through open democratic communication. Put differently, it requires realigning relations among at least four distinct kinds of community that do not map onto one another today:

a. The imagined community, or nation
b. The political (or civic) community, or citizenry
c. The communications community, or public
d. The community of fate, or the parties affected by various developments

The picture I envision encompasses multiple publics, corresponding to the picture of multilevel structure of sovereignty I sketched earlier. Here the multiplicity is not horizontal, as in my earlier effort to rethink the public sphere, which assumed an array of publics and counterpublics. Rather, the multiplicity envisioned here is vertical.

In general, then, I am stressing the need for institutional renovation. This focus contrasts with two other emphases that often dominate discussions of globalization. One is a consumerist response (found not only in unabashed liberals such as Tom Friedman but also in relatively critical thinkers such as Ulrich Beck). This approach envisions the mobilization of transnational consumer movements to curb transnational corporate power through boycotts. It targets communicative power directly on corporations, effectively bypassing the state. Thus, it inadvertently cedes the political terrain instead of seeking to remake it.

A second common emphasis puts its hopes rather in transnational social movements. Certainly, such movements do represent an important response to the mismatches of scale I have identified here; they stretch several of the constituent elements of public communication, including the who, what, where, how, and to whom. But they do not and cannot provide the whole solution. The problem is not only that some of them are reactionary. Nor is it that even the progressive ones are neither fully democratic, nor inclusive, nor accountable. More profoundly, transnational movements, like publics, are counterpowers. Their efficacy requires the existence of institutionalized sovereign powers that can be constrained to act in the general interest. Failing major institutional renovation, neither transnational social movements nor transnational public spheres can assume the emancipatory democratizing functions that are the whole point of public sphere theory.

In general, then, there is no substitute for major institutional renovation. If public sphere theory is to become relevant to the current postnational constellation, it is not enough for cultural studies and media studies scholars to map existing communications flows. Rather, critical social and political theorists will need to rethink the theory's basic premises, both institutional and normative. Only then will the theory recover its point and its promise as a concept that can contribute to emancipation.

NOTE

1. Nancy Fraser, "Rethinking the Public Sphere: Toward a Critique of Actually Existing Democracy," in *Habermas and the Public Sphere*, ed. Craig Calhoun (Cambridge, Mass.: MIT Press, 1991), 109–42.

4

Toward a Critical Theory of Globalization: Democratic Practice and Multiperspectival Inquiry

James Bohman

One of the central ideas of both critical theory and pragmatist theories of knowledge is that epistemic claims are embedded in some practical context that in large part determines their relevant standards of justification and normative conditions of success. A truth claim is thus to be judged in light of its practical consequences. This "practical turn" of epistemology is especially relevant for the social sciences, whose main practical contribution, according to pragmatism, is to supply methods for identifying and solving problems—admitting that there are many ways in which knowledge can work toward these ends.[1] From this perspective, there are many ways in which knowledge can be practical. Certainly, political science may inform the art of statecraft, and international relations theory could consider itself to be a subset of the practical disciplines governing the relations of statesmen and citizens to each other. These disciplines are characterized by a further and important dimension of practical knowledge that is exercised with others in communication and problem solving: second-order and reflective forms of practical knowledge; that is, the knowledge of practical knowledge, or the science of practical knowledge itself. When practical knowledge is put in the service of democratic and emancipatory goals—and thus goals dependent on deliberation and judgment—they also may improve the reflexive practical knowledge exercised together with others. Informed by a clear distinction between instrumental forms of activity such as labor and noninstrumental forms such as communication and interaction, critical theory since Habermas has been interested in a distinct form of praxis as the reflective analysis of how it is that norms may be realized in interaction and intersubjective processes of democratic politics, or "praxeology" in Andrew Linklater's sense.[2] Most of all, critical social science has had a practical orientation toward the analysis of how it is that democratic ideals could be realized in undamaged structures of intersubjectivity given the social facts and constraints of modern societies, including those of world politics.

Critical theory and pragmatism are thus united in a particular democratic conception of practical social science, even if critical social science pursues this broad, democratic impulse as part of a larger project of human emancipation.[3] My goal here is to explore the ways in which it may be applied in a practical theory, the goal of which is to analyze the realizability and feasibility of democratic ideals under the special conditions that apply in contemporary globalizing societies. My argument has three steps. First, I develop a pragmatic conception of critical theory as a social theory of practical knowledge. I argue that such a critical theory ought to provide an account of praxis, that is, develop the form of practical knowledge or praxeology that might orient democratic political activity in the age of globalization.

In developing a social science that provides the practical knowledge of praxis, it is better to offer a pragmatic interpretation of critical social inquiry rather than to endorse any particular version of social theory as distinctly critical or democratic. That is, the accent shifts from theories to methodology with the pragmatist emphasis on methodological pluralism helping critical theory become more practical; the missing term for such a practical synthesis of the two is what I call "multiperspectival theory." In order to illustrate the necessity of this understanding of a theory of practical knowledge, in the second step of the argument I turn to debates about the role of social facts in a practical theory of democracy, including pluralism, complexity, and finally globalization. If globalization is the highly uneven and even contradictory process that recent social scientific analysis describes, a proper theory must capture the ways in which the same complex social process can be experienced in different and even conflicting ways from many different social perspectives. Rather than viewing the complexity of these processes as a collective coordination problem, such a practical theory is "multiperspectival" in providing a framework within which the differential impacts and consequences of globalization can be interpreted as aspects of a "problematic situation" for democratic deliberation, not the least of which is the lack of many of the institutional and noninstitutional bases for democracy at the international level. The third step argues that a democracy that takes these facts seriously must be fundamentally rethought in some of its basic norms and ideals. The place to start is to see democracy as both a multiperspectival mode of social inquiry and a discursive practice in which various perspectives can join and intersect in fruitful ways. An ideal of democracy that is adequate to globalizing societies is feasible only if it is "multiperspectival" in its organizational form and in its form of social inquiry.

While the standard theories of globalization deal with large-scale and macrosociological processes, my argument aims at showing that such theories can be practical if they are "multiperspectival," that is, if they seek to include the perspectives of all those who are affected by such processes. Such a critical and multiperspectival theory of democracy could begin to organize the diversity of forms of social inquiry that are necessary if transnational institutions are to be democratic. Institutional forms of inquiry are democratic if they are open to the wider public deliberation of citizens. A central problem for transnational institutions is the lack of any clear idea of the potentially global public sphere that is not overly diffuse and simply the aggregation of world public opinion. A critical theory of globalization must therefore solve two pressing problems: first, it must show how to make social inquiry within and among transnational institutions more democratic, and, second, it must show the salient differences between national and transnational institutions and public spheres so that the democratic influence over globalization becomes a more tractable problem with feasible solutions. After discussing how theories of globalization can become more critical, I develop just such a critical, democratic theory of globalization, focusing on globalization not primarily as imposing constraints on democratic institutions but as also thereby opening up new institutional possibilities and new forms of publicity.[4]

CRITICAL THEORY, PRAGMATISM, AND PRACTICAL SOCIAL SCIENCE

Social inquiry can be practical in a variety of senses, most typically when it is concerned with issues of feasibility. Critical theory has from the beginning regarded itself as practical in the sense of striving to realize the particular normative goal of human emancipation, or, as Horkheimer puts it, the goal of "liberating human beings from all circumstances that enslave them."[5] If it is both to address all such circumstances and to develop an appropriate ideal of emancipation or freedom from domination, critical theory must employ explanations and interpretations informed by a variety of methods, theories, and perspectives. Sometimes the critic who has this aim must employ practical knowledge in adopting a stance that goes beyond the limits of agents' local practical knowledge and self-interpretations. Such a stance is often called "objective." Most proponents of critical theory in the broad sense of the term, both inside and outside the Frankfurt School, now see the characterizations of this stance as solely objective to be misleading at best, given the epistemic situation of the observer as simply one practical agent among others. The question then is not merely how inquiry can be both interpretive and explanatory, but also how it can be oriented to normative goals. Such inquiry assumes neither a pure "insider" and participant standpoint (in the manner of hermeneutics) nor a pure "outsider" or observer standpoint (in the manner of naturalistic social theories). This distinctively normative standpoint characteristic of critical social inquiry, which may include moral theory, has been called the "perspective of a critical-reflective participant."[6] This is not some particular perspective or the exclusive domain of the social theorist or even the social critic but rather a combination of various perspectives, methods of inquiry, and forms of practical knowledge at different levels.

Historically, there have been two common and not necessarily exclusive answers to the question of what defines the distinctive features of critical social inquiry—one practical and the other theoretical. The latter approach claims that it is a distinctive theory employed by critical social inquiry that unifies its diverse approaches. From this view, critical theory constitutes a comprehensive social theory that will unify the social sciences and underwrite the scientific authority of the critic. The first generation of Frankfurt School critical theory sought such a theory in vain before dropping claims to social science—that is, objective social inquiry—as central to their program in the late 1940s.[7] By contrast, the practical approach holds that the theories of critical social inquiry are distinguished and unified by the form of politics in which they are embedded and the method of verification that this politics entails—namely, democracy and democratic inquiry. But to claim that critical social science is best unified practically and politically rather than theoretically or epistemically is not simply to reduce it to democratic politics. Democracy becomes rather the mode of inquiry that participants adopt in their cooperative social relations to others. The latter approach has been developed by Jürgen Habermas and is now favored by critical theorists.

Given the sort of large-scale and long-term processes at stake in the emergence and changes of international society, it might be tempting to seek some sort of macrotheory of global processes as the new comprehensive basis for criticism. This theory might be a theory of capitalism or of imperialism. While not denying that current globalization is structured around market processes and organized politically by hegemony, such a theory would not issue in the appropriate sort of normatively oriented practical knowledge. Pragmatism has developed quite a different conception of normative social inquiry. Rather than assuming this sort of theoretical stance, pluralistic inquiry answers to a different norm of practical correctness: that criticism must be verified by those participating in the practice and that this demand for practical verification is part of the process of inquiry itself.

This idea of practical verification is a central part of pragmatist epistemology and theories of democracy. A plurality of methods are in this view required not only to grasp social facts in all their complexity but also, and more important, because social facts are from the start taken as "problematic situations" by a variety of actors from a variety of different positions and perspectives. According to Dewey's pragmatism, social facts are neither merely given nor simply constructed. Rather, they represent the problems and conflicts that are the hard realities that agents encounter in any set of social practices, institutions, and arrangements. When sufficiently broad in scope, their resolution requires changing such practices and institutions and thereby transforming the feasible set of possibilities. The problematic character consists at times in the facts being perceived to be constraints on the feasibility of various ideals where feasibility is itself a subject for multiperspectival practical social inquiry.

Rather than to look for something epistemically and theoretically distinctive in the universal and necessary features of social scientific knowledge, critical theory has thus shifted to focus on inquiry and the social relationships between inquirers and other actors in the social sciences. These relationships can be specified epistemically in terms of the perspective taken by the inquirer on the actors who figure in their explanations or interpretations, with the dominant perspective of social scientists being that of the third person or first person—that is, the perspectives of instrumental or interpretive social knowledge, respectively, notably the perspectives at play in the theoretical approach. Some versions of the interpretive approach favor a second-person perspective, and this has been the account of interpretation favored by critical theorists for methodological as well as egalitarian, normative reasons. Although justification is a second-person attitude of giving reasons that others could accept, even social science as collaborative problem solving requires complex perspective taking and the coordination of various points of view, minimally that of the social scientists and the subjects under study.

Even when inspired by the pragmatism of Dewey and Mead, critical theory has insisted that the shift to social interaction requires a further distinction that such an expressivist theory elides, that between communication and discourse at levels of reflection. Communication contains within it the reflexive possibility of testing its own presuppositions and thus of shifting from first-order, everyday communication to second-order discourse, the communication about communication that begins when first-order communicative practice breaks down. It is discourse that is institutionalized in democracy, a discourse that enables all to have equal access to influence on discourses that emerge in such problematic situations. The discursive ideal of democracy presupposes pragmatic symmetry among speakers as the self-originating sources of claims, a symmetry institutionalized in constitutional practices that give all participants the status of free and equal citizens in political discourse, a status that they may not have in first-order communication or in modern practices of art and poiesis. The social sciences play a special role not only in reconstructing such communicative capabilities but also in developing reflexivity sufficient to allow speakers to make manifest the limitations of existing discursive practices.

Yet at the same time, this pragmatic symmetry of participant and theorist in discursive practices of justification and verification of practical knowledge may also underestimate the multiperspectival character of social scientific knowledge. The role of even the reflective participant in a practice does not exhaust the possible social positions of a theorist—here thought of as a critic who does not adopt the third-person stance of epistemic superiority. Rather than assuming singular authority, what the critic does is introduce a new perspective, whether it be that of an outsider who criticizes the implicit assumptions of a practice or that of the observer who sees unintended consequences. The critically reflective participant in a discursive practice must take up all available stances; she assumes that no single normative attitude fully captures all critical inquiry. Only such an inter- and multiperspectival stance is fully dialogical, giving the inquirer and agent equally authoritative practical standing. If indeed all cooperative activities "involve a moment of inquiry," then they also need a moment of self-reflection on the assumptions of such inquiry itself.[8] It is this type of reflection that calls for a distinctively practical form of critical perspective taking. If critical social inquiry is inquiry into broadening the possibilities of cooperative practices such as democracy, it must take practical inquiry one reflective step further. The inquirer carries out this step not alone but rather with the public whom the inquirer addresses. As in Thomas S. Kuhn's distinction between normal and revolutionary science,[9] second-order critical reflection considers whether the framework for cooperation itself needs to be changed and thus whether new terms of cooperation are necessary to solve problems.

When understood in this second-order way, it is clear that various perspectives for inquiry are appropriate in different critical situations in which the terms of cooperation are at issue. If critical reflection is to identify as many of the problems with cooperative practices of inquiry as possible, it must be able to occupy and account for a variety of perspectives. Only then will it enable public reflection among free and equal participants. Such problems have emerged, for example, in the practices of inquiry surrounding the treatment of AIDS. The continued spread of the epidemic and lack of effective treatments brought about a crisis in expert authority, a particular sort of "existential problematic situation" in Dewey's sense.[10] By defining expert activity through its social consequences and by making explicit the terms of social co-operation between researchers and patients, lay participants reshaped the practices of gaining medical knowledge and authority.[11] Or feminist accounts have shown how supposedly neutral or impartial norms have built-in biases that limit their putatively universal character with respect to race, gender, and disability.[12] A critical theory of globalization has to recognize these epistemic limitations and reflexively make them the basis of a new sort of practical and normative theory of complex and large-scale social processes.

The introduction of a new perspective does not, then, necessarily require theories but may be simply a matter of excluded actors making vivid the biases and limitations of traditions that have collective authority by showing how the contours of their experiences do not fit the self-understanding of an institution as fulfilling standards of justice. The introduction of such perspectives may have the effect of initiating second-order deliberation in which participants begin an inquiry into norms as they are actually realized in cooperative practice. An essential feature of democracy is that it institutionalizes the expectation of discursive testing as a mechanism for learning and change. Such learning makes possible the introduction of new perspectives that can transform a democratic polity's normative and institutional framework. As an institutionalized discourse taking up problematic situations and their reflexive justification, democracy is a multiperspectival practice. Within this practice, with its ongoing discursive testing of decisions, policies, institutions, and even the interpretation of various ideals, it is the role of the critic to locate and introduce new perspectives. This is no small task given the inherently problematic nature of democracy. Within the terms of practical inquiry that I have been developing here, social facts concern constraints on the feasibility and possibility of the realization of normative ideals; within this consideration, the social fact of globalization concerns such constraints on the ideal of democracy. If indeed a pragmatic and critical social inquiry has anything to contribute, it should at least help clarify what is at stake in globalization as a problematic situation for democracy and the realization of its ideals.

The social fact of globalization proves exemplary here also in that, contrary to many accounts of social facts, globalization is by definition a fact that can be experienced from many different perspectives and as such can best be understood in a multiperspectival practical inquiry into the framework of decision making and problem solving.[13] As this fact cannot be reconstructed from the internal perspective of any single democratic political community, it requires a certain kind of practically oriented knowledge about the possibilities of realizing norms and ideals in praxis and is thus a theory of democratization, of creating a political space where none now exists.

SOCIAL FACTS, NORMATIVE IDEALS, AND
MULTIPERSPECTIVAL THEORY

In what respect can it be said that this novel sort of practical and critical social science should be concerned with social facts? A social scientific praxeology understands facts in relation to human agency rather than independent of it. Pragmatic social science is concerned not merely with elaborating an ideal in convincing normative arguments but also with its realizability and its feasibility. In this regard, any political ideal must take into account general social facts if it is to be feasible, but it must also be able to respond to a series of social facts that ground skeptical challenges suggesting that circumstances make such an ideal impossible. With respect to democracy, these facts include expertise and the division of labor, cultural pluralism and conflict, social complexity and differentiation, and globalization and the fact of increasing social interdependence, to name a few. In cases where "facts" challenge the very institutional basis of modern political integration, normative practical inquiry must seek to extend the scope of political possibilities rather than simply accept the facts as fixing the limits of political possibilities once and for all. For this reason, social science is practical to the extent that it is able to show how political ideals that have informed these institutions in question are not only still possible but also feasible under current conditions or modification of those conditions. As I have been arguing, the ideal in question for pragmatism and recent critical social theory inspired by pragmatism is a robust and deliberative form of self-rule—also a key aspect of critical theory's wider historical ideal of human emancipation and freedom from domination.

The issue of realizability has to do with a variety of constraints. On the one hand, democracy requires voluntary constraints on action, such as commitments to basic rights and to constitutional limits on political power. Social facts, on the other hand, are nonvoluntary constraints or, within our problematic, constraints that condition the scope of the application of democratic principles. Taken up in a practical social theory oriented to suggesting actions that might realize the ideal of democracy in modern society, social facts no longer operate simply as constraints. For Rawls, "the fact of pluralism" (or the diversity of moral doctrines in modern societies) is just one such permanent feature of modern society that is directly relevant to political order because its conditions "profoundly affect the requirements of a workable conception of justice."[14] However, facts such as pluralism become permanent in that modern institutions and ideals developed after the wars of religion, including constitutional democracy and freedom of expression, promote rather than inhibit their development. This fact of pluralism thus alters how we are to think of the feasibility of a political ideal but does not touch on its realizability or possibility. Similarly, the "fact of coercion," understood as the fact that any political order created around a single doctrine would require oppressive state power, concerns not the realizability or possibility of a particular ideal but its feasibility as "a stable and unified order" under the conditions of pluralism.[15] Thus, for Rawls, regardless of whether they are considered in terms of possibility or feasibility, they are considered only as constraints—as restricting what is politically possible or what can be brought about by political action and power. In keeping with the nature of pluralism, not all actors and groups experience the constraints of pluralism in the same way. Different perspectives on the fact of pluralism result not only from occupying different places in the social relations among groups but also from the determination of the political ideal that such actors may seek to realize.

If this were the only role of facts in Rawls's "political theory," then it would not be a full practical theory in the sense that I am using the term here. Rawls's contribution is that social facts differ in kind, maintaining that social facts such as the fact of pluralism are permanent and not merely to be considered in narrow terms of functional stability. Social facts related to stability may indeed constrain feasibility without being limits on the possibility or realizability of an ideal as such; in the case of pluralism, for example, democratic political ideals other than liberalism might be possible. Without locating a necessary connection between its relations to feasibility and possibility, describing a social fact as "permanent" is not entirely accurate. It is better instead to think of such facts as "institutional facts" that are deeply entrenched in some historically contingent, specific social order rather than as universal normative constraints on democratic institutions. Thus, what Rawls calls "permanent" facts about modern societies are rather those determinations that are embedded in relatively long-term social processes, whose consequences cannot be reversed in a short period of time—such as a generation—by political action. Practical theories thus have to consider the ways in which such facts become part of a constructive process that might be called "generative entrenchment."[16] By "entrenchment of social facts," I mean that the relevant democratic institutions promote the very conditions that make the institutional social fact possible in assuming those conditions for their own possibility. When the processes at work in the social fact then begin to outstrip particular institutional feedback mechanisms that maintain it within the institution, then the institution must be transformed if it is to stand in the appropriate relation to the facts that make it feasible and realizable. All institutions, including democratic ones, entrench some social facts in realizing their conditions of possibility.

Consider Habermas's similar use of social facts with respect to this. As with Rawls, for Habermas pluralism and the need for coercive political power make the constitutional state necessary so that the democratic process of lawmaking is governed by a system of personal, social, and civil rights. However, Habermas introduces a more fundamental social fact for the possibility and feasibility of democracy: the structural fact of social complexity. Complex societies are "polycentric," with a variety of forms of order, some of which, such as nonintentional market coordination, do not answer to the ideals of democracy. This fact of complexity limits political participation and changes the nature of our understanding of democratic institutions. Indeed, this fact makes it such that the principles of democratic self-rule and the criteria of public agreement cannot be asserted simply as the proper norms for all social and political institutions, and this seems ideally suited to understanding how globalization limits the capacity of democracy to entrench itself. As Habermas puts it, "Unavoidable social complexity makes it impossible to apply the criteria [of democratic legitimacy] in an undifferentiated way."[17] This fact makes a certain kind of structure ineluctable since complexity means that democracy can "no longer control the conditions under which it is realized." In this case, the social fact has become "unavoidable," and certain institutions are necessary for the social integration for which there is "no feasible alternative."[18] However, Habermas overestimates the constraining character of this "fact," which says little about the field of indirect and institutionally mediated institutional design that are still possible and feasible. These mediated forms of democracy would in turn affect the conditions that produce social complexity itself. The consequences of the fact of social complexity is thus not the same across all feasible, self-entrenching institutional realizations of democracy, and some ideals of democracy may rightly encourage the preservation of aspects of complexity, such as the ways in which the epistemic division of labor may promote wider and more collaborative problem solving and deliberation on ends. What is the alternative conception of social facts that might guide a critical theory of globalization?

When seen in light of the requirements of practical social science and the entrenchment of facts and conditions by institutions, constructivists are right to emphasize how agents produce and maintain social realities, even if not under conditions of their own making. In this context, an important contribution of pragmatism is precisely its interpretation of the practical status of social facts. Thus, Dewey sees social facts always related to "problematic situations," even if these are more felt or suffered than fully recognized as such. The way to avoid turning problematic situations into empirical-normative dilemmas is, as Dewey suggests, to see facts themselves a practical: "facts are such in a logical sense only as they serve to delimit a problem in a way that affords indication and test of proposed solutions."[19] They may serve this practical role only if they are seen in interaction with our understanding of the ideals that guide the practices in which such problems emerge, thus where neither fact nor ideal is fixed and neither is given justificatory or theoretical priority. In response to Lippmann's insistence on the preeminence of expertise, Dewey criticized "existing political practice" for completely ignoring "occupational groups and the organized knowledge and purposes that are involved in the existence of such groups," which betrays "a dependence upon a summation of individuals quantitatively."[20] At the same time, he recognized that existing institutions were obstacles to the emergence of such a form of participatory democracy in an era when "the machine age has enormously expanded, multiplied, intensified and complicated the scope of indirect consequences" of collective action and where the collectives—affected by actions of such a scope—are so large and diverse "that the resultant public cannot identify and distinguish itself."[21] Dewey saw the solution in a transformation both of what it is to be a public and of the institutions with which the public interacts. Such interaction will provide the basis for determining how the functions of the new form of political organization will be limited and expanded, the scope of which is "something to be critically and experimentally determined" in democracy as a mode of practical inquiry about social facts.[22]

The pragmatist conception thus clearly suggests an understanding of social facts for a social scientific praxeology, namely, that it is better to think of social facts as creating a new space of democratic possibilities, opening up some while foreclosing others. A praxeology becomes critical to the extent that it sees among these opportunities the possibility of a structural transformation of basic institutions. "Given the limits and possibilities of our world," Dahl asks, "is a third transformation of democracy a realistic possibility?"[23] This challenging situation could very well call into question the current normative conception of democracy itself; perhaps its array of possibilities is too restricted or forces too many hard choices on us. The question is not just one of current political feasibility but also of possibility, given that we want to remain committed in some broad sense to democratic principles of self-rule even if not to the set of possibilities provided by current institutions. How do we identify such fundamentally unsettling facts? I turn next to the discussion of a specific social fact, the "fact of globalization," and interpret it not as a uniform and aggregative process but as a problematic situation that is experienced in different and even contradictory ways from a variety of perspectives and is differently assessed with respect to different normative ideals of democracy.

THE FACT OF GLOBALIZATION AND
THE POSSIBILITY OF DEMOCRACY

For some, the fact of globalization permits a direct inference to the need for new and more cosmopolitan forms of democracy and citizenship. Whatever the specific form these assume in future institutions, the usual arguments for political cosmopolitanism are relatively simple despite the fact that the social scientific analyses employed in them are highly complex and empirically differentiated in their factual claims. In discussions of theories of globalization, the fact of global interdependence refers to the unprecedented extent, intensity, and speed of social interactions across borders, encompassing diverse dimensions of human conduct from trade and cultural exchange to migration.[24] The inference from these facts of interdependence is that existing forms of democracy within the nation-state must be transformed and that institutions ought to be established that solve problems that transcend national boundaries.[25] Thus, globalization is taken to be a macrosociological, aggregative fact that constrains the realization of democracy as long as the proper congruence between decision makers and decision takers is lacking. Globalization is taken as a constraint on democracy as it is realized in existing liberal representative systems. The Deweyan alternative is to see that facts "have to be determined in their dual function as obstacles and as resources," as problems that also hold out the conditions that make the transformation of the situation possible.[26] The "mere" fact of the wider scale of interaction is thus inadequate on its own and does not capture what role globalization may play as a problematic situation for the emergence of new democratic possibilities.

A pragmatic interpretation of social facts in this way encourages us to see globalization as Janus-faced, as an obstacle and as a resource for the realization of democratic ideals. This sort of theory sees globalization not as a unitary but rather as a multidimensional process. Even the notion of "complex interdependence" can be misleading insofar as it falsely suggests the telos of an increasingly integrated world or an increasingly homogeneous culture or political community.[27] A pragmatic analysis is better served by a concept such as "interconnectedness" as opposed to interdependence to the extent that interdependence suggests convergence and levels the differences in the ways in which globalization is experienced. Rather, it is important here, as in the case of the fact of pluralism, to see that this process can be experienced in different ways by different peoples or political communities, given that it is a multifaceted and multidimensional process producing "differential interconnectedness in different domains."[28] In some domains such as global financial markets, globalization is profoundly uneven and deeply stratified, reinforcing hierarchies and distributive inequalities. Inequalities of access to and control over aspects of globalizing processes may reflect older patterns of subordination and order even while the process produces new ones by excluding some communities from financial markets and by making others more vulnerable to its increased volatility.[29] The fact of globalization is a new sort of social fact whose structure of enablement and constraint is not easily captured at the aggregative level. It is even experienced in contradictory ways to the extent that its consequences and impacts differ.

How can we understand its practical significance in a normative theory concerned with the feasibility and realization of the democratic ideal? Given the sort of fact that globalization is, there are a number of possible responses to it. The lack of effective global institutions suggests that many of its practical consequences can be seen as suboptimal outcomes of collective coordination problems, solved to the mutual benefit of all by the appropriate application of technical knowledge or expertise. This understanding of the fact of globalization leads, for example, to investing greater authority in international financial institutions in which experts are guided by economic theories of proper market functioning that suggest the policies necessary to avoid instability and volatility in global financial markets. While admitting that expert theoretical knowledge has its role to play, critical theory suggests that such an understanding of the problematic situation of globalization as a coordination problem ignores the way in which such institutions create the potential for domination. Institutions can manage the problems of globalization in ways that consider the interests of everyone only by having mechanisms that ensure that the full range of perspectives is available for inquiry. This requires a kind of second-order testing and accountability not yet available in international financial institutions, as they do not yet fully consider the social disintegration that globalization may bring.[30]

The example of global financial markets raises the question of the sort of practical knowledge employed in institutions and how the method of inquiry in them may promote or inhibit democratic alternatives. The practical alternative to such a solution through *techné* must be multiperspectival in that it considers all the variety of experiences and perspectives in a variety of dimensions and domains. If globalization is profoundly uneven, then the most interconnected locations and domains of the global structure may be enabled in a variety of ways to achieve various political and economic ends, while those that are less connected may experience the global structure as deeply constraining. In this way, the increased scale and extent of interconnectedness across borders increase the possibilities of domination and for this reason require some process of democratization in which the freedom of all may be possible given the consequences of interconnectedness.

One further question about the fact of globalization must be raised in order to understand the inherent possibilities for democracy in it. Is globalization a "permanent" fact for democracy as Rawls described the fact of pluralism for liberalism in that it is deeply embedded in its possible realizations? As many social theorists have argued, globalization is part of long-term social processes beginning in early modernity; as Anthony Giddens put it, "modernity is inherently globalizing."[31] Even if it is modernity rather than democracy that is inherently globalizing, then reversing such processes is possible although not feasible in any short time span and under the normative constraints of democracies and their social preconditions. That is, as long as "globalizing" societies are democratic, we can expect such processes and their impacts to continue. This is not to say that globalization in its current form is somehow permanent or unalterable if we want to realize democratic ideals. Indeed, just how globalization will continue and under what legitimate normative constraints become the proper questions for democratic politics as citizens and public vigorously interact with those institutions that make globalization a deeply entrenched and temporally stable social fact. Reversing globalization rather than restructuring the institutions that maintain it will likely dramatically undo important normative features of democracy as well. In the political activity attending issues related to globalization, the currently existing yet overly weak normative constraints are reconstituted along with the institutions themselves. The social fact of globalization remains open to democratic reconstruction should creative reinterpretation of democracy come about. In the next section, I argue that only in this way can we account for the realization of democracy under the current conditions of globalization, namely, by achieving a new institutional equilibrium between the ideal of democracy and the conditions of its feasibility.

THE IDEAL OF A MULTIPERSPECTIVAL DEMOCRACY

The analysis thus far has taken a robust ideal of democracy for granted consisting of self-rule by the public deliberation of free and equal citizens—the ideal of deliberative democracy that informs both pragmatism and critical theory. Given the uneven and potentially contradictory consequences of globalization, it seems clear that current democratic institutions themselves cannot be responsive to all the dimensions of domination and subordination that are possible considering the scale and intensity of interconnectedness. What are the alternatives? It is not just a matter of exercising an institutional imagination within broadly understood democratic norms and ideals. Informed by democratic ideals of nondomination, the practical knowledge

needed to promote the democratizing of uneven and hierarchical social relations requires an empirical analysis of current transformations and its embedded possibilities. The democratic ideal of autonomy leads David Held
and others to emphasize the emerging structures of international law that
produce a kind of binding power of collective decisions.[32] Others look to
ways of reforming the structures of representation of current international institutions.[33] Still others look to the emergence of various institutions in the
European Union to discuss the trend toward international constitutionalism
or supranational deliberation.

According to the sort of plurality of perspectives endorsed by a pragmatist
philosophy of social science, a historical account of the emergence of single
and multiple institutions would be helpful. In Gerald Ruggie's masterful
analysis of the development of a global order beyond the nation-state, he
shows that the modern sovereign state and the social empowerment of citizens emerged within the same epistemic era as the single point perspective in
painting, cartography, or optics. "The concept of sovereignty then represented
merely the doctrinal counterpart of the application of single point perspective
to the organization of political space."[34] Unbundling sovereignty would lead
to new political possibilities, including the rearticulation of international political space in a new way that cannot be anticipated in dominant theories of
international relations. Focusing on the shifts in the authority of states and the
development of the European Union, Ruggie sees the "EU as the first multiperspectival polity to emerge in the modern era" and thus the emergence of a
new political form. The concept of "the multiperspectival form" does seem to
offer "a lens through which to view other possible instances of international
transformation today."[35] Such an account also applies to the theory of practical knowledge that might inform reflection on the possibilities of democracy
in an era of uneven globalization.

If the political authority that now promotes globalization is to answer to
democratic will formation, the institutions in which such public deliberation
takes place must seek to become explicitly multiperspectival. The positive
conditions for such an extension of current political possibilities already exist in the fact of interdependence—the emergence of greater social interaction
among citizens who participate in vibrant transnational civil societies and in
emerging global public spheres. In order to develop the framework for such
a normative-practical praxeology for emerging multiperspectival institutions,
pragmatism and critical theory once again suggest themselves: here Dewey's
conception of the interaction of public and institutions that not only is responsible for the democratic character of both but also is the plausible feedback mechanism for their structural transformation. Thus, a critical theory of
globalization looks for innovative forms of publicity and democracy not only

because they are feasible but also because they are based rather on normatively robust and democratic interactions between publics and institutions.

THE MULTIPERSPECTIVAL PUBLIC SPHERE: THE CRITICAL AND INNOVATIVE POTENTIAL OF TRANSNATIONAL INTERACTION

How might new forms of inquiry emerge that are able to accommodate a greater number of perspectives and also remain democratic? Here we need again to distinguish between first- and second-order forms of deliberation, where the latter develop in order to accommodate an emergent public with new perspectives and interests. Dewey sees the normal, problem-solving functioning of democratic institutions as based on robust interaction between publics and institutions within a set of constrained alternatives. When the institutional alternatives implicitly address a different public than is currently constituted by evolving institutional practice and its consequences, the public may act indirectly and self-referentially by forming a new public with which the institutions must interact. This interaction initiates a process of democratic renewal in which publics organize and are organized by new emerging institutions with a different alternative set of political possibilities. Of course, this is a difficult process: "to form itself the public has to break existing political forms; this is hard to do because these forms are themselves the regular means for instituting political change."[36] This sort of innovative process describes the emergence of those transnational publics that are indirectly affected by the new sorts of authoritative institutions brought about by managing "deregulation" and globalization. This account of democratic learning and innovation seems to be limited not by the scope of the institutions but only by the presence or absence of a public sphere and civil society through which such potentially transformative interaction can occur, even as the potential for domination increases under current arrangements. Thus, globalization is transformative of political structures, and a critical theory of globalization assesses these transformations in terms of domination and nondomination.

What sort of public sphere could play such a normative role? In differentiated modern societies (in whatever institutional form), one role of the distinctive communication that goes on in the public sphere is to raise topics or express concerns that cut across social spheres: it not only circulates information about the state and the economy but also establishes a forum for criticism in which the boundaries of these spheres are crossed, primarily in citizens' demands for mutual accountability. But the other side of this generalization is a requirement for communication that crosses social domains: such a generalization is necessary precisely because the public sphere has become less socially and culturally homogeneous and more internally differentiated into diverse normative perspectives and social positions. It is certainly the case that the relative absence of state regulation in cyberspace means that censorship is no longer the primary means of inhibiting the formation of public spheres. The powerful social institutions that may inhibit the formation of a broader public sphere in electronic space are now multinational media corporations and other market actors who increasingly design and control its architecture. Publics now develop in new and politically unbounded social contexts, some of which may even be global in scope as civil society and the supporting institutions of the public sphere become more transnational.

In this sort of public sphere, how would actors exhibit their concern for publicity or employ the self-preferentiality of the public sphere to criticize others? Instead of appealing to an assumed common norm of "publicity" or set of culturally specific practices of communication, a cosmopolitan public sphere is created when at least two culturally rooted public spheres begin to overlap and intersect, as when translations and conferences create a cosmopolitan public sphere in various academic disciplines. Such culturally expansive yet socially structured, rather than anarchic, public spheres emerge as political institutions and civic associations and come to include previously excluded groups. Instead of relying on the intrinsic features of the medium to expand communicative interaction, networks that are global in scope become publics only with the development and expansion of transnational civil society. The creation of such a civil society is a slow and difficult process that requires the highly reflexive forms of communication and boundary crossing and accountability typical of developed public spheres. Thus, we can expect that under proper conditions and with the support of the proper institutions, existing vibrant global publics will expand as they become open to and connected with other public spheres. On the basis of their common knowledge of violations of publicity, their members will develop the capacities of public reason to cross and negotiate boundaries and differences between persons, groups, and cultures.

In such boundary-crossing publics, the speed, scale, and intensity of communicative interaction facilitated by the Internet provides a positive and enabling condition for democratic deliberation and thus creates a potential space for cosmopolitan democracy. Such a development hardly demands that the public sphere be "integrated with media systems of matching scale that occupy the same social space as that over which economic and political decision will have an impact."[37] But if the way to do this is through networks rather than mass media, then we cannot expect that the global public sphere will no longer exhibit features of the central and unified form of the national public sphere but will be a public of publics, a decentered public sphere that permits many different levels without an implied universal audience suggested in the idealization of the print-mediated public sphere. Disaggregated networks must always be embedded in some other set of social institutions rather than an assumed unified national public sphere. This suggests that they will be embedded in different, disaggregated political institutions if they are to be the institutions that transform the deliberation of such public spheres in the communicative power of collective action.

The emergence of transnational public spheres is informative for the practical goals of a critical theory of globalization. Once we examine the potential ways in which the Internet can expand the features of communicative interaction, whether or not the Internet is a public sphere is a practical question of possibility rather than a theoretical question about the fact of the matter. It depends not only on which institutions shape its framework but also on how participants contest and change these institutions and on how they interpret the Internet as a public space. It depends on the mediation of agency, not on technology. With the proliferation of nongovernmental organizations (NGOs) and other forms of transnational civil society organizations, it is plausible to expect that two different and interacting levels of multiperspectival innovation may emerge: first, new institutions, such as the European Union, that are more adapted to multiple jurisdictions and levels of governance, and, second, a vibrant transnational civil society that produces public spheres around various institutions with the goal of making their forms of inquiry more transparent, accessible, and open to a greater variety of actors and perspectives. This approach does not limit the sources of the democratic impulse to transnational civil society. Rather, the better alternative is to reject both bottom-up and top-down approaches in favor of vigorous interaction between publics and institutions as the ongoing source of democratic change and institutional innovation.

According to a pragmatically inspired democratic experimentalism, attempts at democratization and reform need not wait for publics to emerge; they can be constructed in various practices. Consultative NGOs may generally become too intertwined with institutions and thus do not generatively entrench their own conditions in this way. This practical difficulty is evident in the official civil society organizations of the European Union that fail to promote public deliberation. Without further conceptual and normative clarification, the appeal to various "bottom-up" strategies of democratization remains normatively underdeveloped.[38] Even when informed by democratic aims, this form of politics cannot capture the complex interrelationships of civil society, the state, and the market, especially given the background of inequalities and asymmetries that operate in processes of globalization. Apart from powerful corporate actors in civil society, NGOs from economically advantaged regions possess significant resources to influence and shape the formation of civil society in other contexts, thus revealing a strong connection between their powers in civil society with market forces.[39]

More models that do not simply designate some organizations as the agent for others have emerged at more local levels, in particular the use of "minipublics" that are empowered to deliberate and make decisions.[40] Here we can include a variety of experiments, from participatory budgets to citizen boards and juries, that have a variety of decision-making powers. Properly empowered and self-consciously constructed, minipublics offer a strategy to get beyond the dilemma of insider consultation and outsider contestation that is a structural feature of civil society activity in currently existing international institutions, with their reliance on expert authority and knowledge as the basis for their legitimacy. Since minipublics seek to include all relevant stakeholders, they do not rely on representation as the mode of communicating interests or even the inclusion of well-organized actors a way to achieve effective implementation. Rather than simply consult, this form of influence would require that institutions transfer some of their authority to the minipublic whose deliberation it empowers, opening up a directly deliberative process within the institution that includes as many perspectives as possible and can be repeated when necessary. This authorization would require the constitutional reform of many of these powerful institutions to make them more open to the decentering power of deliberation across publics. If the minipublic genuinely includes relevant perspectives, it would also go beyond the selectiveness and epistemic limitations of consultation procedures. The minipublic is then an institutionally constructed intermediary, although it could act in such as way as to become an agent for the creation of a larger public with normative powers. In this capacity, they may become open and expandable space for democratic experimentation. While many are issue or domain specific, such experiments often become models for democratic governance in dispersed and diverse polities. As Cohen and Rogers put it, while the more specific and episodic practices aim at mutual benefits through improved coordination, the experimental deliberative practices tied to larger political projects may redistribute power and advantage and in this way secure the conditions of democracy more generally.[41]

The same point could be made about taking existing democratic institutions as the proper model for democratization. To look only at the constraints of size in relation to a particular form of political community begs the question of whether there are alternative linkages between democracy and the public sphere that are not simply scaled up. Such linkages might be more decentralized and polycentric than the national community requires. The issue here is the standard of evaluation, not whether some other public sphere or form of community "is totally or completely democratic, but whether it is adequately democratic given the kind of entity we take it to be."[42] For a nation-state to be democratic, it requires a certain sort of public sphere sufficient to create a strong public via its connections to parliamentary debate. For a transnational and thus polycentric and pluralist community, such as the European Union, requires a different sort of public sphere in order to promote sufficient democratic deliberation. Once a transnational and postterritorial polity rejects the assumption that it must be what Rawls calls "a single cooperative scheme in perpetuity," a more fluid and negotiable order might emerge with plural authority structures along a number of different dimensions rather than a single location for public authority and power. Without a single location of public power, a unified public sphere becomes an impediment to democracy rather than an enabling condition for mass participation in decisions at a single location of authority.

The problem for experimental institutional design of directly deliberative democracy is to create precisely the appropriate feedback relation between disaggregated publics and such a polycentric decision-making process. When compared to the nation-state democracies that are members of the European Union, such a proposal is based on two different forms of disaggregation: the disaggregation of both representative democracy and the national public sphere in order to promote a more deliberative form of transnationalism. At the European level, this would require an innovative form of a symmetrical federalism that would go beyond the hierarchy of territorial federalism along the model of the United States. Most of all, it would require experimentation in reconciling the dispersed form of many-to-many communication with the demands of the forum. Rather than merely seek to determine some institutional formula, the aim of such a design is to enable direct and vigorous interaction among dispersed publics at various levels of decision making. Accordingly, each case of democratization requires the emergence of a vibrant, transnational civil society in which organizations and groups create publics of various kinds to be transnational sites within which various sorts of decisions are debated and discussed, similar to the sort of Internet counter–public sphere that emerged around the Multilateral Agreement on Investment.

Appropriately designed decision-making processes and the existence of a suitable form of publicity to enable access to influence speak at least in favor of the feasibility of such a proposal. The lesson for a critical theory of globalization is to see the extension of political space and the redistribution of political power not only as a constraint similar to complexity but also as a open field of opportunities of innovative, distributive, and multiperspectival forms of publicity and democracy.

CONCLUSION: THE PRAXIS OF GLOBAL DEMOCRACY

A critical theory of globalization is a practical or praxeologically oriented theory that sees the "fact of globalization" in relation to the goal of realizing the norms of human emancipation and democracy. The central questions for such a practically oriented social science are the following: What available forms of praxis are able to promote the transformations that could lead to new forms of democracy? What sort of practical knowledge is needed to make this possible, and how might this knowledge be stabilized in institutionalized forms of democratic inquiry? What are the possibilities and opportunities for democracy at a higher level of aggregation that globalization makes possible? How might the public sphere be realized at the global level? The argument here suggests that such inquiry and institutions must go beyond single-perspective understandings of democracy that dominate national political life as well the various administrative *techne* that are common in the international sphere. If its political realization is not itself to become a means for domination, cosmopolitan democracy requires multiperspectival institutions with forms of inquiry based on interaction with distributive public spheres. A critical praxeology of multiperspectival institutions might add that it is also a reflexive question of putting such organization in the larger context of a project of human emancipation in which all are free from domination to the extent that their perspectives are recognized and contribute to the solution of common problems. The central challenge of globalization for democracy is to have the new forms of interconnectedness without increasing the possibilities for domination.

Given the wide diversity of international society, we might expect the institutional forms of a multiperspectival polity to unlink some aspects of democratic authority from its single-perspective institutions and to begin to open deliberation and inquiry by reflecting the enriched possibilities of a new, dispersed, and increasingly wider politically relevant public. The value of such deliberation is that it at least permits the sort of reflection and inquiry necessary for the transformation of democracies into multiperspectival polities that include states, transnational civil society networks, and the cosmopolitan public sphere. In a pluralist, complex, and unevenly interconnected world, this includes the creation of transnational democratic institutions with forms of inquiry that are accountable to those new transnational publics whom they influence and are influenced by in robust interaction. Such an interactive account of public and institutions gives a plausible practical meaning to the extending of the project of democracy to the global level. It also models in its own form of social science the mode of inquiry that this and other publics may employ in creating and assessing the possibilities for realizing democracy.

NOTES

1. See John Dewey, *Logic: The Theory of Inquiry*, in *The Later Works, 1938*, vol. 12 (Carbondale: Southern Illinois University Press, 1986), 489–95. For an application of pragmatist pluralism to critical social science, see James Bohman, "Theories, Practices, and Pluralism: A Pragmatic Interpretation of Critical Social Science," *Philosophy of the Social Sciences* 28, no. 4 (1999): 459–80.

2. Andrew Linklater, "The Changing Contours of Critical International Relations Theory," in *Critical Theory and World Politics*, ed. Richard W. Jones (London: Lynne Rienner, 2001), 38–41.

3. On the "democratic impulse" as a feature of "critical international relations theory" and how it ties to older forms of international relations theory before neorealism, see Craig Murphy, "Critical Theory and the Democratic Impulse: A Century-Old Tradition," in Jones, *Critical Theory and World Politics*, 62–65.

4. In developing the theoretical sides of this tasks, I rely on my "How to Make a Social Science Practical: Critical Theory, Pragmatism and Multiperspectival Theory," *Millennium* 21, no. 3 (2003): 499–524.

5. Max Horkheimer, *Critical Theory* (New York: Seabury Press, 1982), 244.

6. Jürgen Habermas, *The Theory of Communicative Action, Vol. 1* (Boston: Beacon Press, 1984), 111–19; see also Thomas McCarthy, *Critical Theory* (London: Blackwell, 1994), 81.

7. Rolf Wiggershaus, *The Frankfurt School* (Cambridge, Mass.: MIT Press, 1994), 302–49.

8. Hilary Putnam, *Words and Life* (Cambridge, Mass.: Harvard University Press, 1994), 174.

9. Thomas Kuhn, *The Structure of Scientific Revolutions* (Chicago: University of Chicago Press, 1970).

10. Dewey, *Logic*, 492.

11. Stephen Epstein, *Impure Science: AIDS, Activism and the Politics of Knowledge* (Berkeley: University of California Press, 1996), part II; see also James Bohman, "Democracy as Inquiry, Inquiry as Democratic: Pragmatism, Social Science, and the Cognitive Division of Labor," *American Journal of Political Science* 43 (1999): 590–607.

12. Examples of this sort of social inquiry include Jane Mansbridge, "Feminism and Democratic Community," in *Democratic Community*, ed. John W. Chapman and Ian Shapiro (New York: New York University Press, 1993), 339–96; Charles Mills, *The Racial Contract* (Ithaca, N.Y.: Cornell University Press, 1997); and Martha Minnow, *Making All the Difference* (Ithaca, N.Y.: Cornell University Press, 1990).

13. Multiperspectival inquiry is common in feminist and other critical social inquiry in international relations theory. See, for example, Brooke Ackerly's conception of "the multisited critic" in *Political Theory and Feminist Social Criticism* (Cambridge: Cambridge University Press, 2000). See also Charlotte Bunch, "Women's Rights as Human Rights: Toward a Revision of Human Rights," *Human Rights Quarterly* 12 (1990): 489–90. For a general account of multiperspectival inquiry as essential to practical and

critical social science, see James Bohman, "Critical Theory as Practical Knowledge," in *Blackwell Companion to the Philosophy of the Social Sciences*, ed. P. Roth and S. Turner (Oxford: Blackwell, 2002), 91–109.

14. John Rawls, "The Idea of an Overlapping Consensus," in *Collected Papers*, ed. Samuel Freeman (Cambridge, Mass.: Harvard University Press, 1999), 424.

15. Rawls, "The Idea of an Overlapping Consensus," 225.

16. William Wimstatt, "Complexity and Organization," in *Proceedings of the Philosophy of Science Association 1972*, ed. R. S. Cohen (Dordrecht: Riedel, 1974), 67–86.

17. Jürgen Habermas, *Between Facts and Norms* (Cambridge, Mass.: MIT Press, 1996), 305.

18. Jürgen Habermas, *The Postnational Constellation* (Cambridge, Mass.: MIT Press, 2001), 122.

19. Dewey, *Logic*, 499.

20. John Dewey, *Liberalism and Social Action*, in *The Later Works, 1935–1937*, vol. 11 (Carbondale: Southern Illinois University Press, 1991), 50–51.

21. John Dewey, *The Public and Its Problems: The Later Works, 1925–1927*, vol. 2 (Carbondale: Southern Illinois University Press, 1988), 255, 314.

22. Dewey, *The Public and Its Problems*, 281.

23. Robert Dahl, *Democracy and Its Critics* (New Haven, Conn.: Yale University Press, 1989), 224.

24. On the various positions in the controversies over globalization, see David Held, Anthony McGrew, David Goldblatt, and Jonathan Perraton, *Global Transformations: Politics, Economics, and Culture* (Stanford, Calif.: Stanford University Press, 1999).

25. See David Held, *Democracy and the Global Order* (Stanford, Calif.: Stanford University Press, 1995), 98–101, for an argument of this sort that emphasizes the scope of interconnections and its consequences for the realization of autonomy as the key problem for democratic governments.

26. Dewey, *Logic*, 499–500.

27. On complex interdependence, see Robert Keohane, "Sovereignty in International Society," in *Global Transformation Reader*, ed. D. Held and A. McGrew (Cambridge: Polity Press, 2000), 117.

28. Held et al., *Global Transformations*, 27.

29. Held et al., *Global Transformations*, 213. For various dimensions of this issue, see Andrew Hurrell and Ngaire Woods, eds., *Inequality, Globalization, and World Politics* (Oxford: Oxford University Press, 1999).

30. Dani Rodrik, *Has Globalization Gone Too Far?* (Washington, D.C.: Foreign Affairs Press, 1994); see also Ngaire Woods, "Making the IMF and the World Bank More Accountable," *International Affairs* 77, no. 1 (2001): 83–100.

31. Anthony Giddens, *Consequences of Modernity* (Stanford, Calif.: Stanford University Press, 1990), 63.

32. Held and Habermas have argued for such a fundamentally Kantian, legal interpretation of cosmopolitan democracy.

33. See Thomas Pogge, "How to Create Supranational Institutions Democratically," *Journal of Political Philosophy* 5, no. 2 (1997): 163–82. Pogge argues that rep-

resentation should be based not merely on state membership but also on "deep identification" with a group. Similarly, Habermas argues that a reformed Parliament will be crucial for the further development of the European Union. See Habermas, "Why Europe Needs a Constitution," *New Left Review* 3 (2001): 22.

34. Gerald Ruggie, *Constructing the World Polity* (London: Routledge, 2000), 186.

35. Ruggie, *Constructing the World Polity*, 196.

36. Dewey, *The Public and Its Problems*, 255.

37. Nicholas Garnham, "The Mass Media, Cultural Identity, and the Public Sphere in the Modern World," *Public Culture* 5 (1995): 265.

38. See John Dryzek, *Democracy in Capitalist Times* (Oxford: Oxford University Press, 1997); for a different criticism of such approaches, see Alison Jaggar, "Feminism and Global Citizenship," in *Women and Citizenship*, ed. M. Friedman (Oxford: Oxford University Press, in press).

39. See, for example, Jael Silliman, "Expanding Civil Society, Shrinking Political Spaces: The Case of Women NGOs," in *Dangerous Intersections: Feminist Perspectives on Population, Development and the Environment*, ed. Y. King and J. Silliman (Boston: Southend Press, 1998). A complex account of the NGO as an organizational form for social movements is found in Alison Jaggar, "Feminism and Global Citizenship."

40. See Archon Fung, "Recipes for Public Spheres," *Journal of Political Philosophy* 3 (2003): 338–67.

41. For the criticism of the democratic aims of the more discrete sorts of deliberative experiments and the advantages of a larger political project, see Joshua Cohen and Joel Rogers, "Power and Reason," in *Deepening Democracy*, ed. A. Fung and E. O. Wright (London: Verso, 2003), 251 ff.

42. Neil MacCormick, "Democracy, Subsidiarity and Citizenship," *Law and Philosophy* (1997): 345. Contrary to the spirit of MacCormick's claim, however, a democracy that is "adequate" to transnational institutions of this sort will not thereby be more minimal than democracy in the national state but robust in different ways.

5

Democratic Institutions and Cosmopolitan Solidarity

María Pía Lara

In this chapter, I would like to rescue the term "globalization" from its common understanding among "globaliphobics"[1] and "globaliphilics"[2] and propose the development of a "normative framework" for such a concept. I claim that if globalization is understood as a further stage of social complexity, we must provide a normative understanding of the measures needed against the devastating effects of social injustice and poverty and against the iron logic of the market. My aim is to point out the practical paths needed to establish such a normative link between processes of globalizing democratic institutions of law and rights and the growing trend of a democratic culture of cosmopolitanism. I wish to show how certain processes of "globalization" can be used to bring to light the necessity of worldwide cooperation in helping poor countries establish democratic institutions and defend their constitutions by recognizing the basic rights of all persons living in those countries. In my view, the only way we can rescue Kant's insight into the possibility of an age based to a greater extent on peaceful coexistence as a result of correlating a respect for rights of inclusion with the goals of justice and solidarity is if we use the term "globalization" in a normative way.[3] The normative term I will use in order to understand this normative insight is "globalizing justice."

Two hundred years ago, Kant conceived of a second foundational moment for democratic politics. He thought of "perpetual peace" and its pacifying effects as a second "social contract," which establishes a new political agreement between individuals in order to make possible a strong defense of human rights, along with a peaceful coexistence within a growing cosmopolitan culture. When Kant envisaged a "world public sphere" and a "world civil society," he was pointing to the need for an internationalization of democracy by applying the concept of international law—cosmopolitan law, that is—to create what he called "a peaceful global order." Following his proposal today, Habermas and other theorists[4] have tried to further develop his concept of global peace with relation to globalization processes. By using them to create a contemporary normative view, these theorists have addressed significant issues that relate to Kant's ideas. This new conceptualization of democratic expansion during our times needs to be considered as we focus on globalization. Thus, I will deal first with a critical recovery of Kant's legacy, valuable in terms of solidaristic efforts from the global community to help impoverished countries build democratic institutions. Second, I will address the normative categories needed in order to make the concept of "globalization" central to the development, and I will examine concrete examples of retroactive justice as devices used to link events that have already occurred, along with their historical consequences, with globalization processes of building up democratic institutions and regulations. By recognizing that this link represents an important connection between the radical democratization of human rights and processes of democratic globalization, I will further envisage what Kant had in mind when he spoke of a cosmopolitan global era.

RETHINKING KANT'S NORMATIVE GROUNDS FOR A "COSMOPOLITAN ORDER"

When we review globalization processes according to a normative framework, it becomes clear that poverty is now a global problem. Hunger, injustice, and limited opportunities for economic and political survival have led to massive migration from poor countries into developed countries. People who remain in poor nations face the cruel reality of needing policies that better redistribute wealth and that, in turn, will enhance the justice of such policies. The term "democratization" cannot refer only to ensuring the legality of electoral democracy since a qualitative leap would require—in terms of justice—that the political system be fundamentally transformed. I propose that only a rights-protective regime makes it possible to deepen a democratic order. The transformation of democratic governments is concerned not only with who is in power but also with how and within what limits a government exercises that power. Thus, electoral democracy may be a necessary condition for developing a democratic order, but it cannot be the only condition for entering into the process of broadening democratic goals and institutions. Electoral democracy can be extremely vulnerable to populist, protofascist demagoguery. The recent experiences of the former president of Peru, Alberto Fujimori, provide a clear example. Fujimori was first democratically elected but then managed to stay in power by changing the laws to suit his aim of becoming a dictator. Therefore, if both of these processes are now perceived as problems that concern all humanity, then there are important reasons to consider Kant's normative framework for a peaceful order with globalization processes of solidarity and justice.

By globalizing rights, we should succeed in closing the gap between markets and economic and social rights—between electoral democracy and civil and political rights. Markets seek only economic efficiency and to maximize the quantity of goods. When markets produce more overall, they do not necessarily produce more for all. This is because, for one thing, economics alone cannot offer social benefits to all and, second, because the laws of free market and trade cannot provide better ways of living in a more humane order—an order that presupposes coping mechanisms for inequalities such as poverty, hunger, and injustice. Free markets necessarily produce drastic market inequalities.[5] Thus, the idea that countries can overcome their social, economic, and political difficulties by simply entering into the international competitive arena of the free market is proven wrong—particularly if we turn our attention to what happened in Asia during the 1980s and 1990s.[6] Many countries implemented policies that they claimed improved their economies with aggressive efforts to become competitive according to the standards of international markets. As they pursued this narrow path of economic growth and international competition, they argued, their countries participated in a collective effort to find ways to improve the quality of life without transforming their political institutions. As is now clear, not only did they fail to improve living conditions in terms of distribution of wealth and standard of living; rather, their political institutions showed signs of corruption, an absence of respect for human rights, and a highly restricted sense of freedom. Recently, the Asian regimes' economic standards have suffered, while political crises seem to be leading their authoritarianism into new and critical stages.

Believing Asia's path to be a good example of economic growth, some Latin American countries—such as Brazil, Argentina, and Mexico—embraced strong policies to facilitate their entry into the world market and to ameliorate their standard of living by means of world trade agreements. Their efforts, however, have made us aware that the market alone will not build modern democratic countries that seek a more cohesive development. If civil and political rights keep democracy within its proper limits, economic and social rights set the proper limits on markets. Thus, the global trend of recognizing the benefits of privatizing state enterprises in underdeveloped countries and the pursuit of aggressive policies to compete internationally are certainly not the only means to a real transformation of societies whose basic inequalities and low standard of living are tied to an unfair distribution of wealth.[7] The measures needed to attain economic stability and increase opportunities for all can be achieved only by dismantling authoritarian states and building up democratic institutions.[8] These democratic institutions can provide the means for a healthy redistribution of wealth and a fairer social order that would greatly improve not only their standard of living but also their quality of life.[9] Thus, there is no real possibility of integral development without democracy. Only democratic institutions, with their goal of counterbalancing the rigid rule of the markets, can provide a healthy equilibrium that leads to a fairer society—a much-needed process that would allow those countries to fight against their own unjust traditions of corruption, clientelism, and daily practices of disregard for human rights. A global democratic understanding of the law should begin with the assumption that individuals bear all basic rights. If this is true, however, then we need to consider a global space—such as the one Kant envisaged—that could take the lead in the protection of rights beyond the boundaries of nation-states.

Thus, one important aspect of the need of Third World countries to build democratic institutions is their ties with First World countries and their responsive solidarity in achieving democratic transformations. In this stratified world society, however, it is certainly true that there are irreconcilable interests that arise out of the asymmetrical interdependency between developed countries, countries that are growing quickly, and countries that are underdeveloped. The only way to link internal democratic demands and external procedures that can foster the building up of democratic institutions to an agreed coordination with other countries that would be supported by an institutional space of global politics and governance is to create global democratic institutions and collective agreements that support the new global era.[10]

There is yet another good reason to recognize that globalization must be framed according to Kant's normative grounds. Economic experiments have helped us appreciate the need for the democratization of poor countries along with the need to spread global democratic measures and institutions that will counterbalance the rigid blindness of the market's logic. Yet we must also have democratic institutions to stop the civil, ethnic, and nationalistic wars that have produced the horrors of genocide, ethnic cleansing, and all types of crimes against humanity that have been perpetrated during civil wars in the last hundred years. Experience has led us to an important stage in which we have learned a great deal from the tragic wars that have proliferated as civil and ethnic wars in the twentieth century. If what we have learned about moral crisis is pointing us in the direction of new institutions wherein cosmopolitan law is possible, there is also an evident need to help those countries that have suffered such traumatic events overcome their tragedies by reeducating their societies in democratic ways and to develop legal procedures for the accountability of crimes committed against their fellow humans. The burden of the past is something countries that have suffered civil, political, and ethnic warfare do not know how to overcome, and there is growing evidence that the more a country learns from its past mistakes, the greater the possibility of fostering a conscious understanding of democratic duties and responsibilities.[11] Countries that have recovered from a traumatic event are now facing a basic social concern about what to do with the people who committed such crimes and for their victims. Two important things are at stake here. First, there are the legal procedures that democratic institutions grant for accountability and individual responsibility in committing crimes against humanity or in any violation of human rights. Second, there is a significant moral effect on society when there is an effort to disclose the "truth" about what happened during repression and state violence once the murderers are subject to public trials.[12] The creation of a collective moral consciousness of past deeds and the fostering of a collective space where moral learning produces a collective consciousness provide essential links between nondemocratic countries and those that historically possess democratic traditions. Furthermore, in order to find a process to evaluate what happened in countries that are undergoing transitions to democracy, we need international tribunals. They offer the only hope for those countries whose constitutions and political agreements impede the prosecution of their criminals because of the power and support they continue to hold.[13] Thus, the internationalization of human rights, along with the creation of a New Human Rights Court,[14] would allow for accountability of crimes against humanity and war crimes beyond nation-state sovereignty.[15] As Ruti G. Teitel argues, "The increasingly dynamic relation of the individual and the state in a fast changing public sphere affects understandings of personal and collective responsibility, thus bringing about related changes in the conception of democracy."[16]

It is for this reason that Axel Honneth has called our attention to this historic moment as an important political stage of a new kind—a new social contract following Kant's idea "of international relations to the situation in world politics: states ought to be able to emerge 'from a state of lawlessness, which consists solely of war' by giving up 'their savage (lawless) liberty, just as individual persons do, and, by accommodating themselves to public coercive law, form a polity of all peoples (*civitas gentium*) that would necessarily continue to grow until it embraced all the peoples of the earth.'"[17] The normative framework of globalization should begin by recognizing this as the historical frame of a new social contract to pursue a peaceful coexistence within societies.

NORMATIVE CATEGORIES FOR THE
DISCUSSION OF GLOBALIZATION

With the establishment of a horizon for democracy based on human rights with this new social contract, there are some important conceptualizations that must be considered here. The first is the development of our notion of human rights as inherent to a democratic order and the shift from the initial concept, in which human rights were protected by nation-states, to the more current, revised idea that human rights can be protected only by the existence of international law and international courts that warrant accountability to individuals independently of their nation-states. Jürgen Habermas has addressed this issue fully in his essay "Kant's Idea of Perpetual Peace, with the Benefit of Two Hundred Years' Hindsight."[18] Here, Habermas discusses the need to conceive the idea of human rights on different levels: the moral one—that is, the moral content and validity of the idea of human rights; the political one—in other words, the policies that allow the idea of human rights to pursue some concrete political goals; and the legal one—which is to say the positivization of the idea of human rights attributed to each person as a human being into laws that bind individuals to respect them on the grounds of international laws. Habermas argues, however, that "the conception of human rights does not have its origins in morality," but, rather, he points out, "it bears the imprint of the modern concept of individual liberties and is therefore distinctly juridical in character." Habermas rightly suggests that "what gives human rights the appearance of being moral rights is neither their content nor even their structure but rather their form of validity, which points beyond the legal order of the nation-state."[19] Thus, the connection between human rights and globalization must come from this link between the validity of the idea of human rights with its expanding scope beyond the political framework of the nation-state and the globalization of democratic institutions.

The second principle that will allow us to fully grasp the normative framework of globalization within the connection of human rights and democracy is the way in which moral learning processes implemented since 1945 have led to the emergence of new social factors that made possible the positivization of international law. Allow me to address this historic issue with a brief reconstruction of the idea of human rights. It is true that one can trace the notion of human rights back to the Virginia Bill of Rights and to the American Declaration of Independence of 1776. We can also look to the 1789 *Declaration des droits de l'homme et du citoyen* of the French Republic. These kinds of declarations were inspired by the political philosophies of John Locke and Jean-Jacques Rousseau. Human rights were immediately linked to the democratic concept of the nation-state. They, therefore, depended on how concretely constitutions regarded the protection and their sanction thereof.[20] The concept of human rights, however, bears a peculiar feature that must be examined: the most important characteristic of human rights is that they are "constructions" that consider individuals to be the bearers of rights. Because of their universal scope, whether or not these rights are defined and protected by a specific constitution of a nation-state, their validity depends on the fact that they can be applied to *every human being as such*. Therefore, the concept of human rights shares the kind of universal power that moral norms possess.[21] This category of human rights possesses universality and requires enforcement beyond the territory of the nation-state. The normative idea of human rights has been used by many groups of civil societies where they see this connection linked immediately to the idea of democratic institutions and universal acccountability.[22] Non-state participants, therefore, became the most important ingredient in the transformation of the Universal Declaration of Human Rights into an obligatory international law. This could happen only after the traumatic events of World War II allowed them to understand the significance of such rights.

A historical reconstruction of this transition allows us to stress the fact that the creation of a concept of human rights—along with its universal validity—was not fully understood until the catastrophic events of the Holocaust took place. Crucial measures were taken afterward to revise the historical experiences of World War II. The concept of human rights has been associated with the normative idea of humanity and, as such, has received criticism that focuses on the "moral" content of the idea of humanity. For some theorists this is merely an excuse to justify their fights against one another or as the embodiment of "evil." Through his concept of the "political,"[23] Carl Schmitt developed the strongest criticism of the concept of humanity. Schmitt first claimed that the politics of human rights were set to enhance the natural struggles between nations as struggles against "evil," and, thus, the idea of "humanity" was a vehicle for "bestiality." Habermas has tried to address Schmitt's criticisms by differentiating between morality, politics, and legality. Habermas correctly pointed out that the concept of human rights cannot be confused with morality. Rather, violations of human rights can be condemned and battled from the moral point of view only via mediation—that is, within the framework of a legal order and according to institutionalized legal procedures that protect us from a moral dedifferentiation of law and that guarantee full legal protection even to those accused of committing crimes against humanity. According to Habermas, therefore, a position like the one taken by Carl Schmitt against a politics of human rights can aim to "civilize" war only through international law and protects, above all, the sovereignty of states to conduct wars without any legal restrictions.

Issues such as Schmitt's criticism of humanity as a moral concept can help us understand the complexities that lie at the heart of the positivization of human rights. Hannah Arendt's answer to this problem, for example, took the wrong approach to solving such a difficulty. It is interesting to notice, however, that she insightfully recovered the concept of the term "humanity" in her study of totalitarianism, which focuses on the Nazi technique for the dehumanization of persons. By "deconstructing"[24] the concept of humanity, Arendt gave a description of what happened to the Jews in concentration camps and what were the features that those humans lost in order to define "humanity." She claimed that humanity means plurality, spontaneity, the capacity to initiate action, and an enlarged mentality. In a section called "The Perplexities of the Rights of Man," Arendt stated that

> the declaration of the Rights of Man at the end of the eighteenth century was a turning point in history. It meant nothing more nor less than that from then on Man, and not God's command or the customs of history, should be the source of Law. Independent of the privileges which history had bestowed upon certain strata of society, certain nations, the declaration indicated man's emancipation from all tutelage and announced that he had now come of age. Beyond this, there was another implication of which the framers of the declaration were only half aware. The proclamation of human rights was also meant to be a much-needed protection in the new era where individuals were no longer secure in the estates to which they were born or sure of their equality before God as Christians. . . . Therefore, throughout the nineteenth century, the consensus of opinion was that human rights had to be invoked whenever individuals needed protection against the new sovereignty of the state and the new arbitrariness of society.[25]

Arendt also wrote in "Ideology and Terror: A Novel Form of Government" that the methods that blame the historical disappearance of humanity (becoming superfluous) on totalitarian terror were inaugurated with the creation of concentration camps—places where people were taken away from society.[26] By individually describing every step by which terror was used to erode the capacity to react, to move, and to act, Arendt found that "dignity" and, with it, all traces of our common humanity were erased. Dana Villa understands Arendt's work as a new kind of moral awareness, saying that she "wants us to take in—slowly, painfully, miserably—not merely man's inhumanity to man, but the fact that psyche, character, and the moral life were all largely destroyed by the camps"—thus leaving humans without any moral trace in which to give any meaning to their actions. Furthermore, Arendt was seeking a description that allowed us to comprehend that human power can transform people into animals. Indeed, the experiences that took place inside concentration camps revealed the appearance of a new kind of "perverted animal,"[27] one that lacked a capacity to morally react. Thus, Arendt's legacy of defending the term "humanity" as a normative category played an important role in linking historical experiences to moral lessons. Though Arendt's efforts gave us useful insight into the meaning of the word "humanity" in the political and moral context by which we appraise historical experience, she did not succeed in differentiating the moral content of the term "humanity" in connection with the idea of human rights as the world's response to the moral collapse during the Holocaust and as positive law within the normative territory of democratic institutions. She did, however, connect the idea of human rights to a global order when she described the confusion caused when the Jews became "stateless" persons. In fact, Arendt claimed that the ingredient missing from our normative views in the first declarations of the rights of man was the idea that protection beyond the protection of the nation-state is necessary. This is because people can easily create nondemocratic laws and become murderers to our compatriots, just like the Nüremberg racial laws of 1935 reversed the German process of social inclusion. Thus, between the notion of "humanity" and the defense of "human rights," we needed the mediation of positive democratic law—that is, the positivization of human rights as a basic legal concept regardless of an individual's citizenship. As Jean Cohen has correctly argued,[28] one can defend stateless persons only through the positive globalization and enforcement of human rights and with policies and agreements implemented by international institutions. Cohen also suggests that "by institutionalizing new connections and relations, by articulating international codes, especially if these are protected by independent supranational courts to whom individuals could appeal, international law has a key role to play in a wide range of domains."[29] In short, law at an international level would play a role parallel to that of the nation-state when rights were first part of the constitutions of democratic nations. Yet to make this a realistic possibility, one must first focus on the way in which subjects see themselves involved in the positivization of a democratic rule of law by protecting human rights. In order to accomplish this successfully, however, we—the subjects of a global order who create and obey the laws needed for a world constitution—must reflect ourselves in its very creation. What we need now is to focus on the need to exert pressure on the already "changing consciousness of citizens" to see "globalization" as an important process for democratizing the world as well as on its impact on all domestic and international affairs. Citizens of the world today must understand that when they perceive themselves as global subjects, they become members of a global community that leaves them no choice but to cooperate and compromise.

Only through the efforts of the international civil society that took the Nüremberg trials as its scenario for public debate was it possible to launch a remarkable worldwide movement for human rights that was founded in the rule of law. This movement also inspired the development of the United Nations and the creation of nongovernmental organizations (NGOs) around the world and encouraged national trials in response to human rights violations. These, in turn, formulated rules about human entitlement that circulate in local, national, and international settings. These new participants in international civil society were the NGOs.[30] The year 1945 became a turning point that led to new alternatives in the pursuit of positivization of human rights with a broader scope than the one originally offered when the nation-state was created. As Martha Minow has argued, "Especially when framed in terms of universality, the language of human rights and the vision of trials following their violation equip people to call for accountability even where it is not achievable."[31] The aftermath of World War II created a public arena in which new crimes were identified and discussed. A few practical measures were then implemented in response to the morally significant experiences of the twentieth century—events that we call now "the Holocaust" or "Shoah"—as well as to the totalitarian regimes that ignored basic understandings about our normative ideas with regard to humanity.[32] Unfortunately, the international community had to wait decades before a significant advancement in setting norms became possible.

The open debate about the moral debacle caused by the Nazi regime led to a reconsideration of our understanding of the connection between morality and law. William Korey suggests that "it was the NGOs who would take on the challenge of transforming the words of the Declaration from a standard into reality; it was they who would assume the function of implementing the demands of international morality."[33] The impact of international civil society and its influence in creating a global setting for human rights can be seen clearly when we consider the available data.[34] After 1945, the NGOs were few and held the responsibility for symbolic tasks that were consultative in nature. Approximately twenty years later, in 1968, the total number of NGOs reached 500; then, twenty-five years later, in 1992, that figure grew to 1,000 groups. Thus, the international civil society that the NGOs appeared to represent played a decisive role in transforming the phase from an article of declaration "into a critical element of foreign policy discussions in and out of governmental or intergovernmental circles."[35] At first, NGOs held the responsibility of fact-finding and setting standards. Later, they became a type of ombudsman that could intervene on behalf of the oppressed. And finally, they participated in the creation of various agencies and institutions. In this way, international civil society allowed us to create international law.

LEARNING FROM THE PAST: RETROACTIVE JUSTICE, A NECESSARY INGREDIENT IN THE BUILDING OF DEMOCRACIES

The traumatic experiences of the twentieth century, particularly after 1945, have clarified some of the problems related to our initial understanding of human rights and of the political institutions needed to support the policies that protect them. One of the first lessons was that only those countries with no democratic institutions have participated in the commission of fratricidal crimes. Two mechanisms, therefore, are clearly essential to aid those in need of protection. First, we need democratic institutions both inside and outside of nation-states. Second, some form of international law must address the political aims of nations and limit, by means of some authoritative coercion, their power in the event that they violate human rights. Until now, however, even our weakest global institutions have shown limitations in dealing with these issues. A public forum of nations would allow the promulgation of such violations and open new forums in which to recognize and defend the claims of the dispossessed.[36] These forums are not simply a normative condition but, rather, seem today to be empirically possible if we examine the recent events of our times.[37]

Carlos Nino[38] maintains that "retroactive justice"—which is a necessary step that connects the phases of helping countries become democratic with making them begin the process by redressing their past—presents a variety of difficulties. The transition a country can make from having an authoritarian regime to adopting a democratic one creates a conflict of interests. On the one hand, a peaceful transition into democratic order is secured by entering into many political agreements with various groups, often including the leaders of the authoritarian dictatorships. On the other hand, it is impossible to define democratic processes without acknowledging the crimes that violated those very human rights that now should be at the basis of their constitutions. Such is the case with many countries in Latin America, Africa, and Asia. Often, their transitions into democracy required the granting of amnesty and pardons to murderers who still felt justified in the commission of their crimes. A third issue that concerns the legal and moral spheres relates to the "diffusion of responsibility." It is impossible to commit massive human rights violations without the acquiescence of a great many people.[39] How, then, do countries that are negotiating democracy judge their past leaders and the people who helped them commit their crimes? Furthermore, how does a legal system prosecute criminals who were protected by their own authoritarian laws and who pressed for further amnesties?

These question are not easily answered. As Ruti Teitel has argued, "Transitions are vivid instances of conscious historical production."[40] There is, however, a positive view of past experiences that can help us clarify some possible solutions. It is important to focus on the fact that if such crimes occur only in authoritarian or totalitarian regimes, the most important political response to mass violence is to change the political structure. Because they can occur wherever there is no democracy, Carlos Nino believes it is important to develop a theory of "retroactive justice" for cases of large-scale human rights violations. By implementing a political process of "retroactive justice," Nino argues, we can help societies protect democratic values and stress the moral learning process of disclosing the accountability of a crime. "An aggressive use of the criminal laws," he writes, "will counteract a tendency toward unlawfulness, negate the impression that some groups are above the law, and consolidate the rule of law." In order to restore or build a democracy, "some degree of investigation and prosecution of massive human rights violations is necessary for consolidating democratic regimes."[41] Because it "plays a pivotal role in shaping social memory,"[42] the law is vital for the expansion of other democratic institutions. Retroactive justice is also a key to opening public spaces for many different democratic tasks. Just as Martha Minow has written,

> Potential responses to collective violence include not only prosecutions and amnesties, but also commissions of inquiry into the facts; opening access to secret police files; removing prior political and military officials and civil servants from their posts and from the roles for public benefits; publicizing names of offenders and names of victims; securing reparations and apologies for victims; devising and making available appropriate therapeutic services for any affected by the horrors; devising art and memorials to mark what happened, to honor victims, and to communicate the aspirations of "never again"; and advancing public educational programs to convey what happened and to strengthen participatory democracy and human rights.[43]

Therefore, in shaping the future of a country that aims to build up democratic institutions, it is the framework of the law, the language, and the procedures and vocabularies of justice that become key.[44]

Even throughout the past century, however, silence and impunity have been the norm rather than the exception. The tendency to forgive or forget such crimes has always been related to the threat that earlier regimes will interrupt the transition with a military coup. These societies face a double-edged sword. On the one hand, they must become democratic societies regulated by the rule of law and come to terms with their past. On the other hand, they are forced to issue legal pardons and amnesties and remain silent. Instead of redressing their past, they foster impunity and oblivion. Thus, countries such as Argentina, Brazil, Chile, and Uruguay have been forced to create the most bizarre laws of forgiveness and impunity. We need a law of global citizens, for only such laws can protect individuals from state arbitrariness. A rule of international law will succeed only if it can penetrate the sovereignty of states and prosecute individuals (functionaries) for crimes they committed within their political and military service.

The evident collision of state interests and juridical initiatives must be considered here. State sovereignty will hardly allow the further development of individual accountability beyond the nation's scope. Thus, it is important to seek ways in which accountability can be coordinated through the strengthening of legality throughout countries. Clearly, only with the help of an international legal system and of public figures such as judge Baltasar Garzón, who has played such an important role as a guiding member of the "strong public,"[45] can we expect to successfully prosecute criminals such as Pinochet. His case was not solved by a legal course of action, as international civil society expected, but Pinochet's return to his country created the possibility for Chilean civil society to reassume the task of redressing its past. As the debate is now opened and newspapers have shown a growing interest in these issues over the past few years, it is not impossible to see that Kant's "global order" is not merely a utopian ideal but a needed new normative framework in which to consider globalizing democracy.

NOTES

1. A term used recently by former Mexican President Ernesto Zedillo to label those who oppose globalization as imperialist forces of domination.

2. Leftist Mexican newspapers immediately responded to Zedillo's use of the term by creating its opposite to describe those who place globalization at the center of neoliberalism.

3. James Bohman and Matthias Lutz-Bachman argue that "'perpetual peace' means that human beings can solve the problem of violence for a second time and emerge from the state of nature among nations with a new form of cosmopolitan law and a 'peaceful federation among all the peoples of the earth.'" James Bohman and Matthias Lutz-Bachman, eds., *Perpetual Peace: Essays on Kant's Cosmopolitan Ideal* (Cambridge, Mass.: MIT Press, 1997), 1.

4. See, for example, David Held, *Democracy and the Global Order: From the Modern State to Cosmopolitan Governance* (Stanford, Calif.: Stanford University Press, 1995).

5. Amartya Sen, *Inequality Reexamined* (Cambridge, Mass.: Harvard University Press, 1992).

6. We have already received important information about the empirical evidence of what I claim here in the books by people who have been involved directly with international economic institutions and with the international market. See Joseph E. Stiglitz, *Globalization and Its Discontents* (New York: Norton, 2002); see also George Soros, *On Globalization* (New York: Public Affairs, 2002).

7. This claim is justified in light of Amartya Sen's research that links famines to nondemocratic governments. See Amartya Sen, *Poverty and Famines* (Oxford: Clarendon Press, 1981).

8. As John Rawls suggests, famines and other problems related to distribution of wealth and justice "are attributable to faults within political and social structure, and its failure to institute policies to remedy the effects of shortfalls in food production." John Rawls, *The Law of Peoples* (Cambridge, Mass.: Harvard University Press, 1999), 109.

9. See Sen, *Inequality Reexamined*.

10. David Held argues that "cosmopolitan democratic law could be promulgated and defended by those democratic states and civil societies that are able to muster the necessary political judgment and to learn how political practices and institutions must change and adapt in the new regional and global circumstances." Held, *Democracy and the Global Order*, 232.

11. See Ruti G. Teitel, *Transitional Justice* (Oxford: Oxford University Press, 2000).

12. In her important new research, Ruti G. Teitel claims that "social knowledge of the past is constructed through public processes. These proceedings generate a democratizing truth that helps construct a sense of societal consensus. The processes are also performative: they assume a profoundly critical and transformative aesthetic—a ritual that inverts the prior repression's knowledge policy. While impunity reigned under repressive rule and the military regimes were known for their cover-ups, by contrast, successor regimes are known for their due process. The right to a hearing, a traditional part of governmental administrative procedures, publicly affirms rights to political participation and individual dignity." Teitel, *Transitional Justice*, 82.

13. The case of Pinochet is but one example of this problem.

14. In April 2002, the new International Criminal Court was ratified by sixty-six countries. As a journalist from the *New York Times*, Barbara Crossete, argues, "The court closes a gap in international law as the first permanent tribunal dedicated to trying individuals, not nations or armies, responsible for the most horrific crimes, including genocide and crimes against humanity." See Barbara Crossette, "War Crimes Tribunal Becomes Reality, without U.S. Role," *New York Times*, April 12, 2002.

15. As Teitel has well argued, "Twentieth-century successor justice further reconstructed the individual's relation to the state: thus, the postwar Nuremberg trial's generative principle of individual responsibility emphasized the role of the individual as

subject of a sovereign international law. . . . In the contemporary transitional phenomena, the postwar democratic vision is now in the process of being superceded by more complex and fluid understandings of sovereignty and responsibility that mediate the individual and the collective, national and international orders." Teitel, *Transitional Justice*, 226.

16. Teitel, *Transitional Justice*, 226.

17. Axel Honneth, "Is Universalism a Moral Trap? The Presuppositions and Limits of a Politics of Human Rights," in Bohman and Lutz-Bachman, *Perpetual Peace*, 155–78, 155–56.

18. Jürgen Habermas, "Kant's Idea of Perpetual Peace, with the Benefit of Two Hundred Years' Hindsight," in Bohman and Lutz-Bachman, *Perpetual Peace*, 113–54.

19. Habermas, "Kant's Idea of Perpetual Peace," 137.

20. Habermas clarifies this idea by explaining that "the model of constitution making is understood in such a way that human rights are not pre-given moral truths to be discovered but rather are constructions. Unlike moral rights, it is rather clear that legal rights must not remain politically non-binding. As individual, or 'subjective,' rights, human rights have inherently juridical nature and are conceptually oriented toward positive enactment by legislative bodies." Jürgen Habermas, "Remarks on Legitimation through Human Rights," *Philosophy and Social Criticism* 24, no. 2/3 (1998): 157–71, 164.

21. Habermas clarifies that "it is constitutive to the meaning of human rights that, according to their status as basic rights, they belong within a framework of some existing legal order, whether it be national, international, or global, in which they can be protected. The mistake of conflating them with moral rights results from their peculiar nature: apart from their universal validity *claims*, these rights have had an unambiguously positive form only within the national legal order of the democratic state. Moreover, they possess only weak validity in international law, and they await internationalization within the framework of a cosmopolitan order which is only now emerging." Habermas, "Kant's Idea of Perpetual Peace," 140.

22. Many theorists consider the idea and value of human rights not as enough to display a strong conception of democratic justice. However, I urge those theorists to observe the importance that the ideals of human rights have had in emergent civil societies and their tasks according to them. For countries that have enjoyed strong democratic institutions, there is no originality in stressing the need of this connection, but it is the most important connection for countries that aim at succeeding in the process of becoming democratic.

23. Carl Schmitt, *The Concept of the Political,* trans. G. Schwab (Chicago: University of Chicago Press, 1996), 54.

24. I am using not Derrida's conception of deconstruction but rather an ordinary sense of what deconstruction means, namely, the possibility of understanding the different semantical meanings that configured a term.

25. Hannah Arendt, *The Origins of Totalitarianism* (New York: Harcourt Brace Jovanovich, 1975), 291.

26. Dana Villa explains that "the horror of totalitarianism, its 'radical evil,' is the creation and treatment of masses of human beings as superfluous, then it presents us with a new danger to the human status, one which darkens our moral horizon." See Dana R. Villa, *Politics, Philosophy, Terror: Essays on the Thought of Hannah Arendt* (Princeton, N.J.: Princeton University Press, 1999), 15.

27. Villa, *Politics, Philosophy, Terror*, 21.

28. See Jean L. Cohen, "Rights, Citizenship, and the Modern Form of the Social: Dilemmas of Arendtian Republicanism," *Constellations* 3, no. 2 (1996): 164–89.

29. Cohen, "Rights, Citizenship, and the Modern Form of the Social," 177.

30. See Jeffrey C. Alexander, "From War Crime to Holocaust Trauma: Progressive and Tragic Narrations of the Nazis' Mass Murder of the Jews," in *Cultural Trauma*, ed. Jeffrey C. Alexander and Neil Smelzer (Berkeley: University of California Press, in press).

31. Martha Minow, *Between Vengeance and Forgiveness: Facing History after Genocide and Mass Violence* (Boston: Beacon Press, 1998), 48.

32. Jonathan Glover has written a book that attempts to connect the idea of humanity to the moral history of the twentieth century. See Jonathan Glover, *Humanity: A Moral History of the Twentieth Century* (London: Jonathan Cape, 1999).

33. William Korey, *NGOs and the Universal Declaration of Human Rights* (New York: St. Martin's Press, 1998), 2

34. Korey, *NGOs and the Universal Declaration of Human Rights*.

35. Korey, *NGOs and the Universal Declaration of Human Rights*, 3.

36. Iris Marion Young suggests that we should consider the United Nations an institution for the promotion of global justice: "Although the General Assembly imperfectly represents the diverse peoples of the world, it is the only institution that in principle represents nearly all the world's people. . . . The United Nations has also sometimes served as an instrument for principled co-operation among states to confront domination or promote well-being." Iris Marion Young, *Inclusion and Democracy* (Oxford: Oxford University Press, 2000), 272.

37. Teitel argues that "these legal developments coincide with an increase in theorizing about the increasingly dense obligations of humanitarian intervention, again raising ultimate questions about moral and legal responsibility for atrocities. Whether this is a case of law shaping history or of history shaping law, what is evident is the overall dynamic—that juridical and historical understanding have moved in similar directions over time." Teitel, *Transitional Justice*, 75.

38. Carlos Santiago Nino, *Radical Evil on Trial* (New Haven, Conn.: Yale University Press, 1996).

39. See Marguerite Feitlowitz, *A Lexicon of Terror: Argentina and the Legacies of Torture* (New York: Oxford University Press, 1998), and Martha K. Huggins, Mika Haritos-Fatouros, and Philip G. Zimbardo, *Violence Workers: Police Torturers and Murderers Reconstruct Brazilian Atrocities* (Berkeley: University of California Press, 2004).

40. Teitel, *Transitional Justice*, 70.

41. Teitel, *Transitional Justice*, x.

42. Teitel, *Transitional Justice*, 71.

43. Minow, *Between Vengeance and Forgiveness*, 23.

44. It is precisely this connection between "human rights" as ideals and as positive law with democratic transitions that has inspired most of the important democratic transitions of the late twentieth century.

45. I am using here Nancy Fraser's terminology to describe those members of the judicial system that configure and make laws. See Nancy Fraser, "Rethinking the Public Sphere," in *Justice Interruptus*, 69–98 (New York: Routledge, 1998).

6

The Transnational University and the Global Public Sphere

Peter Uwe Hohendahl

This chapter examines the role and function of the advanced research university against the backdrop of a globalized public sphere. For this purpose, I propose to introduce a new notion, namely, the concept of a transnational university, a concept that is presently not a familiar one. It is needed, I believe, to define more recent developments in higher education that can no longer be discussed within a national paradigm.[1] In other words, it is an attempt to distinguish the advanced research university from an older model of the university that was closely linked to the nation-state. From a different perspective, Bill Readings has tried to determine the nature of these recent transformations by calling the new university a "university of excellence," but the purpose of his analysis is different from mine since his primary interest is the formalization of education through the loss of the cultural referent and its consequences for the curriculum and the methodology of teaching.[2] My own interest, however, is focused on the relationship between the university and the public sphere. The question that I want to address is, What happens to the idea and the practice of the research university when the public sphere has openly transcended national borders and reflects global concerns? Put differently, what happens to the university when it has to define its mission in transnational terms? I argue that this relatively new situation has changed the way the university looks at and assesses its resources as well as its achievements. It can no longer be satisfied with the task of serving the nation. Instead, it develops a global map for its mission and negotiates its role within a broader international public sphere. This transition entails not only new opportunities but also new and different responsibilities that could possibly conflict with the idea of a traditional, national university.

The idea of a transnational university does not yet have a positive content; it can only be derived negatively from the idea of a national university. Therefore, my analysis will start with the traditional link between the nation-state and the university. This relationship can be defined in a variety of ways, such as administrative and financial links in the modern German university; however, they are neither exhaustive nor exclusive. The private American research university of the twentieth century was also defined in national terms, although the state had no direct administrative power over its governance and only a very limited responsibility for its operation. The relationship between the university and the nation-state, which began in the early nineteenth century, was defined along three different but interconnected axes: 1) the training of students for advanced positions in the state bureaucracy or the civil society (professionals); 2) the production of advanced knowledge through research that would, directly or indirectly, serve the national community; and 3) the development of an ethos of self-cultivation and intellectual identity formation for which the German idealists introduced the term *Bildung*.[3] They held the practice of exclusive training in a specialized discipline, such as law or medicine, in low esteem since it was oriented primarily toward practical goals without raising the intellectual self-consciousness of the student. It was Fichte in particular who connected the goal of higher education with the larger task of nation building and thereby forged a strong link between university and nation outside the mundane task of training civil servants.[4] In America, the general liberal education and professional training were differentiated when the traditional college was supplemented with professional schools and the graduate school for the specific purpose of training future members of the academy.[5] While German university reformers considered these two dimensions to be integrated, they were institutionally separated in the American reform of the late nineteenth century.

As noted, the paradigm of the national university cannot simply be reduced to the state university or the question of funding by agencies of the state. Rather, it is more important to consider the national university in terms of its complete integration into the intellectual life of the nation. Put differently, the national model defines itself vis-à-vis a national public sphere, both in cultural and in political terms. For this reason, the most radical of the German reformers rejected the old university that had supplied the state with competent civil servants. Instead, they wanted the university's commitment to the nation to come from epistemological and moral principles that in turn guided the actual organization of the new university.[6] In their view, the students are perceived as academic citizens whose education is related not only to the needs of the state (administration) but also to the needs of the civil society. Martha Nussbaum's recent proposal to reinvigorate the American undergraduate curriculum clearly invokes the idea of the education of citizens, and although she is quite critical of older definitions of the national community, she reconnects her project to the political nation that is, however, defined in multicultural terms.[7] The *Bildung* of citizens rather than utilitarian knowledge is at the center of her project.

While the discourse of the early and mid-nineteenth century focused on the ethos of the university (both in Germany and in England), the research university of the late nineteenth and twentieth centuries placed greater emphasis on the link between the production of empirical knowledge and the economic and social gains of the national community.[8] The organization of research at the university became a national project where advanced knowledge would be transformed into useful technology.[9] Around 1900, the nationalization of research took on the form of a competition between Western nations that was clearly reflected in the public discourse. It redefined the function of the research university as an integral part of a larger economic and political as well as military project that responds to vital needs of the nation-state.[10]

Here we can observe a shift in the structure of the national model of the university. During the twentieth century, the research university functioned as an instrument of the nation-state in different ways. While it continues to proclaim its autonomy vis-à-vis the state, it is realized only under specific circumstances (during times of peace) and in particular areas of knowledge.[11] The turning point appears to be World War I, when the war effort impacted the university in significant ways—not only in Germany but also in the United States.[12] Now it is the armed nation-state that shapes the mission of the university in terms of military strategy. The radical refunctioning of the university denied the traditional autonomy of the institution and thereby served as an index for the essential elements that had to be guaranteed by civil society. It is the extreme stress of war that brings to the fore the role of the public sphere for the moral and epistemological legitimization of the university. I will return to this issue later.

Before I examine the role of the classical university in the national public sphere, I have to address a number of empirical issues that are relevant for the assessment of the modern national university. They concern 1) the composition of the faculty and the student body, 2) the development of the curriculum, and 3) the question of funding. In his analysis of the development of the German university, Peter Moraw has rightly emphasized the fundamental transformation of the German university during the nineteenth century.[13] It is a transition from regional universities founded and supported by regional princes (*Landesherren*) to institutions with national aspirations, even when the support structure does not significantly change. Furthermore, Moraw has demonstrated that faculty recruitment changed after 1810. Local and regional recruitment based on social networks was increasingly replaced by national recruitment based on expertise in specific scientific fields. Specifically, the development of specialized disciplines and the trend toward national recruitment went hand in hand. The struggle of a research university for excellence encouraged the development of national standards with respect to recruitment. Similarly, the emergence of research universities in the United States required a different type of faculty, namely, researchers who made their mark in a special discipline. While the older college assessed its faculty primarily in terms of teaching, the new research university stressed qualifications in research.[14] This shift consequently impacted the recruitment policy. Local and regional recruitment patterns gave way to national searches and, if necessary, international appointments. Given the initial lack of training opportunities in America, universities looked for talent in Europe if they could not find it at home. In the foreign languages, for instance, it was and still is quite common to appoint foreign nationals. The fact that according to European standards the American research university is a latecomer, encouraged from the beginning a broadening of recruitment patterns beyond national borders and thereby prepared the way for the internationalization of the faculty in the late twentieth century.

The trend toward nationalization can also be observed in the composition of the student body. While student migration was common in the seventeenth and eighteenth centuries, Germany's regional universities served primarily students from the same region. It was in the interest of the prince to keep the *Landeskinder* at the university that he funded and controlled. Questions concerning religious affiliation, of course, played an important role. Since many students were preparing themselves for employment in the civil service, they had to prove their qualifications and their loyalty to the regional bureaucracy by attending regional universities. These patterns continued to play a role in the nineteenth and early twentieth centuries. At the same time, however, one can discern a growing nationalization of the student body, especially at the leading research universities, such as Berlin, Bonn, and Breslau.[15] The outstanding quality of their faculty also attracted students from other parts of Germany. Similarly, the composition of the student body of all major American research universities reflected the move away from regional recruitment. Admissions policies carefully consider the geographic composition as an important factor among others. However, there is a notable difference between state and private schools. The mandate of state schools privileges the admission of in-state students, a fact that decisively influences the composition of the student body. Here, as in the German case, regional and national concerns compete with each other. But when it comes to the recruitment of graduate students, local and regional criteria do not play a major role since the state university expects to be measured by the same criteria of excellence as the private schools.

While the development of a national faculty and a national student body are fairly obvious, the evolution of a national curriculum is more difficult to demonstrate. There are two reasons. First, curriculum decisions were mostly left to the faculty of the individual university and therefore were less exposed to outside pressure; second, they were increasingly dictated by the research of the individual disciplines that came out of particular universities. At the same time, however, there were also strong forces that supported national standardization. The formation of scientific disciplines and the ensuing development of research agendas within specific scientific communities transcended the local and regional arena—consequently, the curriculum moved toward national standards. This is true not only for the natural sciences but also for the humanities.[16] The ongoing scientific dialogue enhanced the nationalization of the curriculum. American graduate schools around the turn of the century, for instance, were clearly engaged in building competitive disciplinary programs with standardized curricula that would allow the young PhD to compete in a national market.[17] The resistance to this trend came, as Gerald Graff has shown, from the undergraduate college that was teaching oriented and highly suspicious of specialization.[18] But even in this arena of undergraduate teaching where questions of values and moral norms were considered more important, the preoccupation with local and regional concerns was replaced with larger agendas. The radical revamping of Harvard's undergraduate program by president Charles William Eliot in the 1870s, although initially a local issue, also changed the mission of the American college. The introduction of electives that gave students more freedom transformed the ethos of the college by breaking down the fairly rigid curriculum of the older college. Of course, Eliot's reforms did not make an immediate national impact, but by the turn of the century they were widely accepted as a significant improvement.[19] One should note that it was not a federal bureaucracy that introduced this transformation from above; rather, the successful reforms were the result of intensive debates in the public sphere. These discussions centered around fundamental questions of *Bildung*, that is, questions of self-realization and self-formation. Hence, in the long run, the idea of undergraduate education emerged as a national project and converged with the idea of a research university based on a national scientific community. In the German case, this convergence occurred already in the early nineteenth century in Humboldt's and his coreformers' idea that a university begins with an integrative concept of critical knowledge (philosophy) that precedes more specialized disciplinary knowledge. Ideally, therefore, the university is a *universal* institution that must look for the broadest organizational foundations available. For these reformers, the emerging modern nation-state was the best solution. (It is noteworthy that Schelling's lectures *On University Studies* of 1802 remain so detached from any practical considerations that they did not even mention the state as the possible engine of reform.)

As soon as the German reformers began to focus on the material side of their ideas, they looked to the state for help, which meant that they rejected strictly local arrangements (cities) or other institutions (church). The notion of private universities based on donations remained beyond their horizon. In Germany, the idea of a national university was and has remained until today clearly linked to the state through its funding and administrative supervision. This integration into the bureaucracy of the state (financial dependence, civil servant status of the faculty) defined the limits of the university's autonomy. Given the scale of the growing financial needs of the new research university in the nineteenth century, the state was better suited than any other institution to provide the necessary funds.[20] However, the development of the American research university in the twentieth century demonstrates that different patterns were possible and ultimately even more successful. In other words, it proved that the national mission of the university does not depend on state funding. It can be defined in terms of the public service of a private school under the leadership of a president who monitors and guides the curriculum and especially the direction of research. Still, ongoing involvement with the federal bureaucracy is part of this process, at least since the mid-twentieth century. The national mission of the American research university, its commitment to public service, was, to a greater extent, the result of its exposure to and participation in the national public sphere. This also applies to state universities.

Yet this exposure and participation deserves closer scrutiny. To what extent can we talk about the formation of national standards through the public sphere? While the reform of the Prussian university system was carried out by Wilhelm von Humboldt and his successors as a high-ranking administrator (*Sektionsleiter*), one must remember that the actual reorganization was preceded by almost a decade of public discussions spearheaded by the leading intellectuals of the time, beginning with Kant's late essay *The Conflict of the Faculties* (1798).[21] Humboldt's proposals could draw on numerous suggestions and recommendations, among them Friedrich Schleiermacher's *Occasional Thoughts on Universities in the German Sense* (1808). It is crucial to note that the general direction of this discussion tended toward a definition of the university as a national mission, specifically the revival of the nation. The public addressed in the writings of the reformers is not limited to university faculty and state administrators. It is a broader audience for whom the defeat of Prussia and Austria and the occupation of parts of Germany by

French troops demand a cultural and political response. For this reason, Fichte's *Addresses to the German Nation* of 1808 turn to issues of education as vital elements of nation building. Only through a completely new system of education, Fichte maintains, can the German nation be saved. Pedagogical and moral measures that can be communicated within the public sphere, not political and military ones, will overcome the loss of autonomy.

Therefore, the relationship between the public sphere and the idea of the university (understood as a norm) becomes crucially important around 1800. There are two dimensions that must be distinguished. On the one hand, the university as an institution of the state faces the public sphere of the private citizens who are discussing the decisions and actions of the state in terms of their rationality and legality. This critique could be applied to the existing university as well—its organization, its effectiveness, and its ethos. This is precisely the arena of the university reformers. Their critique of the contemporary university refers back to the concept of reason in order to develop an entirely new institution for which even a new name (*Akademie*) might be necessary. This critique is launched, so to speak, from the outside and has to be distinguished from a critique from within. It is the second form in which university and public sphere are related. The university contains its own, specifically academic, public sphere in which faculty and students take part. Kant's *Conflict of the Faculties* postulates such an internal public sphere insofar as the philosophical faculty is assigned the task of monitoring and criticizing the upper faculties (theology, law, and medicine). Yet this internal academic public sphere, although it is located within a particular university, is by no means merely local. Through the medium of print, it becomes national and links up with the general public sphere that faces the university from without. Still, their discourses are not identical. Whereas the internal public sphere examines and challenges the concept of *Wissenschaft*, that is, the scientific production and mediation of knowledge, the external public sphere investigates the function of the university as an institution with respect to the national community. Around 1800, this discourse fundamentally challenged the older regional university as outdated and ineffective for the idea of a nation.

It is important to note that the liberal concept of the public sphere, as it was developed in the second half of the eighteenth century and then reinforced in the nineteenth century,[22] is essential for the emergence of the modern national university. Although the modern European university remains connected to the state, it participates in the development of constitutional freedom. It claims, as part of its public status and mission, freedom of speech, freedom of opinion through print, and freedom of meeting (*Versammlungsfreiheit*). In fact, the university becomes a vital instrument for the development of freedom since the ideal concept of science (*Begriff der*

Wissenschaft) has been deduced from reason. Through the internal public sphere and the production of knowledge at the university, the critical debate advances in the general public sphere. In other words, for the reformers, the university was a critical instrument for political education (*Bildung*)—not in the sense of training for specific political activities but in the sense of creating an ethos of addressing political problems. For the realization of this goal, academic freedom was indispensable. So it is not accidental that both in nineteenth-century Germany and in twentieth-century America, the definition and defense of academic freedom became a critical issue.[23]

I

The concept of a critical public sphere entails universal claims that could rarely be materialized in the nineteenth and twentieth centuries.[24] Its institutional form was largely the civil society of the nation-state. The model of the national university reinforced this structure. On the one hand, it transcended the regional origin of the university; on the other, it was tied to the nation-state through the composition of its faculty and students as well as the conception of scientific research. At the same time, we have to note that this structure was based on a compromise. Both the universal claims of a critical academic public sphere and the conception of research as a methodological production of knowledge potentially challenge the institution of the national university. In particular, the emergence of disciplines that develop theories and methodologies for research cannot be contained within national boundaries. Even the humanities, already in the nineteenth century, underwent transnational configurations (positivism in literary criticism was by all means a European phenomenon). Institutionally, the national university dealt with these elements by experiencing and defining them in terms of competition with other nations. In some areas, such as the natural sciences, this situation, especially when the political stakes were high, attracted the attention of the state. In these cases, the emergence of an international research community was checked and possibly controlled by state agencies that also undermined the autonomy of the university. Research for the military follows different standards; it is, for example, not open to public scrutiny.

During the late twentieth century, it became increasingly difficult to maintain the pure model of the national university. The reasons for the breakdown are manifold. In most general terms, one must acknowledge that both the classical nation-state and the research university have been challenged and put under stress. As a result, they no longer converge as easily as they did in the nineteenth and early twentieth centuries. Not only in America but also in

Europe, the state has decreased its commitments to the university and encouraged reconfigurations so that the university has a different place and different function within the social system. I believe that this marks the emergence of a new type of academic institution, the transnational university. At this point, it can already be described as an ideal type, although there is possibly not a single university that fulfills all the criteria. I believe that the emergence of a globalized public sphere is an important, supportive element but not a cause. Rather, globalization is a more suitable environment for the success of a transnational university that can no longer automatically rely on the state and faces economic conditions that demand significant repositioning. Leading research universities, mostly located in the United States, have found themselves increasingly as part of a transnational grid and have responded by redefining their role accordingly.

In administrative terms, the transnational university has followed the example of the corporate world.[25] As is well known, since the 1980s university administrations have been restructured according to the corporate model with its strong emphasis on efficiency and financial accountability. This restructuring of the university as an economic enterprise with a more precise calculation of its resources and a sharper definition of the desired product in the arenas of teaching and research has redefined the faculty as workers and the students as clients/customers who have to be serviced. The fiscal policy of the corporate university must seek as much autonomy as possible since the state is no longer available as a dependable partner.[26] As Bill Readings and others have observed, this shift has also changed the ethos of the university.[27] The commitment to a substantive concept of culture has decreased and been replaced by more formal standards of professionalism that can be applied across disciplines. The classical element of *Bildung* as it was cultivated by the humanities has declined significantly in value. As we have seen, cultural values were indispensable for the concept of a national university. For the corporate university, on the other hand, they are probably more of a supplement to professional training. They are seen as enriching but not essential element of the education. The symbiosis of the university and the nation-state reinforced the role of the university as both the locus of culture and its critical assessment. The corporate university, insofar as it favors professional training, shows less interest in national agendas per se. Instead, its logic leads to norms and standards that can be used in a process of international self-understanding. In other words, the model of the corporate university does not depend on the concept of the nation. While it may negotiate national values and the expectations of the state, its self-assigned mission is different. Its propensity is to move toward an international environment. The reasons for this propensity become clear when we examine its faculty and student body, its research agenda, and its funding patterns.

What differentiates leading American research universities from their European counterparts is the composition of their faculties. They are much more inclined to hire nonnationals when they are needed to fill gaps in specific disciplines. By and large, leading American universities favor scientific qualifications over national affiliation because they must compete with other universities in order to maintain their ranking. This hiring pattern has resulted in the internationalization of the faculty at major American research universities, which stands in contrast to the composition of the faculty at leading European universities that have continued to define their labor market in national terms. There may be legal reasons for this policy (senior faculty members must be citizens) or simply the impact of conventions since there is (with the exception of the United Kingdom) no explicit understanding of competition among universities.

A similar change can be observed in the composition of the student body. Especially within the past decade, the internationalization of the student body at leading American research universities has increased dramatically both at the college level and at the level of the graduate school. One can speak of a global arena for the selection of the brightest students. The imposition of restrictions for student visas after the events of 9/11 suddenly made it obvious to the public that training of foreign students has become a vital financial resource for American universities and a significant part of the American economy. Foreign students either pursue training in particular disciplines (graduate students) or seek a diploma from a prestigious American university (undergraduates). Largely, their desire to study at an American university has more to do with the acquisition of professional knowledge than culture. Hence, the tie between nationally defined cultural values and scientific studies is less important. The students are less interested in *Bildung* than preprofessional or professional training, a fact that is reflected in their choices within the university curriculum.

The curriculum of the traditional liberal arts college as well as the research university has been under pressure for the last two decades to foreground preprofessional training at the expense of humanistically oriented courses, as much as American academic institutions have resisted this tendency. Martha Nussbaum's study of curriculum development at American colleges must be understood as a report on attempts to oppose the trend toward a utilitarian concept of education.[28] Although she rightly emphasizes the importance of humanistic studies, she overlooks the source of the pressure to redefine the curriculum in utilitarian terms. We are dealing with a complex cluster of interrelated causes that cannot be eliminated by the good intentions on the part of the faculty. They range from the expectations of the parents who have to pay high tuition to the structure of the labor market and the concept of science and research. The slow but unmistakable marginalization of the humanities reflects this transformation of the American university. Both in terms of enrollment and degrees and in terms of funding, the humanities have been in state of relative decline since the 1970s.[29] The corporate university has accommodated these changes without major difficulties since it is not deeply committed to the idea of *Bildung*; instead, it treats these issues strategically. They are seen as enrollment problems. The more students are perceived as clients and consumers rather than as academic citizens, the less meaningful the link to the nation as a cultural community. The ongoing internationalization of the student body that I discussed previously will possibly reinforce this tendency.

While changes in the structure of the curriculum are meaningful indicators of long-term transformations, they are not the primary cause for the origin of the transnational university. Two factors play a crucial role, namely, the new concept of science and research and the question of financial resources, that is, the problem of funding. They are, to be sure, interrelated since the funding of advanced research, especially in the natural sciences, has determined basic policy decisions of the research university. Under the conditions of the Cold War, it was understood that the federal government would fund many major science projects ("big science"). They were, to a large extent, projects that either directly or indirectly supported American defense. The alliance between the university and the state was built on the idea of decisive national interests that were shared by both sides. The strength of this alliance gave a crucial advantage to leading American research universities in comparison with their European counterparts, where the financial resources of the state were more limited and the will to invest in university research was more restricted. As a result, we could observe a reorientation of the national university in the direction of applied science and technology.

II

The end of the Cold War affected this relationship. With the demise of the Soviet Union, the federal government decreased funding for big science. Therefore, academic research either had to cut back and think small or had to find other sources for its projects. This meant that the leading research universities had to share a larger part of the cost or else find a new partner. During the 1990s, they pursued both strategies energetically.[30] As a result of the economic boom and more generous donations, they could invest more financial resources and at the same time form alliances with private industry. Hence, the selection of research projects would be codetermined by the interests of private industry. This shift, which originally was a marginal phenomenon in limited areas of research, became, I believe, structurally significant during the 1990s. When the private sector supplanted the state as a major partner in the organization of research and the allocation of funds, the concept of a national university begins to erode, and a new type of university emerges, the transnational university.

One can also look at this process from the perspective of the conception and organization of research, not only in the natural sciences but also to a lesser extent in the humanities and the social sciences. The theoretical work and the development of methodologies have become more international. The flow of ideas and theories from one country to another has increased and accelerated to an extent that the notion of a national science has lost its validity. Even in the humanities today, the community of scholars defines itself in international terms and is by no means restricted to Western countries. However, a closer look reveals that this global network is not evenly spread. Its nodal points are major research universities or academies that dominate the communication. Although their majority is located in the United States, they do not function any longer as purely national institutions. They have learned to operate in a globalized environment with respect to their faculty and student body, their research policies, and their funding. Specifically, they have realized that they cannot count on the state for their financial needs. This has given private universities with large endowments and efficient development offices the advantage over state schools. It is also the reason why countries with a long tradition of exclusive state funding, such as France and Germany, have fallen behind. They find it difficult to adjust to an environment dominated by international corporations with agendas that transcend the nation-state. They still define their position primarily vis-à-vis the state on the one hand and a national public sphere on the other. It is only very recently that the European debate has moved beyond this parameter when private foundations began to discuss the need for and viability of private universities. It is noteworthy that Jürgen Habermas's 1989 essay "The Idea of the University: Learning Processes" focuses exclusively on the idea of a national university that develops its critical potential in a dialog with a nationally conceived public sphere.[31] Although he distances himself from the idealism of traditional German definitions of the university ("organizations no longer embody ideas," 102) and moves away from his radical democratic program of the 1960s, he basically holds on to a national model of the university and defends its critical potential against functionalist interpretations of the university. He situates the university at the intersection of the social system and the life-world and insists on the importance of general education, that is, *Bildung*, as part of the university's mission. In other words, he insists that there must be communication between the university and the public sphere: "The process of acquiring scientific knowledge is intertwined not only with technical development and preparation for the academic profession but also with general education, the transmission of culture, and enlightenment in the public political sphere."[32] Although Habermas remains wedded to a national frame, this link is less important for his analysis. Drawing on Talcott Parsons, he distinguishes four functions of the university, namely, 1) research and scientific training, 2) academic preparation for the profession, 3) general education, and 4) contributions to cultural self-understanding, as separate but equally important for the concept of the university.[33] Only the final section of the essay moves in the direction of a universal concept of the university by keeping the level of abstraction high. This strategy avoids most empirical questions of existing historical and cultural differences. While Habermas begins with a national model, ultimately this constellation fades away and opens a generalized perspective. Yet it is not clear whether he talks about a transnational university since neither economic nor geographic issues enter his discussion. This is not altogether surprising since the German discourse is still closely tied to a national model.[34]

III

The transnational university will continue to negotiate research contracts with the state and make its resources available to projects of national interest, but it will not want to position itself in such a way that it will depend exclusively on state funding. Instead, as the 1990s have clearly shown, it will choose a strategy where the risk is carefully balanced. Both government agencies and private industry are and will continue to be partners for the organization and funding of major research projects. The maintenance and development of big science in particular will require a higher degree of flexibility.[35] For this reason, fund-raising campaigns play an increasingly central role. In its practical institutional existence, the transnational research university defines its loyalty as a commitment to its own strength and a responsibility to its own international or even global agenda. As I will discuss later, this shift contains the need for new and different ethical commitments on the part of the university. The fact that the nation and the nation-state are no longer the ultimate horizon for the university also changes its mission or idea.[36] In general terms, the transnational university has to legitimize its position in the context of an international and globalized public sphere. This means that we have to reexamine the relationship between the university and the public sphere or, more properly, various competing public spheres.

The modern national university was conceived in the early nineteenth century vis-à-vis an emerging national public sphere that was determined largely by the interests of the bourgeoisie and provided the concepts of rational critique and *Bildung* as its ideal model of self-regulation; its transnational variant faces a more complex structure that defies an easy synthesis.[37] When we call this public sphere international or global, we must realize that these terms cover a host of phenomena that do not readily fit together.[38] To some extent, this new public sphere continues to propagate elements of the classical liberal public sphere; in other respects, however, it aligns itself with social and political interests that are incompatible with liberal ideas. The mass public of the late nineteenth century already undermined the idea of enlightened discourse, and the existing globalized mass media of the late twentieth century are not well suited to propagate a mission of universal criticism.[39] Neither international entertainment programs nor international news services are defined primarily in critical or normative terms, although they can sometimes be used for those purposes. Moreover, this global communications network is only one layer of competing networks at the national, regional, and local levels. It is as much determined by an international market and the commodity form as older variants of the public that were at the center of the critique by the Frankfurt School during the 1940s (Adorno) and 1960s (Habermas). But in comparison with these forms, the use and function of the globalized version are even more difficult to ascertain. Its connection to the global expansion of the financial market and corporate capitalism is obvious, but the effect is more ambiguous. The political opposition to global capital has strategically and effectively used the new networks. Radical movements with very different goals (some democratic, some definitely antidemocratic) have been participating in the new globalized public sphere to pursue heterogeneous and conflicting agendas. Frequently, religious and regional ethnic identity claims have shaped their understanding of publicity. The refunctioning of the medium of television by the terrorists on 9/11 as a gruesome spectacle is only the most extreme definition of publicity within a globalized public sphere. It is important to note that the news media turned out to be willing participants and showed no restraints in the repeated display of the horrible images.

On the other hand, there is also the public sphere of international organizations, such as the United Nations or the International Court in The Hague, to consider as an important structural element. Unlike the electronic media, they play a significant albeit contested role in the composition of the globalized public sphere. Attempts at seeking lawful solutions to international political conflicts in the United Nations and looking for justice in the international court (when it cannot be found within the nation-state) continue the agenda of the older liberal public sphere on a larger scale. The normative core of these attempts is clearly indispensable for the configuration of a global public sphere. At the same time, the normative claim is also the reason why these international institutions frequently fail in the world of power politics where correct judgments and insights cannot be translated into actions because they clash with particular political or economic interests.

The university as a national institution has been affected by these recent developments, but mostly indirectly. The transnational university, however, because of its faculty and student body as well as its research agenda, would be more directly involved. Since its mission is oriented toward an international environment, the emergence of a globalized public sphere, both on the empirical and on the normative level, determines its practices more immediately. It will, among other things, enhance the trend toward corporatization that began in the 1980s. Just as major corporations have positioned themselves outside the nation-state (while still cooperating with nation-states), the transnational university is driven in the same direction and will define itself in similar terms. The latest trend of major research universities in the United States to seek out highly visible logos can be interpreted as a symbolic move to create not only national but also international visibility; it is, in other words, an attempt to impact the public sphere in the same way that a major corporation creates its global image. The transnational university wants to signal that it is open to clients and partners in other parts of the world. A small number of American research universities have been quite successful in creating a broad network of relationships, ranging from faculty- and student-exchange programs to international research projects financed either by government agencies or private capital. From the point of view of the university, it is not in its interest to focus its teaching and research activities exclusively on the interests and needs of the nation. The transnational university is committed to a cosmopolitan agenda, especially in the area of research. This tendency is most obvious in the natural sciences but also recognizable in the humanities, where today national cultural traditions clearly play a less important role than fifty years ago.[40]

IV

Ideally, the research imperative, first institutionalized by the German university of the nineteenth century, follows a universal logic. Disciplines such as mathematics and physics are driven by theoretical problems and developments that cannot be contained within national borders. But even philology, where the study of particular national traditions dominated scholarly work, was determined by transnational theoretical and methodological considerations. The more recent emergence of transnational universities has enhanced these trends. What is called "theory" in the humanities today is produced and disseminated primarily at major research universities with little regard to the interests of the national environment. The transfer of humanistic theories has become largely independent of a particular national agenda, which does not exclude the possibility that a specific theory will assume a particular ideological function in its new environment. What is more important in our context is the fact that the transnational university functions as a nodal point for an international academic network. Within this network, research is more public now than fifty years ago. As remarked earlier, the exchange of results is faster and more efficient. At the same time, we have to note that access can also be more limited to the general public of the region and the nation where the new knowledge is produced. The greater speed does not automatically translate into wider access and participation. While the model of the national university in its evolution from the nineteenth to the twentieth century moved in the direction of democratic participation, the transnational university seems to be more ambiguous in this respect. On the one hand, it opens broader transnational concerns and removes the shackles of a national ideology; on the other, it can take on elitist features, thereby widening the gap between the general mass public and its own internal communications.

The relationship of the national university and the public sphere was, as we saw, a dual one. On the one hand, the university had to negotiate its role vis-à-vis the general public sphere—both its cultural and its political side; on the other, it was committed to the creation of an internal dialogue within and between disciplines, a self-regulating critical function through which the intellectual autonomy of the university was established and maintained. The internal public sphere could be threatened by the nation-state when the latter tried to control the academic affairs of the university—therefore the strong emphasis on freedom of teaching and research as an ongoing theme of the institutional self-definition. Has the emergence of a transnational concept of the university changed the structure of this relationship? If the corporate university is the only form of the transnational university, the answer has to be affirmative since the corporate university defines itself to the outside world in terms of publicity (it offers knowledge and methods of knowledge production to its clients) and to itself in terms of efficiency. But it is not plausible to assume that the corporate university is the only form of the transnational university. It can also be conceived as an institution with a commitment to the production of knowledge that serves the common good and self-critical internal dialogue.[41] But there is a difference. The academic public sphere, that is, the critical internal dialogue, opens itself to a transnational network receiving feedback from other parts of the world. This is, as we will see, equally important for empirical problems and normative issues. This space, guaranteed by academic freedom, influences the way in which the university deals with the outside world—in the way it selects its faculty and its students, profiles and organizes its research projects, and communicates with institutions on the outside. In short, as an idea, the transnational university is compatible with the concept of a critical and self-reflective university.

V

Of course, the question arises whether the existing research university has any similarity with the idea. If we follow Bill Readings's analysis, there is no hope for the resurrection of the national university of culture or the emergence of a new type of university. Yet I believe that his assessment underestimates both the challenges and the opportunities for a transnational university. He clearly sees the dangerous path, namely, the corporatization of the university and its privatization as part of a growing service industry, but he does not examine the public and political aspects that lie beyond the boundaries of the nation-state. The transnational university can draw on older traditions but define them within a globalized context. The nineteenth-century university was, as commentators have noted, a catalyst for social change in two respects. First, through its research imperative, it supported and enhanced the production of knowledge that accelerated modernization. Second, although not yet democratic itself, the idea of an academic community devoted to the pursuit of knowledge and *Bildung* ultimately fostered the democratization of the social system. The result was the mass university of the late twentieth century. Both aspects are relevant for the idea of a transnational university. The transfer of knowledge in the specific sense of theoretical knowledge and research methodologies from advanced transnational research universities to other parts of the globe is an important tool for scientific equality and the possibility of scientific exchange.[42] We should not think of this transfer exclusively in terms of useful technology. It is equally vital for the humanities and the social sciences insofar as they develop forms of critical knowledge. In short, the transnational university can function as an engine of social and political change.

Second, the internationalization of the faculty and the student body, with an influx from all parts of the globe, opens up opportunities for democratization. Again, this is more an indirect result of an academic community devoted to critical learning and methodological research. While the transnational research university is elitist in terms of its selection process and its funding, it propagates an ethos of scientific work that is hostile to traditionalism and ideological dogmatism. As a result of its international relations and commitments, the transnational university is, I believe, in the long run, on the side of global de-mocratization. The very fact that the transnational university has distanced it-self from the nation-state and national ideologies favors processes of rethink-ing research goals and commitments in the arena of teaching. Postcolonial studies would be just one example of such reexamination.

While the idea of a transnational cosmopolitan university holds the prom-ise of transformation in a globalized context, actually existing research uni-versities are of course determined by highly complex economic and social constellations where regional and national obligations and commitments have by no means disappeared. Today they are expected to perform under difficult financial conditions that invite solutions of the kind that Readings has labeled as "the university of excellence." To put it differently, the transnational uni-versity is prone to corporatization because it can no longer count on the firm commitment of the nation-state. Therefore, it has to finance its public role in private terms. This is the reason why major American research universities have been considerably more successful in sustaining their mission than Eu-ropean state universities. They have been able to build resources that have outstripped their European counterparts.[43] At the same time, they are faced with the danger of compromise, of turning critical discourse into the service of extrinsic goals. It appears that presently this tension cannot be removed.

The idea of a transnational cosmopolitan university with a commitment to a globalized public rests in material terms on specific economic and social conditions that determine its actual opportunities. Yet these conditions do not rule out the development of an intellectual community engaged in a critical and ethically responsible definition of teaching and research. In two ways, the transnational university is challenged to overcome its present compromise. The first impact comes from the globalized public sphere. In this arena, in-ternational social and environmental movements put pressure on the concep-tion of knowledge production. University research is exposed to international criticism when its global effects are harmful to people in other parts of the world. The second challenge comes from the internal public sphere of the academy. This public sphere has clearly changed during the past two decades. Faculty and student participation in governance has decreased. Today, faculty meetings rarely produce the political energy that characterized the 1960s and 1970s. At the same time, the struggle for recognition of programs and de-partments engaged in competition with each other has ambiguous effects. While it can lead to intellectual conformity with the administration in order to receive desired funding, it can equally enhance critical innovation for the purpose of ensuring survival. Briefly stated, internal competition also rein-forces a critical self-understanding of knowledge production. The methods of advanced university management, in principle endorsed by the transnational university, seem to develop their own dialectical movement. By enforcing cost management through competition, the university must constantly challenge itself in its own struggle for public recognition.

As a consequence, the transnational university finds itself in a peculiar position. The will to preserve its independence, not only in financial but also in intellectual and political terms, implies a fundamental contradiction. In order to retain its intellectual autonomy in the arena of teaching and research, it has to insist on its financial autonomy. Yet this very move endangers its intellectual autonomy since it can be preserved only by commercializing the university through applied research. This dilemma contains, I believe, a *productive* ethical challenge for the members of the academic community. They must call into question the very material foundation on which their work is built insofar as these foundations undermine the university's freedom. At the same time, they must also question their own affirmation of autonomy and their critique as abstract. In this mode of a double critique, the transnational university permanently deconstructs itself, gaining its own momentum out of this act. Therefore, it is less stable than the national university but more flexible and adaptable.

NOTES

1. However, I do not assume that the nation-state has disappeared or lost its relevance for the definition of global politics. Rather, I want to stress the disengagement of the transnational university from the nation-state.

2. Bill Readings, *The University in Ruins* (Cambridge, Mass.: Harvard University Press, 1996).

3. Wilhelm Richter, *Der Wandel des Bildungsgedankens* (Berlin: Colloquium Verlag, 1971); Walter H. Bruford, *The German Tradition of Self-Cultivation: Bildung from Humboldt to Thomas Mann* (London: Cambridge University Press, 1975).

4. Johann Gottlieb Fichte, *Addresses to the German Nation*, trans. R. F. Jones and G. H. Turnbull, ed. George Armstrong Kelly (New York: Harper & Row, 1968).

5. See Nathan Rheingold, "Graduate School and Doctoral Degree: European Models and American Realities," in *Scientific Colonialism: A Cross-Cultural Comparison*, ed. Nathan Rheingold and Marc Rothenberg (Washington, D.C.: Smithsonian Institution Press, 1986), 129–49; James Turner and Paul Bernard, "The German Model and the Graduate School: The University of Michigan and the Origin Myth of the American University," in *The American College in the Nineteenth Century*, ed. Roger L. Geiger (Nashville: Vanderbilt University Press, 2000), 221–41; and Roger L. Geiger, "The Era of Multipurpose Colleges in American Higher Education, 1850–1890," in Geiger, *The American College in the Nineteenth Century*, 127–52.

6. See F. W. J. Schelling, *On University Studies*, trans. E. S. Morgan, ed. Norbert Guterman (Athens: Ohio University Press, 1966).

7. Martha C. Nussbaum, *Cultivating Humanity: A Classical Defense of Reform in Liberal Education* (Cambridge, Mass.: Harvard University Press, 1997).

8. See Rüdiger vom Bruch, "A Slow Farewell to Humboldt? Stages in the History of German Universities 1810–1945," in *German Universities Past and Future: Crisis or Renewal?*, ed. G Ash Mitchell (Providence, R.I.: Berghahn Books, 1997), 3–27; Rüdiger vom Bruch and Rainer A. Müller, eds., *Formen ausserstaatlicher Wissenschaftsförderung im 19. und 20. Jahrhundert: Deutschland im europäischen Vergleich* (Stuttgart: Steiner, 1990).

9. In his 1910 report *Academic and Industrial Efficiency*, sponsored by the Carnegie Foundation, Morris Cooke strongly advocated national searches for academic positions. In his opinion, this procedure would increase the efficiency of the university. We have to note, however, that his recommendation is closely linked to a concept of a university where the faculty is no longer involved in governance and administration. The national search was part of a new system of functional differentiation that looks at professionals as laborers. Cooke's proposal by far exceeds Weber's assessment of the American university around 1900. Cooke opted for the university as a mental factory. In this context, faculty visibility becomes an asset for the whole enterprise rather than a quality of the individual professor. For the transnational university, this model is of limited use since it is based on a mechanical model of mass production. This rigid model leaves not much space for intellectual creativity and flexibility. Contemporary business interests would not be served by Cooke's model. When the transnational university favors international visibility of its star faculty, it wants to highlight "uniqueness" rather than the typical. In other words, it is looking for highly noticeable interventions that produce global effects. See Morris L. Cooke, *Academic and Industrial Efficiency: A Report to the Carnegie Foundation for the Advancement of Trading* (New York, 1910).

10. See Reinhard Riese, *Die Hochschule auf dem Wege zum wissenschaftlichen Grossbetrieb: Die Universität Heidelberg und das badische Hochschulwesen 1860–1914* (Stuttgart: Klett, 1977).

11. In 1909, Max Weber vigorously defended academic freedom against interventions by the state. In particular, he criticized the tendency of the Prussian state to impose its political and religious preferences on faculty appointments. "The freedom of science, scholarship, and teaching in a university certainly does not exist where appointment to a teaching post is made dependent on the possession—or simulation—of a point of view which is 'acceptable in the highest circles' of church and state." His defense is based on a sharp distinction between religious and political worldviews that cannot be demonstrated objectively on the one hand and scientific analyses that can be demonstrated in an objective manner on the other. For him, academic freedom means the protection of the scientific approach not only for the purpose of scholarship but also as a way of educating students to accept "the obligation of intellectual integrity." The transnational university will have to revisit this question. While Weber's distinction between belief systems and objective science would not be as persuasive as a century ago and while the state is possibly not the most dangerous threat to academic freedom anymore, there is one aspect that will be central, namely, Weber's insistence on the worldliness of the university. This may be more important to-

day than in the Europe of 1909. See Max Weber, "The Power of the State and the Dignity of the Academic Calling in Imperial Germany: The Writings of Max Weber on University Problems," *Minerva* 11, no. 4 (October 1973): 570–632.

12. See Clyde W. Barrow, *Universities and the Capitalist State: Corporate Liberalism and the Reconstruction of American Higher Education 1894–1920* (Madison: University of Wisconsin Press, 1990); see also Christopher Jahr, "Die 'geistige Verbindung von Wehrmacht, Wissenschaft und Politik': Wehrlehre und Heimatforschung an der Friedrich-Wilhelms-Universität zu Berlin 1933–1945," *Jahrbuch für Universitätsgeschichte* 4 (2001): 161–76.

13. Peter Moraw, "Aspekte und Dimensionen älterer deutscher Universitätsgeschichte," in *Academia Gissensis: Beiträge zur älteren Giessener Universitätsgeschichte*, ed. Peter Moraw and Volker Press (Marburg: Elwert, 1982), 1–43.

14. For the development of English literature departments, see Gerald Graff, *Professing Literature: An Institutional History* (Chicago: University of Chicago Press, 1987), 55–64, 121–44.

15. See Konrad H. Jarausch, *Deutsche Studenten 1800–1970* (Frankfurt am Main: Suhrkamp, 1984), 13–34.

16. In addition, professional organizations played an important role in the process of nationalization. They provided their members with a disciplinary identity that transcended the local and regional levels.

17. See John S. Brubacher and Solomon W. Rudy, *Higher Education in Transition* (New York: Harper & Row, 1976), 174–97; Burton J. Bledstein, *The Culture of Professionalism: The Middle Class and the Development of Higher Education in America* (New York: Norton, 1976); and Laurence Veysey, *The Emergence of the American University* (Chicago: University of Chicago Press, 1965).

18. Graff, *Professing Literature*, 81–97.

19. See W. B. Carnochan, *The Battleground of the Curriculum: Liberal Education and American Experience* (Stanford, Calif.: Stanford University Press, 1993).

20. The national university around 1900 (the second phase) prefigures in certain ways the transnational university around 2000; especially in the United Sates, universities such as Johns Hopkins, Chicago, and Stanford owed their existence to private entrepreneurs who acted as sponsors. Without major input of capital, the research university could not be maintained. It is worth noting that German planners around 1900 realized that in the long run even the strongest German state university would not be able to compete with the private universities in America. Their response was the foundation of the Kaiser-Wilhelm-Gesellschaft, a research academy that would also seek private funding.

21. Charles McClelland, *State, Society, and University in Germany 1700–1914* (London: Cambridge University Press, 1980), 68–79, 106–10.

22. See Jürgen Habermas, *The Structural Transformation of the Public Sphere* (Cambridge, Mass.: MIT Press, 1989); see also Peter Uwe Hohendahl et al., *Öffentlichkeit: Geschichte eines kritischen Begriffs* (Stuttgart: Metzler, 2000).

23. One of the interesting questions in regard of the new research university in the early nineteenth century is the exclusive focus on the state as the best provider and benefactor, although some of the reformers (Schleiermacher, Humboldt) were aware

of the potential dangers. Why was there no discussion of the free association (*Verein*) as an alternative? It would have mobilized civil society as the protector of the autonomy of the university. Humboldt believed that academies could be organized this way and suggested the possibility of *Privatgesellschaften* for scholarly communication in the empirical sciences. Today, private foundations are large enough to consider the foundation of a university, but by and large they do not have the support of civil society. There seems to be no forum for a discussion similar to that around 1800. While there is a globalized public sphere, there seems to be no transnational civil society.

24. See Craig Calhoun, ed., *Habermas and the Public Sphere* (Cambridge, Mass.: MIT Press, 1992).

25. See Readings, *The University in Ruins*, 21–43; more recently, see also Henry A. Giroux and Kostas Myrsiades, eds., *Beyond the Corporate University: Culture and Pedagogy in the New Millennium* (London: Rowman & Littlefield, 2001).

26. For the transnational university, the relationship to the corporate world is probably the equivalent of the relationship of the university of the nation-state to the state. Note Schleiermacher's cautious attempt to define the boundaries between state and university. While he is aware that the new university cannot do without the state, he wants to preserve as much internal autonomy as possible. The transnational university finds itself in a similar position vis-à-vis the corporate world. It needs the support of corporations but cannot allow them to dictate the terms of the cooperation. Thus, drawing the boundaries is as difficult as it was for the national university in the early nineteenth century. Yet the pressure points seem to differ. While Schleiermacher was concerned about funding and faculty appointments, the impact of the corporate world would be felt more in the arena of research, including the selection of projects. See Friedrich Schleiermacher, *Occasional Thoughts on Universities in the German Sense* (San Francisco: EMText, 1991).

27. See Janice Currie and Janice Newson, eds., *Universities and Globalization. Critical Perspectives* (Thousand Oaks, Calif.: Sage, 1998).

28. Nussbaum, *Cultivating Humanity*, esp. 293–304.

29. See Walter Cohen, "The Economics of Doctoral Education in Literature," *Proceedings of the Modern Language Association* 115 (October 2000): 1164–87.

30. See Sheila Slaughter and Larry L. Leslie, *Academic Capitalism: Politics, Policies, and the Entrepreneurial University* (Baltimore: Johns Hopkins University Press, 1997).

31. Jürgen Habermas, "The Idea of the University: Learning Processes," in *The New Conservatism: Cultural Criticism and the Historians' Debate* (Cambridge, Mass.: MIT Press, 1989), 100–27.

32. Habermas, "The Idea of the University," 107.

33. Talcott Parsons and Gerald M. Plott, *The American University* (Cambridge, Mass.: Harvard University Press, 1973).

34. Fritz Ringer gives a good account of the cultural pessimism of the leading German professors, mostly in the humanities, after 1890. Their complaints about the lack of serious learning and deep *Bildung* sharply contrasts with the strength and the success of the German university system around 1900. Unlike 1800, this crisis was felt as an intrinsic ideological event. For this reason, no major institutional changes oc-

curred. As an institution, the university of the nation-state remained unchanged. Today's crisis in Germany reminds us of the constellation around 1800. Both the institution and the idea of the university are in jeopardy. It is not certain that the German university will survive in its present form. Similarly, the present American crisis includes both the institution and the ideological legitimation. Just as in Germany, the nexus between the nation-state and the university has become weak. At this point, the idea of a transnational university opens up a new perspective. See Fritz K. Ringer, *The Decline of the Mandarins: The German Academic Community 1890–1933* (Hanover, N.H.: University Press of New England, 1990).

35. Ronald G. Ehrenberg, ed., *The American University: National Treasure or Endangered Species?* (Ithaca, N.Y.: Cornell University Press, 1997).

36. It is noteworthy that the essays in the volume *Universities and Globalization: Critical Perspectives*, ed. Janice Currie and Janice Newson, still discuss the development of postsecondary education mostly within national frameworks. Globalization is seen primarily as a new economic environment that impacts national educational systems. They do not focus on the globalization of education as intrinsic to education (universities).

37. See Oskar Negt and Alexander Kluge, *Public Sphere and Experience* (Minneapolis: University of Minnesota Press, 1993).

38. For a good summary of these tendencies, see Sheila Slaughter, "National Higher Education Policies in a Global Economy," in Currie and Newson, *Universities and Globalization*, 45–70.

39. See Michael Warner, "The Mass Public and the Mass Subject," in Calhoun, *Habermas and the Public Sphere*, 377–401.

40. There are strong indications that the transnational university depends on a lingua franca for its internal as well as external communications. Under the present conditions, this can only be English as the common bond of the former British Empire and the national language of the United States. Obviously, political dominance coincides with academic preeminence. It is noteworthy that in a number of European countries, projects to found international universities are under way where English is either the exclusive language of instruction or at least an option. From the perspective of the university of culture, these projects are destructive since they undermine the connection between the medium of instruction and the culture to be studied. The national culture becomes objectivized and loses its traditional authority.

41. The claim that the transnational university is apt to serve the common good describes a horizon of possible thought and engagement but not a necessary outcome. In structural terms, the transnational university appears to be indifferent although not hostile to social expectations. By contrast, the pure university of reason would not tolerate such indifference. How and to what extent can the transnational university develop an ethos of social commitment? The obvious answer is, with the help of the members of the academic community. Yet this answer is insufficient because it is individualistic and voluntaristic. The more important aspect would be the grounding of any praxis in the institution itself. In this regard, the activity at the level of programs and centers might be more effective than that of the central administration. By setting up these centers and programs, the central administration delegates its responsibility

to smaller units with the possible caveat that support can be withdrawn in an adverse situation. It seems, therefore, that the transnational university offers opportunities but no guarantees.

42. As Francis B. Nyamnjoh and Nantang B. Jua demonstrate, the epistemological playing field is not even. Compared with the West, African universities are disadvantaged because of the hegemony of Western knowledge, especially theories and methodologies produced at American universities. Collaboration between Western and African universities therefore favors Western epistemologies (with predictable results). Similar arguments can be made for the Middle East or South America, for instance. This means that even a well-funded transnational university in Africa or South America remains attached to and penetrated by Western forms of knowledge production. Its intellectual power carries a structural bias that has little to do with the consciousness and interests of the resident scholars and researchers. Yet we have to take this bias into consideration when we discuss the critical potential of the transnational university. As a hegemonic institution, the transnational research university is caught up in the dialectic of the production and dissemination of knowledge that enables exchange but at the same time reproduces inequality. Critical thought can access this inequality, but can it change it? See Francis B. Nyamnjoh and Nantang B. Jua, "African Universities in Crisis and the Promotion of a Democratic Culture: The Political Economy of Violence in African Educational Systems," *African Studies Review* 45, no. 2 (September 2002): 1–26.

43. To compensate for its lack of flexibility, German universities have resorted to a model of research institutes that are only formally controlled by the university but independent in the definition and execution of their research projects. These institutes attract projects with applications in industrial production. See Bernd Hüppauf, "Research and Higher Education—Reforming the Reforms: The Example of the Federal Republic of Germany," *European Studies Journal* 7, no. 2 (fall 1990): 1–31, esp. 10–11.

III

RACE, MEMORY, FORGETTING

7

Beyond Eurocentrism: The Frankfurt School and Whiteness Theory

Clay Steinman

People make their own history, but they do not make it out of whole cloth; they do not make it out of conditions chosen by themselves, but out of such as they find close at hand. The tradition of all past generations weighs like an alp on the brains of the living.

—Marx, *The Eighteenth Brumaire of Louis Bonaparte*[1]

As a white and mostly European enterprise, the critical theory of the Frankfurt School has reparations to pay. The reasons are structural, not biographical. The wealth—the spectacular economic growth—of Europe and later the United States made possible critical theory's development, providing the conditions that supported its practice as well as its objects of analysis. Yet the colonial basis of much of this wealth remained distant, suffering peripheral to critical theory's explicit concerns.[2] The debt and its accumulated interest endure, to be repaid if in small measure with engaged theoretical work, particularly work that introduces critical race theory to critical theory, of which the essay by Susan Buck-Morss discussed in this chapter should be considered exemplary. This engagement would reinvigorate critical theory as "minor" theory, in the language of Gilles Deleuze and Félix Guattari, theory alive as "crystals of becoming whose value is to trigger uncontrollable movements and deterritorializations of the mean or majority," theory reverberating with the voices of silenced or subdued minorities, articulated through forms conscious of their recombinations.[3] These are terms true to critical theory's emancipatory project.

Reparations would first acknowledge the dispossessed, their specific historical presence, and then take seriously their claims on Western intellectual culture. Such efforts would ask whether critical theory can *in theory* adequately

115

address issues of race, of colonial domination and its residual toxicity, of an emancipation that decenters Enlightenment conceptions of the good life in favor of an openness to what centuries of thinkers conceived of as the animal barbarism of the dark and unwashed. If "cultural criticism must become social physiognomy,"[4] then critical theory must illuminate the white barbarism on which Enlightenment culture and its own critique in the last instance rest.

This seems more productive than, for example, yet again indicting Theodor W. Adorno for his hostility to jazz. Instead, it might be possible to see what critical theory itself can contribute to its own assessment, by working through the critique of Adorno on jazz while examining the racial politics of *The Authoritarian Personality*, for decades in the United States the most widely known work of the Frankfurt School.[5] *The Authoritarian Personality* sought to measure and account for domestic racism after World War II, concentrating on the relationship between anti-Semitism and psychological and social structures of domination. Adorno played a major role in the project; Max Horkheimer was its key administrator.

Richard Leppert, Evelyn Wilcock, and others have maintained against ad hominem dismissals that Adorno's essays on jazz were fundamentally antiracist in their attention to appropriation and domination.[6] Permeated by dialectical thought, Adorno's essays, argued in nonlinear form, are rarely of simple character. Product of an elite German education, Adorno wrote with prejudice against the commercial, and he did not know jazz to anything like the extent he knew the music of high art. His writing—most of it dating from the 1930s and the early 1950s, when long-playing records with extended improvisation were just appearing—is, as Leppert says, "missing" a half century of composition and performance available today.[7] Adorno's writings on jazz reproduce the cardinal sin of his critiques of commercial music generally: they overemphasize standardization, and this accounts for the essays' own "formulaic aspect."[8] Yet I suspect this was as much a matter of Adorno's individual taste and conjunctural tactics (for whom and against what was he writing?)—taste and tactics that we can assess without resort to evaluation of the underlying theory. For that theory, as a dialectical theory, is distinctively a theory of contradiction. It would argue that each work of jazz is both the product of a "commercial business driven by the pursuit of profit and a site of creative human activity from which some very great popular music has come and continues to emerge."[9] Yet here the analysis only begins. Whatever Adorno's individual remarks, for critical theory generally this hybridity becomes reconceptualized as a dynamic symptom of human potentiality blocked—and reenvisioned. Jazz is seen against a field of the heterogeneity of its own potentiality, the potential of musical choices governed by its historical development as a musical form. It is this potential that becomes illuminated as denied, the ghost of lost chances in a landscape of industrial gray.

Because of jazz's origins primarily in Afro-diasporic history and its crucial status as a site of superior accomplishment, because of jazz's own performance of the dialectic of creativity and oppression, indeed creativity against oppression in the Afro-diaspora, arguments about the politics of jazz have for almost a century been inseparable from arguments about the politics of race. In the 1930s, when Adorno's first major article on the subject appeared, whites tended to speak and write of jazz as black music in an essentialist sense, entertaining but primitive and perhaps even dangerous, its refinement best left to whites—providing all-too-apt examples of what bell hooks calls "eating the other."[10] Record companies forced black groups to call themselves by such names as "The Jungle Band" and "Chocolate Dandies" even though the groups wanted to call themselves by the names of their leaders and musicians; songs themselves were given such labels as "Ethiopian Nightmare" and "Thick Lip Stomp."[11] In England and Germany, critics described jazz as degenerate black and Jewish culture, deserving wary approach or, as for the Nazis, suppression.[12]

Mostly writing about "German dance-band music" and against the racist essentialism of most jazz critics and many fans, Adorno argued in the mid-1930s that the best jazz performances were not extensions of a primitive racial nature but that they "in virtuoso pieces yield an extraordinary complexity."[13] Nevertheless, the jazz he heard suffered from being "dominated by the function" of being "dance music" rather than being "dominated . . . by an autonomous formal law," as was the modern serial music he championed as beacon of emancipated creativity.[14] As for its connection to African music, because of its commercial standardization, the "extent to which jazz has anything at all to do with genuine black music is highly questionable; the fact that it is frequently performed by blacks and that the public clamors for 'black jazz' as a sort of brand-name doesn't say much about it, even if folkloric research should confirm the African origin of many of its practices."[15] When he argued that the "skin of the black man [who plays jazz] functions as much as a coloristic effect as does the silver of the saxophone," Adorno did so to criticize "the capitalist requirement that [the formal elements of jazz] be exchangeable as commodities."[16] As part of this commodification, the "European-American entertainment business" uses black musicians as "figures in advertisements, . . . their triumph . . . a confusing parody of colonial imperialism."[17] To the extent that jazz did have black origins, he said, they were in the "music of slaves," of the "domesticated body in bondage."[18] Any attempt to break out of the modern bondage of capitalist life through the "partial success" of improvisation "counts strictly among those attempts to break out of the fetishized commodity world which want to escape that world without ever changing it, thus moving ever deeper into its snare."[19] By the time he wrote "Perennial Fashion—Jazz" in the early 1950s, Adorno had gained a better sense of the varieties of jazz and its histories.[20] He acknowledged the existence of bebop and said there is "little doubt . . . regarding the African elements in jazz," but he still maintained that the "range of the permissible in jazz is as narrowly circumscribed as in any particular cut of clothes" manufactured by the fashion industry.[21]

This is of course Adorno's standard argument, repeated time and again in different analyses of the white-dominated culture industry and its products, so it might appear that his writing on jazz only happens to be about the problematics of black culture in racist society.[22] Yet to the extent that the argument does not foreground the specific situation and experiences of black performers and black audiences—does not see African American music as a site of struggle—it is not only Eurocentric but also white, an epistemological location neither Adorno nor many other European American thinkers of the time could have seen. The whiteness of Adorno's analyses resides in their assumption that audiences were not significantly raced or, more precisely, that race was at most one aspect of social disadvantage in class society.[23] Adorno's treatment of jazz misses the emancipatory meaning it could have for progressive people of the Afro-diaspora (and for allies such as Herbert Marcuse): concentration on the work's moment of negation, which critical theory considered its task to illuminate in the culture it privileged. Jazz rearticulates elements of the music of African life, torn and reconstituted by the Middle Passage and slavery, music itself originally sung as resistance to slavery, as critique of European domination.[24] Like all music, jazz in any of its varieties concretizes complex and contradictory historical experiences into sounds, and in so doing its texts in their details offer access to a mediated form of that experience, which Stuart Hall and others have called the "diaspora aesthetic."[25] Structurally, this historical struggle Adorno could not see, and so like many listeners he fetishized what Mike Budd has analyzed as the "separation of the sound of jazz from the social relations and functions of which Afro-diasporic music was a part," a separation covered by social ignorance, facilitated by the commodity form.[26]

Yet this aesthetic, a "minor" and hence valorized aesthetic in Deleuze and Guattari's light, was explicitly taken up by Duke Ellington and other African American jazz composers and musicians, if in more nationalist terms. In 1939, Ellington, for example, wrote, "Our aim has always been the development of an authentic Negro music, of which swing is only one element. We are not interested primarily in the playing of jazz or swing music, but in producing a genuine contribution from our race. Our music is always intended to be definitely and purely racial."[27] For Adorno, Ellington's appeal to authenticity might have seemed a denial of the contradictory ways history stamps cultural work. Yet an antiracist critical theory would value the appeal's insistence on the irreducible existence in the music of oppression and resistance, taking up the negative moment of the struggle for self-representation that Ellington's argument represents. Such a reconstructed critical theory would see white efforts to essentialize jazz as the products of what Ella Shohat and Robert Stam have called "ethnicities-in-relation," permeating significant social relations in societies marked by racial histories.[28]

To think "white" is to stake out a position that appears nonracial, to think in ways that do not acknowledge the racial privilege connected to a white position.[29] Tim Wise has put it succinctly: "Being white means never having to think about it."[30] This might seem a perverse way of describing Adorno, a racial refugee from the Nazis, who in 1945 did associate the difficult contemporary situations of blacks and Jews, and in one unpublished version of "On Jazz" "included Jews in his exploration of jazz style and the extent to which individuals may play along with their own stigmatized situation."[31] Yet it is in his treatment of blacks that Adorno became most white. Never a writer cloaked in the discourse of the impartial, Adorno here spoke from a position that neither foregrounds nor acknowledges that it is raced. Despite his own commitment to the "equality of all who have human shape," despite his own losses to the racism of the Nazis, Adorno generally failed to apply critical theory's critique of domination to the history of Afro-diasporic struggles.[32]

Such an assessment, however, risks fetishizing individual thinkers when what matters is discursive context. Even if Adorno's racial politics had been deliberate rather than unwittingly reproductive of the structural, which I do not believe, the expectation that thinkers should somehow be perfect, more politically sensitive than their environment normally would allow, not only rubs up against the insight from Marx with which I began this chapter but also smacks of a childish desire for perfection in one's parents.[33] Throwing rocks at Adorno does not help sort out the value of critical theory for an antiracist emancipatory politics.

A more dialectical approach might start with Susan Buck-Morss's consideration of critical theory and the Enlightenment in light of slavery and colonial domination. As she argues, Enlightenment notions of freedom were developed in a world of slavery that "by the mid-eighteenth century . . . came to underwrite the entire economic system of the West," a contradiction lived by John Locke and black slavery's other freedom-loving investors.[34] Enabling this contradiction was a distinction between the concept of slavery, condemned as a moral wrong, and the practice of colonial slavery, embraced as justifiable. This opposition may have functioned as a metaphor for one less kind and gentle, that between slavery involving whites and slavery involving blacks. "Weak minds exaggerate too much the injustice done to Africans," said Montesquieu.[35] Perhaps no set of Enlightened elites was more inconsistent on the matter than the majority of U.S. revolutionaries who campaigned against what they thought of as their enslavement by royalist Great Britain and then supported the writing of slavery of black people into their founding Constitution.[36] None was more inconsistent—except perhaps for those among the French revolutionaries who supported the keeping of colonial slaves until 1848.[37] Eurocentrism is not just another form of ethnocentrism, not just a matter of paying attention only to what is closest to home, a blind spot so prevalent that it might easily be seen as congenital rather than racist.[38] Because what Buck-Morss calls "really-existing slavery" was essential to the fabric of European economic life into the nineteenth century, internally as well as colonially, its erasure functioned as mystification in the service of domination, the failure of Enlightenment in the service of Enlightenment's self-satisfaction.[39]

This exnomination of blacks takes a curious form in the volumes of the Institute of Social Research–related U.S. project, the Studies in Prejudice[40] series coedited by Max Horkheimer, and specifically in the book on which Adorno collaborated, *The Authoritarian Personality*.[41] These works interrelated ideas and methods from psychoanalysis, empirical social psychology, and critical social theory to study psychological and social causes of bigotry. An analysis of their racial politics might assist the development of an antiracist critical theory. In their foreword to the series, Horkheimer and his coeditor, Samuel H. Flowerman, began by referring to the "full and violent destructiveness" of Nazi anti-Semitism and ended by offering the five volumes in their series as tools for understanding and combating "intergroup prejudice and hatred."[42] The movement from the particularity of the war against the Jews to more general considerations of prejudice reproduces the conceptual confusion in *The Authoritarian Personality* as a whole. A "prominent example of politically committed social research in the American academy,"[43] is it a book about anti-Semitism, or is it about bigotry in general at a specific historical moment? Horkheimer, in the preface to the volume, began by saying, "This is a book about social discrimination."[44] He defined the topic at hand as "the position of minorities in modern society, and more specifically the problem of religious and racial hatreds," which he linked to the development of the "authoritarian type of man" and to "antidemocratic trends."[45] These would be measured by the "F scale," a psychological indicator of potential for fascistic behavior, for a personality that "fawns before admired authority (representing strength) and loathes weakness—in Jews, women, homosexuals, or other outgroups."[46] Aside from a reference to the Institute's 1939 work on anti-Semitism,

Horkheimer says nothing to indicate that this would be largely a study of big-otry against Jews.[47] The project, including its subsidized publication by Harper and Brothers, was funded by the American Jewish Committee, whose Depart-ment of Scientific Research Horkheimer was hired to head after a two-day planning conference in New York in May 1944.[48] Yet I do not believe that the concentration on anti-Semitism was an effect only of its funding.[49] Rather, for Horkheimer, Adorno, and their social-psychologist colleagues on *The Author-itarian Personality* at the University of California, Berkeley, racism against blacks with some exception seems to have fallen through the epistemological net within which they worked, stitched together from ill-fitting Marxist, Freudian, and liberal-instrumental social-psychological approaches.[50] Simi-larly, in chronicling the prejudice studies, neither Jay nor Wiggershaus in their otherwise helpful accounts makes more than passing mention of prejudice against anyone other than Jews.[51]

The concerns of the *Authoritarian* studies also had specific contextual sources. In the shadow of the particularities of the Holocaust, in a moment when the coming decline of U.S. anti-Semitism could not be foreseen, the need to generate critical knowledge of anti-Semitism was understandably ur-gent. Anti-Semitism was still oppressive and threatening to Jews in ways al-most unimaginable today, ways confirmed by the interview material in *The Authoritarian Personality*. One unpublished study led by Frankfurt School re-searchers of 566 factory workers in major U.S. cities during the late war pe-riod, for example, found that more than two-thirds were in some sense anti-Semitic.[52] Well into the postwar era, U.S. right-wing discourse still included openly anti-Semitic elements, and leftists of many political stripes were fear-ful of a resurgent right. At the same time, research universities remained largely segregated by law or in effect, and funding for studies of racism against blacks in particular was miniscule. As telling as it seems now, it should not be startling given the context that in a nearly 1,000-page book about the instantiation of majority ethnocentrism in U.S. individuals, in a se-ries called "Studies in Prejudice," African Americans receive only a handful of mentions. Still, they are worth enumerating.[53]

1. *African Americans and ethnocentrism.* The first reference comes in the conceptual introduction, "The Study of Ethnocentric Ideology," in which Daniel J. Levinson explained that the researchers labeled their object of study ethnocentrism—rather than prejudice or racism—because they considered it a broader term, extending to in-group feelings about out-groups neither racial nor religious (102, 107).[54] These included "Okies," "the insane," and "zoot-suiters."[55] For Levinson, "ethnic" described perceptions of cultures, not body types or nations, a point particularly important in terms of thoughts about Jews (103).[56] "Ethnocentrism," then, involved "a hierarchical, authoritarian

view of group interaction in which ingroups are rightly dominant, outgroups subordinate" (150).

The researchers first measured prejudice against Jews in a separate measure of anti-Semitism, the "A-S scale" (57–101). To analyze the connection between anti-Semitism registered on this scale and other forms of ethnocentrism, they then developed an "E scale" of 34 items (102–50). Subscales of the E scale looked at three other forms of ethnocentrism: hostility toward African Americans, the "N scale";[57] hostility toward other minority groups (Japanese and Filipino Americans, "Okies," "foreigners," "criminals") and women of all backgrounds, the "M scale";[58] and the "P scale," which measured what Levinson called "pseudo-patriotism," conformist attachment to national identity and nationalist hostility to Mexicans, Germans, and Japanese (107). "*Genuine* patriotism" was ascribed to those who identified with their own national values but understood their relativism (107; emphasis in the original).[59]

The purpose of the scales was to find correlations between these different forms of ethnocentrism.[60] The hope was that such correlations would illuminate general psychosocial causes and, ideally, lead to prescriptions for change. Statistically, the E scale was found reliable overall as a measure of an identifiable constellation of attitudes, and the results of the three separate subscales (but not all individual items) correlated with each other and with the E scale with "considerable significance," allowing predictions to be made from one to the other (112–13). The E scale also correlated with the results of the A-S scale (122–23). One conclusion from this might have been that Jews and people of color and women of all backgrounds had a common political project against prejudice since "each facet of ethnocentric ideology as here conceived is accepted by most high scorers, rejected by most low scorers" (146), but there is no indication that this connection ever was made. Ultimately, the E scale questionnaire was reduced to ten items for easier use. The question about women in the postwar era was dropped, hostility to women's rights having been found so strong and widespread that the question failed to discriminate between high and low overall scorers[61] (121). The reduced E scale did include a question about zoot-suiters, but there is no indication that the investigators related its responses to prejudice against Mexican Americans or Latinas/Latinos generally.[62] These results correlated well with what would become the Berkeley group's most famous and enduring instrument, the F scale, designed to measure "implicit antidemocratic trends" and "implicit prefascist tendencies" (222, 224, 222–79). Yet because they wanted an instrument "that would measure prejudice without appearing to have this aim and without mentioning the name of any minority group," the F scale itself did not examine hostility toward disadvantaged groups in the United States (222).

Designed as metonym for racism against African Americans, anti-Semitism, and prejudice among other U.S. minorities, the F scale over time became their metaphor, blotting out the particularities of prejudice, their histories no longer visible as cause.

2. *African Americans and the raced gaze.* Another mention of African Americans comes in Betty Aron's chapter on the value of the Thematic Apperception Test, which asks research subjects to tell the story they see playing out in a series of pictures with a range of plausible meanings. Aron used the test to elicit information about character traits, background, and constellations of prejudice (489–90). For example, subjects who had taken the E scale test were shown a photo of a police officer with a night stick facing a man in a T-shirt whose race seems unspecifiable, his arms outstretched, and his back against the wall (picture 6, between 508 and 509). The picture was "commonly interpreted as [showing] a suspect caught by the police." High E scale scorers tended to describe the man as a "dangerous criminal, a Negro or Mexican with an innately weak character. . . . He may have been involved in a strike or race riot for which he is condemned by the story-teller." For low scorers, "the man has either been striking for higher wages or fighting race prejudice"—a markedly different take on a similar scenario. As Aron says, "The most important differences between stories of high and those of low scorers reflect their attitudes toward minority groups" (527–28). Subjects were also shown a picture of an African American in his early teen years wearing a suit jacket and open-collared white shirt standing next to an elderly African American woman in a chair. Beyond the young man is the bottom half of a photograph; all that can be seen is a group of legs in trousers and shoes. Both are looking at something to the right of the photo's edge. As Aron describes it, they appear "'clean' or 'neat,' and seem to be acting in a socially acceptable way." High scorers tended to construct scenarios in which the two were "different from most Negroes." Low scorers tended to stress a bond of familial love and encouragement between a grandmother and grandson. High scorers said the boy has done well in school, but not very well. Some high scorers thought that the two were looking offscreen at someone dying or being hurt (528–29). These results seem suggestive for research and theory about raced responses to media.

3. *African Americans and the authoritarians.* The highest overall scorers on the ten-question E scale (and in subsequent in-depth interviews) were white non-Jewish prisoners at San Quentin (817–18). They also scored highest on the F scale (844). These prisoners were the most specifically racist against blacks, stressing biological connection to apes and animals generally and to "savages" and "the jungle" (825). Suffering from "intense *status anxiety*," they repeatedly expressed fears of black people not being kept "in their

place" and rising up against whites and then taking advantage of them (826; emphasis in the original). Though they were anti-Semitic, the high-scoring prisoners differentiated clearly between the two groups; for example, they not once connected Jews with the "primitive instincts" they frequently ascribed to blacks (830–35). According to the report of the principal investigator of the San Quentin study, William R. Morrow, "Negroes are almost universally perceived as a very submerged outgroup—as contrasted with an imagined 'dominant' outgroup such as Jews are thought to be" (824). Jews, on the other hand, were routinely characterized as possessing "dominance combined with exclusiveness." For Morrow, "This attitude centers around fantasies of victimization by Jewish power, and a fear of being overwhelmed by that power" (831). It was also sometimes mixed with envy and admiration (832)—feelings rarely mentioned in connection with blacks. Fear and insecurity have been common causes of both anti-Semitism and racism against black people. But like the enormous differences in socioeconomic status and political power of Jews and blacks in the United States at midcentury, the forms of prejudice have been quite distinct. *The Authoritarian Personality* made clear that while there have been connections between symptoms of anti-Semitism and white supremacy, they differ fundamentally in that anti-Semitism has in some measure functioned as perverted populism, resentment against shadowy and illegitimate powers, while racism against blacks has tended to involve contempt and hostility for those of a distant and strange underlife. As one respondent put it, "The Negroes produce so rapidly that they will populate the world, while the Jews will get all of the money" (636).[63] These findings showed that racism against blacks was a different and generally more severe problem than anti-Semitism in the United States. But nowhere does the book analyze this phenomenon or explore its causes and effects.

Despite the work on racism in the body of the book, there is not one word about it specifically in the introduction, which concentrates on using the research to study and combat the "potentially fascistic individual," with a focus on anti-Semitism. In the four chapters he signed, Adorno did mention hostility to African Americans, but always in connection with anti-Semitism or prejudice generally. Although unambiguously opposed to such hostility—clearly here he was antiracist, as Leppert says of Adorno's writings on music—Adorno never analyzed antiblack racism's specific qualities or distinctive harms. He did mention findings that "members of other minority groups, with strong 'conformist' tendencies, were outspokenly antisemitic. Hardly any traces of solidarity among the different outgroups could be found" (611). But he made no mention of prejudice by Jews—with two exceptions involving prejudice of Jews against Jews, the first of a Jewish man of Turkish descent who "indulged in violent anti-Semitic diatribes" and the second of German

Jews against their eastern European counterparts (612, 624). In the chapter he coauthored on the F scale, he did write, "Although anti-Semitism is still to be understood primarily as an aspect of general ethnocentrism, there can be no doubt but that it has some special features of its own" (265). These are described in a chapter (16) signed by Adorno. Yet no such consideration was given to racism against African Americans. At the same time, Adorno anticipated by decades the critique antiracists would make of orthodox Marxism, taking to task those who "belittle the importance of racial discrimination by labeling it simply as a byproduct of the big issues of class struggle," and he went on to say that such a position "may be indicative of repressed prejudice on their own part" (772). No liberal universalist, he argued that people free from stereotypes would "tend to acknowledge differences and to take a positive stand toward differentiation" (773).

In 1943, before working on the project (in English) for the American Jewish Committee, Horkheimer and Adorno wrote (in German) most of what was to become the "Elements of Anti-Semitism: Limits of Enlightenment" chapter of *Dialectic of Enlightenment*.[64] Again a distinction is made between racism against African Americans and anti-Semitism, though here the Nazi terror is invoked: "The blacks must be kept in their place, but the Jews are to be wiped from the face of the earth, and the call to exterminate them like vermin finds an echo among the prospective fascists of all countries" (137). There is of course much already written about the relationship between the two projects.[65] Here I want to use the second, more explicit text to argue, again, that while anti-Semitism is considered in detail and seen as the emblem of domination, racism and colonialism figure only implicitly, as examples of the general "evil senselessly visited on . . . all the persecuted, whether animals or human beings," Enlightenment gone mad (165). Missing, too, is consideration of the specific racial projects that spawned and have revivified oppressions of blacks and Jews (let alone of other racially marked victims of institutional prejudice). In part what makes "Elements of Anti-Semitism" so unlike anything in *The Authoritarian Personality* is its development, especially in the section published after the war, of an argument about the incorporation, the taking up, of the general moment of anti-Semitic irrationalism in the rationalizations of postwar society. "Anti-Semitic views," Horkheimer and Adorno wrote, "always reflected stereotyped thinking. Today only that thinking is left" for "in the world of mass production, stereotypes replace intellectual categories" (166). Later Adorno would write, "We viewed social psychology as subjective mediation of the objective social system, without whose mechanisms it would not have been possible to keep a hold on its subjects."[66] Wiggershaus argues that what mattered to Adorno and Horkheimer was not so much the amount of anti-Semitism in the United States in the

1940s as the terrifying rise of technocratic thinking and its ruthless "attitudes and behaviour which lacked any reverence for living beings, for people, for the victims of discrimination."[67]

Critical theory historically and today, in earlier generations and in our own enterprises, carries with it the responsibility of the well-fed, even though it has opposed racism against blacks and other U.S. minorities, even though it has been sensitive to the misery of the "millions hungering for rice who have fallen through the narrow meshes" in a world in which the "abundance of goods . . . could be produced everywhere."[68] Again, the issue is structural, not biographical. The critique of anti-Semitism in the early twenty-first century requires a more general critique of colonial and postcolonial racism that can be found but is by no means foregrounded in *The Authoritarian Personality* and the "Elements of Anti-Semitism." The critique of instrumental reason must not turn its back on race. Racism is so entangled and difficult that struggles against it could well use critical theory's commitment to the dialectic of possibility. In the chapter of social analysis that he originally intended to include in *The Authoritarian Personality*, Adorno stressed his long-standing interest in the imbrication of the social in the psychological and in his belief that the Berkeley studies pointed the way toward empirical analysis of that process. What he wanted to see next was research designed "to find out how objective economic laws operate, not so much through the individual's economic motivations" as "through his unconscious make-up."[69] He believed such studies "would provide us with the true scientific explanation of the nature of contemporary prejudice."[70] With this turn, the particular suffering of people raced as less than white becomes obscured, just as racial difference was not an issue for Adorno when he discussed the reception of jazz. Yet, again, none of this need be true in theory.[71]

These losses—like the disappearance of women and Mexican Americans from the research of the Berkeley project or the lack of attention paid to other racisms and to homophobia and, indeed, like the minimal attention paid to the effects of prejudice on any of its victims[72]—argue that the first generation of the Frankfurt School left a legacy best served by situating its texts in the moments in which they were written, by declining to see them as philosophical treatises historical only in the sense of a history of ideas—in short, by applying to them the strategies of critical theory itself. One reason the most timely writings of Herbert Marcuse—*An Essay on Liberation, Counterrevolution and Revolt*—may seem more out of date than, say, his "Affirmative Character of Culture" is that they embrace their historical moment, making less sense as that moment rapidly recedes. It may well be that we take too much of critical theory as being beyond its moment, that we can best use critical theory for emancipatory purposes if we insist on that aspect of it that attends to the concrete.[73] Just as the first generation of the Frankfurt School took as a central task the critique of Enlightenment, which thanks to Buck-Morss we can now more clearly situate in a world built on and within different forms of slavery, so it may be that a central task for later generations is to reconceptualize critical theory in ways that take up Anglo-European concepts only following their decentering and to rethink ways theory has been raced white, encumbered in Marx's phrase from *The Eighteenth Brumaire*, by "circumstances existing already, given and transmitted from the past." As Richard Dyer says of white racism, "One must take responsibility for it, but that is not the same as being responsible, that is, [as being] to blame for it."[74] Critical theory can take responsibility by engaging in its own defamiliarization. "White power . . . reproduces itself regardless of intention, power differences [among whites], and goodwill, and overwhelmingly because it is not seen as whiteness, but as normal. White people need to learn to see themselves as white, to see their particularity. In other words, whiteness needs to be made strange."[75]

One work that undermines its whiteness and at the same time seems rooted in critical theory, John Mowitt's *Percussion: Drumming, Beating, Striking* takes its readers (and critical theory) to places earlier generations could not find with their conceptual maps. Mowitt continues critical theory's explorations of music and its social situation, but he does so in a way that allows for multiple perspectives and contexts of production and consumption to be heard. The text refuses to mystify its own situated contribution in its organization of these voices of difference. *Percussion* takes up Adorno's key concepts—immanence, nonidentity, the dialectic of rationalization—as well as his concern with the role of commodified music in people's lives, especially as expressed with Hanns Eisler in *Composing for the Films*.[76] Yet by listening to those who produce and receive and by seeing this production and reception in its social intertextuality, the book is able to make visible musical communication in its physicality, as interpellation of rhythmic sounds, culturally and economically coded to be sure.[77] Mowitt offers an immanent criticism of Chuck Berry's "Rock 'n' Roll Music" that in its close analysis should sweep away any lingering high-culture prejudice that such music lacks any moment of art autonomous from the market.[78] Yet more significant for a race-sensitive critical theory is the way Mowitt allows the work's African American voice to be heard in its mediated form as the performed song "links the being of rock-and-roll to a struggle within the 'contact zone' between the cultures of Africa and the Americas, a struggle that is figured in the song as a conflict of beats."[79] However marked by their commodification, such works carry within them the promise of solidarity, of debts acknowledged and addressed. For Mowitt, as for Buck-Morss and, I hope, increasing numbers of others, to talk about Western culture is to talk about race. Theory, as Mowitt argues, is struck by the recognition of cultures and voices of difference. Such a move, self-consciously raced, becomes necessary if, as we have been promised, "Enlightenment itself, [which] having mastered itself and assumed its own power, could break through," allowing us at last to hear and see a world transformed.[80]

NOTES

For additional readings, critical conversation, and editorial suggestions, I am grateful to the anonymous reviewers and to Sara Austin, Kendrick Brown, Steve Burt, Harry Hirsch, Hsueh Yeh, Nora Ishibashi, Leola Johnson, Sylvia López, Carlos Nelson, Joan Ostrove, Ahmed Samatar, Franz Samelson, Sandy Schram, and Jeff Sklansky and especially Mike Budd, Jim Dawes, Bob Entman, Nan Hanway, David Itzkowitz, Kiarina Kordela, Stephanie Leitch, Richard Leppert, Mark Mazullo, David Chioni Moore, Linda Schulte-Sasse, and Michelle Wright. Thanks to Peter Uwe Hohendahl for organizing and leading the 2001 Cornell Critical Theory Seminar on the Frankfurt School and the follow-up conference in 2002; to their sponsors, Cornell's Institute for German Cultural Studies and the German Academic Exchange Service; and to Aoife Naughton, Max Pensky, Julia Stewart, and all the participants. Finally, I am grateful to the Associated Colleges of the Midwest and to the staff at the Newberry Library for research support and hospitality in the spring of 2004.

1. Karl Marx, *The Eighteenth Brumaire of Louis Bonaparte*, 3rd ed., trans. Daniel De Leon (Chicago: Charles H. Kerr, 1913), 9 (gendered language retranslated).

2. The white supremacist slaughter of the Herero, some 65,000 people, between 1904 and 1907 by German forces in what is now Namibia looms particularly large in this regard, emblem of the barbarism that Walter Benjamin insisted haunts civilized worlds. Benjamin, "Theses on the Philosophy of History," in *Illuminations*, ed. Hannah Arendt, trans. Harry Zohn (New York: Schocken Books, 1968), 256. The standard account of the massacre can be found in Horst Dreschler, *"Let Us Die Fighting": The Struggle of the Herero and the Nama against German Imperialism (1884–1915)*, trans. Bernd Zollner (London: Zed Books, 1980). For an incisive analysis, see Mahmood Mamdani, "A Brief History of Genocide," *Transition*, no. 87 (2001): 26–47. Robert W. Kestling has compared the treatment of blacks during the German imperial and Weimar periods with their treatment by the Nazis. "Blacks under the Swastika: A Research Note," *Journal of Negro History* 83, no. 1 (winter 1998): 84–99. Mamdani and others have connected the mentality of the German colonial genocide in Africa with that of the Nazi extermination of Jews. Most of the Frankfurt writers were Jews, and though all but Benjamin survived the Nazis, they suffered the Holocaust's destruction of family and of friends and of the world in which they were raised.

3. Gilles Deleuze and Félix Guattari, *A Thousand Plateaus: Capitalism and Schizophrenia*, trans. Brian Massumi (Minneapolis: University of Minnesota Press, 1987), 106.

4. Theodor W. Adorno, "Cultural Criticism and Society," in *Prisms*, trans. Samuel and Shierry Weber (Cambridge, Mass.: MIT Press, 1967), 30.

5. T. W. Adorno, Else Frenkel-Brunswick, Daniel J. Levinson, and R. Nevitt Sanford, *The Authoritarian Personality*, Studies in Prejudice (New York: Harper Brothers, 1950).

6. Leppert, in commentaries included in his recent anthology of Adorno's writing on music, has perceptively traced the arguments high and low in Anglo-American cultural criticism. Richard Leppert, "Music and Mass Culture," in *Essays on Music*, by Theodor W. Adorno, ed. Leppert (Berkeley: University of California Press, 2002), 327–72, and Evelyn Wilcock, "Adorno, Jazz and Racism: 'Über Jazz' and the 1934–37 British Jazz Debate," *Telos* 107 (spring 1996): 69–80.

7. Leppert, "Music and Mass Culture," 347.

8. Leppert, "Music and Mass Culture," 346.

9. Keith Negus, *Popular Music in Theory: An Introduction* (Hanover, N.H.: Wesleyan University Press, 1997), 36, quoted in Leppert, "Music and Mass Culture," 346.

10. Theodor W. Adorno, "On Jazz," trans. Jamie Owen Daniel, modified by Richard Leppert, in *Essays on Music*, 470–95, and bell hooks, "Eating the Other: Desire and Resistance," in *Race and Representation* (Boston: South End Press, 1992), 21–39. See, for example, Paul Whiteman, *Jazz* (New York: Sears, 1926). Whiteman was also featured in Universal's 1930 two-color Technicolor musical review *King of Jazz*, which includes a racist cartoon by Walter Lantz imagining Whiteman's comic encounter with the origins of jazz in Africa. See also Leppert, "Music and Mass Culture," 353–54; Ella Shohat and Robert Stam, *Unthinking Eurocentrism: Multiculturalism and the Media* (London: Routledge, 1994), 226; and Wilcock, "Adorno, Jazz and Racism," 71–72. A symptomatic song in this regard is Ray Henderson, Buddy De Sylva, and Lew Brown's "The Birth of the Blues," which begins, "Ohhhh, they say some darkies long ago/Were searching for a different tune/One that they could croon/As only they can./They only had the rhythm, soooo/They started swaying to and fro/They didn't know just what to use/That is how the blues/Really began." This opening verse, recorded by the Revelers on July 14, 1926, was rarely used in subsequent recordings of "The Birth of the Blues" (making the "they" of the song's standard lyrics vague) and cannot be found on the numerous Internet listings postings of the song's words, although the Revelers' 1926 version reached eleventh place on the charts. Ray Henderson, Buddy De Sylva, and Lew Brown, Victor BVE 35770-4, 1926; anthologized on *Breezin' Along with The Revelers*, compact disc, ASV, AJA 5278, 1999 (date and sales information from liner notes). Adorno mentioned the group in his 1927 "The Curves of the Needle" and in his 1933 "Farewell to Jazz." *Essays on Music*, 273 and 499. Given Adorno's familiarity with the Revelers and the popularity of "The Birth of the Blues," it seems almost certain that he heard this longer version. It might well have been one object of his critique, discussed later in this chapter, of the notion that such music had any significant connection to black people or to Africa. See also Frank Kofsky, *Black Nationalism and the Revolution in Music* (New York: Pathfinder Press, 1970), 9–10, 14.

11. Wilcock, "Adorno, Jazz and Racism," 76 n, 76, 77 n.

12. From a critically acclaimed British book of 1933: "Most jazz is written and performed by cosmopolitan Jews. The nostalgia of the Negro who wants to go home has given place to the infinitely more weary nostalgia of the cosmopolitan Jew who has no home to go to." Constant Lambert, *Music Ho: A Study of Music in Decline* (London: Faber & Faber, 1933), quoted in Wilcock, "Adorno, Jazz and Racism," 79 n.

13. Leppert, notes to "On Jazz," 492 n, and Adorno, "On Jazz," 470. Having investigated Adorno's time in England, 1934–1938, Wilcock concluded, "It is difficult to claim that Adorno never heard real jazz" and noted that "it has been suggested that Adorno had no experience of black jazz on which to base his argument. This is untenable." "Adorno, Jazz and Racism," 65, 69.

14. Adorno, "On Jazz," 472. Elsewhere, Adorno opposed the "perennial sameness of jazz" to a "basic organization of the material within which the imagination can roam freely and without inhibition, as within an articulate language" (Theodor W. Adorno, "Perennial Fashion—Jazz," in *Prisms*, trans. Samuel Weber and Shierry Weber (Cambridge: MIT Press, 1981), 122.

15. Indeed, at one point Adorno called jazz "the amalgam of the march and salon music," leaving aside Afro-diasporic influences entirely. "On Jazz," 477, 491.

16. Adorno, "On Jazz," 477.

17. Adorno, "On Jazz," 477–78.

18. Adorno, "On Jazz," 478; also see Adorno, "Perennial Fashion," 122.

19. Adorno, "On Jazz," 478.

20. When he wrote "On Jazz," he later confessed, he had been "suffering painfully from a lack of knowledge about America." "Scientific Experiences of a European Scholar in America," in *Critical Models: Interventions and Catchwords*, trans. Henry W. Pickford (New York: Columbia University Press, 1998), 227.

21. Adorno, "Perennial Fashion," 121–22, 123.

22. For example, with Max Horkheimer, he saw examples of Orson Welles's innovative film style (here he must have been referring to *Citizen Kane* of 1941 and perhaps to *The Magnificent Ambersons* of 1942) as gestures of "calculated rudeness" that "confirm the validity of the system all the more zealously." He criticized "early film comics" (he might well have had Buster Keaton in mind), for whom "individual weakness is proclaimed and revoked in the same breath," and "stumbling is confirmed as a kind of higher skill." Max Horkheimer and Theodor W. Adorno, "The Culture Industry: Enlightenment as Mass Deception," in *Dialectic of Enlightenment: Philosophical Fragments*, ed. Gunzelin Schmid Noerr, trans. Edmund Jephcott (Palo Alto, Calif.: Stanford University Press, 2002), 102, and Adorno, "Perennial Fashion," 129.

23. See, for example, Adorno's otherwise suggestive "Types of Musical Conduct," in *Introduction to the Sociology of Music*, trans. E. B. Ashton (New York: Seabury Press, 1976), 1–20.

24. Being tone deaf to nuances of audience response was a methodological failing Adorno came to recognize after he had begun his difficult encounters with empirical media researchers in the United States, from 1938 to 1941: "It is an open question, which in fact can only be answered empirically, whether, to what extent, and in what dimensions the societal implications disclosed in musical content analysis are also understood by the listeners and how they react to them. It would be naïve simply to pre-

sume an equivalence between the societal implications of the stimuli and the 're-sponses.'" Adorno, "Scientific," 227. However, Adorno's 1953 essay "Perennial Fashion—Jazz" bears no trace of this subsequent insight, one crucial to any contemporary reconstruction of critical theory. "Perennial Fashion—Jazz" was no more concerned with the complexities of audience response, let alone the raced complexities of audience response, than was the 1936 "On Jazz."

25. Stuart Hall, "Cultural Identity and Cinematic Representation," in *Black British Cultural Studies: A Reader*, ed. Houston A. Baker Jr., Manthia Diawara, and Ruth H. Lindeborg (Chicago: University of Chicago Press, 1996), 220. Also suggestive in this regard are George Lipsitz, "Against the Wind: Dialogic Aspects of Rock and Roll," in *Time Passages: Collective Memory and American Popular Culture* (Minneapolis: University of Minnesota Press, 1990), 99–132; Lipsitz, "Albert King, Where Y'at?," in *Dangerous Crossroads: Popular Music, Postmodernism and the Poetics of Place* (London: Verso, 1994), 173–81; and John Mowitt, *Percussion: Drumming, Beating, Striking* (Durham, N.C.: Duke University Press, 2002). Mowitt's work is discussed later in this chapter.

26. Mike Budd, e-mail message to author, July 20, 2003.

27. Duke Ellington, "Duke Says Swing Is Stagnant," *Down Beat*, February 1939, 16–17, quoted in Eric Porter, *What Is This Thing Called Jazz?: African American Musicians as Artists, Critics, and Activists* (Berkeley: University of California Press, 2002), 1.

28. Shohat and Stam, *Unthinking Eurocentrism*, 220–47. Particularly helpful is their discussion of relations between African American and Jewish American ethnicities in Hollywood, most notably and notoriously played out in the 1927 *The Jazz Singer* (220–41). Although widely considered a "Jewish film" by Jews and others, *The Jazz Singer* performs Jewishness in ways designed to appeal to non-Jewish audiences as well as to Jews. Compare it to the 1932 Yiddish American film *Uncle Moses*.

29. Richard Dyer, *White* (London: Routledge, 1997), 29.

30. Tim Wise, "Membership Has Its Privileges: Thoughts on Acknowledging and Challenging Whiteness," in *White Privilege: Essential Readings on the Other Side of Racism*, ed. Paula S. Rothenberg (New York: Worth, 2002), 107.

31. Adorno, "Mélange," in *Minima Moralia: Reflections from Damaged Life*, trans. E. F. N. Jephcott (London: Verso, 1974), 102–3, and Wilcock, "Adorno, Jazz and Racism," 78.

32. Adorno, "Mélange," 102.

33. Leppert, quoting Thomas Adam Pepper, makes a similar argument. Leppert, "Music and Mass Culture," 348 n, and Pepper, *Singularities: Extremes of Theory in the Twentieth Century* (Cambridge: Cambridge University Press, 1997), 23.

34. Susan Buck-Morss, "Hegel and Haiti," *Critical Inquiry* 26 (summer 2000): 821, 826.

35. Quoted in Buck-Morss, "Hegel and Haiti," 828. The quotation is from *The Spirit of Laws*, 1748. A translation by Thomas Nugent, revised by J. V. Pritchard, can be found at www.constitution.org/cm/sol.htm.

36. Buck-Morss, "Hegel and Haiti," 832.

37. Buck-Morss, "Hegel and Haiti," 833.

38. Robert F. Berkhofer Jr. defines ethnocentrism as "judgment of one people's qualities by another in terms of the latter's own ideals and standards" and says that it "has prevailed from ancient times to the present among all peoples." He defines racism as "a specific social doctrine" that was "an invention of the European peoples in the modern period of their expansion around the world." Berkhofer, *The White Man's Indian: Images of the American Indian from Columbus to the Present* (New York: Vintage, 1978), 35, 55.

39. Buck-Morss, "Hegel and Haiti," 833. Buck-Morss indicts "official" "(white) Marxism" as well for its insistence that plantation slavery was premodern and thus not deserving inclusion in narratives of class struggle against capitalism—an exclusion opposed by W. E. B. DuBois as well as by such Caribbean Marxists as C. L. R. James and Eric Williams, the first prime minister of Trinidad and Tobago, who argued that "plantation slavery was a quintessentially modern institution of capitalist exploitation." "Hegel and Haiti," 850, 851 n, 850. See, for example, James, *The Black Jacobins: Toussaint L'Ouverture and the San Domingo Revolution*, 2nd ed. (1938; reprint, New York: Vintage, 1963). Williams, whom James had taught in Trinidad, was an outstanding and well-known student at Oxford around the time Adorno attended Oxford's Merton College in the mid-1930s. Adorno may have known Williams personally; he likely was aware of the racism that Williams and other black students encountered at Oxford. Indications of this can be found in the twin critiques of racial essentialism and denial of lived difference Adorno wrote in 1945. Wilcock, "Adorno, Jazz and Racism," 73 n, 74, and Adorno, "Mélange."

40. According to Rolf Wiggershaus, the use of "Prejudice" instead of "Anti-Semitism" in the series title "stemmed from the caution of a Jewish organization intent on assimilation" and came about "in the hope that democrats would be more likely to respond to a call to fight prejudice and social discrimination in general than they would be to a call to fight anti-Semitism." *The Frankfurt School: Its History, Theories and Political Significance*, trans. Michael Robertson (Cambridge, Mass.: MIT Press, 1994), 409.

41. A comprehensive theoretical analysis of *The Authoritarian Personality*, including what Martin Jay has called its "stress on psychological rather than sociological explanations of prejudice," a stress visible in the text but later seen by Adorno as a result of a "misunderstanding," is beyond the scope of this chapter. Jay, *The Dialectical Imagination: A History of the Frankfurt School and the Institute of Social Research, 1923–1950* (Boston: Little, Brown, 1973), 227, and Adorno, "Scientific," 230. In hindsight, Adorno wrote of the volume, "The work's focus on the subjective moments was interpreted along the lines of the predominant tendency of the times, as though social psychology was used as a philosopher's stone, whereas, in Freud's famous turn of phrase, it was simply trying to add something new to what was already known." "Scientific," 231; see also Anson Rabinbach, "'Why Were the Jews Sacrificed?': The Place of Antisemitism in Adorno and Horkheimer's *Dialectic of Enlightenment*," in *Adorno: A Critical Reader*, ed. Nigel Gibson and Andrew Rubin (Malden, Mass.: Blackwell, 2002), 132–49. Also worth further analysis is the history of the reception and impact of *The Authoritarian Personality* within social psychology. Richard Christie, for example, reports "outrage" by strict disciplinarians at the project's combination of fields,

while Franz Samelson charts hostile responses from within the Cold War academy but also offers a telling critique of the studies themselves—that they failed to investigate the role of anticommunism in authoritarian, racist, and anti-Semitic personalities. One of Adorno's Berkeley colleagues, Nevitt Sanford, has written his own account, which includes a tantalizing reference to using their indicators to measure the antiauthoritarian effects of a college education. For a mainstream, mid-1960s treatment of the project and the reactions it produced within social psychology, see the work of Roger Brown. Lou Turner discusses *The Authoritarian Personality* in terms of Marxist theory. Christie, "Origins and Reactions to *The Authoritarian Personality,*" in *Strength and Weakness: The Authoritarian Personality Today*, ed. William F. Stone, Gerda Lederer, and Richard Christie (New York: Springer-Verlag, 1993), 5; Samelson, "The Authoritarian Character from Berlin to Berkeley and Beyond: The Odyssey of a Problem" (revised version of "Authoritarianism from Berlin to Berkeley: On Social Psychology and History," *Journal of Social Issues* 42, no. 1 [1986]: 191–208), in Stone et al., *Strength and Weakness*, 22–43; Sanford, "A Personal Account of the Study of Authoritarianism: Comment on Samelson," *Journal of Social Issues* 42, no. 1 (1986): 209–14; Brown, *Social Psychology* (New York: Free Press, 1965), 477–546; and Turner, "Demythologizing the Authoritarian Personality: Reconnoitering Adorno's Retreat from Marx," in Gibson and Rubin, *Adorno: A Critical Reader*, 150–71.

42. Max Horkheimer and Samuel H. Flowerman, foreword to the Studies in Prejudice series, *Authoritarian Personality*, by Adorno et al., v, viii.

43. Peter Uwe Hohendahl, *Prismatic Thought: Theodor W. Adorno* (Lincoln: University of Nebraska Press, 1995), 42. The project was also an attempt to realize the bringing together of empirical and critical work Horkheimer had outlined in 1937 in "Traditional and Critical Theory," based on experiences with similar questions (though not particularly concerned with anti-Semitism) in the late 1920s and early 1930s (see "Authority and the Family"). As Horkheimer himself wrote to a Frankfurt School colleague in December 1943, the studies "would constitute what we propagated in our first pamphlets after our arrival in this country: the bringing together of certain European concepts with American methods." Horkheimer, "Traditional and Critical Theory," trans. Matthew J. O'Connell, in *Critical Theory* (New York: Seabury Press, 1972), 188–243, and Horkheimer, "Authority and the Family," trans. Matthew J. O'Connell, in *Critical Theory*, 47–128. The Horkheimer letter is quoted in Wiggershaus, *Frankfurt School*, 360.

44. Max Horkheimer, preface to *Authoritarian Personality*, by Adorno et al., ix.

45. Horkheimer, preface to *Authoritarian Personality*, by Adorno et al., ix, xi.

46. Horkheimer, preface to *Authoritarian Personality*, by Adorno et al., xi. The definition is from Stone et al., *Strength and Weakness*, 4.

47. Horkheimer did, however, tell a colleague in March 1944 that he hoped the project would provide the "scientific proof of antisemitism being a symptom of deep hostility against democracy." Quoted in Wiggershaus, *Frankfurt School*, 361. For an account of *Studies in Prejudice* in the context of Jewish organizational efforts against prejudice within the ongoing national "race relations" project, see Stuart Svonkin, *Jews against Prejudice: American Jews and the Fight for Civil Liberties* (New York: Columbia University Press, 1997), esp. 11–40. For a harsh critique grounded in the

argument that "anti-Semitism gradually all but disappeared from the study of the authoritarian personality and become just one of the many topics under investigation" in the context of "the failure of Critical Theory" to come to terms with anti-Semitism, see Ehrhard Bahr, "The Anti-Semitism Studies of the Frankfurt School: The Failure of Critical Theory," in *Foundations of the Frankfurt School of Social Research*, ed. Judith Marcus and Zoltán Tar (New Brunswick, N.J.: Transaction Books, 1984), 312, 311–21.

48. Svonkin, *Jews against Prejudice*, 37, 211 n, and Jay, *The Dialectical Imagination*, 221.

49. The stress on empirical methods, however, may have been due to pressure from the American Jewish Committee. According to Samelson, in putting together their proposals, the authors believed there was a "need to develop empirical methods in order to reach an American audience as well as receive financial support." This seems consistent with the prevailing faith among liberal intellectuals in social-scientific research as a tool for problem solving. Samelson, "The Authoritarian Character," 34, and Svonkin, *Jews against Prejudice*, 28–40. For an account of the appeal of scientism to U.S. Jews and their allies for cosmopolitanism at midcentury, see David A. Hollinger, *Science, Jews, and Secular Culture: Studies in Mid-Twentieth Century American Intellectual History* (Princeton, N.J.: Princeton University Press, 1996).

50. As late as June 1945, Horkheimer planned to supervise a study connecting anti-Semitism to racism against blacks, including anti-Semitism and racism internalized by its victims. This seems to have resulted in the Bettelheim and Janowitz volume mentioned later, but there racism against blacks in the end played only a secondary role. Wiggershaus, *Frankfurt School*, 378, and Bruno Bettelheim and Morris Janowitz, *Dynamics of Prejudice: A Psychological and Sociological Study of Veterans*, Studies in Prejudice (New York: Harper and Brothers, 1950).

51. Both do mention the discussion of prejudice against blacks by U.S. World War II veterans and its correlation with prejudice against Jews found in Bettelheim and Janowitz, *Dynamics of Prejudice*. Wiggershaus points out that one of many relevant questions elided in a preliminary report on the research in the summer of 1944 was, "What was the status of anti-Semitism in comparison with discrimination against the blacks and the policy of wiping out the American Indians and confining them to reservations?" He also notes that the report made no mention of the "'social anti-Semitism' typical in the United States: unofficial but unquestionably valid and unavoidable regulations such as the exclusion of Jews from certain clubs, hotels or student organizations; or the percentage of positions given to Jews at most of the important universities or in a series of professions." He attributes these omissions in part to "courtesy for the host country and the interests of the Institute's sponsors." Wiggershaus also twice connects the work on anti-Semitism to Gunnar Myrdal's earlier work on racism in the United States, *An American Dilemma*, begun in 1937 with funds from the Carnegie Corporation and published in 1944, to which Horkheimer referred in December 1944 as he developed the Studies in Prejudice series. Wiggershaus notes, too, that one of the measurement scales discussed here, the E scale, included items related to "other minorities." Jay, *The Dialectical Imagination*, 219–52, 236; Wiggershaus, *Frankfurt School*, 350–80, 408–30, 426–27, 365, 350–51, 377, 412, 424; and Myrdal,

with Richard Sterner and Arnold Rose, *An American Dilemma: The Negro Problem and Modern Democracy* (New York: Harper and Brothers, 1944).

52. Wiggershaus, *Frankfurt School*, 368, and Jay, *The Dialectical Imagination*, 225.

53. In what follows, all unmarked citations are to Adorno et al., *Authoritarian Personality*, in general.

54. Levinson's views on race were remarkably consistent with learned views today: biological classifications have been arbitrary and do not exist in the world in pure form; there is nothing defensible about skin color's "misapplication to cultures" (103). His use of ethnocentrism, however, was broader than was conventional at the time in its extension to groups with no common ancestry.

55. Although hostility toward outsiders and class prejudice may as well have been factors, most accounts have linked the 1940s reputation among whites of zoot suits—and the related arrests and beatings in Los Angeles of those who wore them—to racist prejudice against Mexican Americans. See, for example, El Teatro Campesino's brilliant *Zoot Suit*; Mauricio Mazon's *The Zoot-Suit Riots: The Psychology of Symbolic Annihilation*, Mexican American Monograph 8 (Austin: University of Texas Press, 1989); and "Zoot Suit Riots: American Experience," Public Broadcasting Service, June 29, 2003, www.pbs.org/wgbh /amex/zoot/.

56. As has been widely observed, not talking about the continuing and enduring effects of racism in the United States hides its existence; making all groups "ethnic," whatever its ideally antiracist intent, risks marginalizing the particular forms of racial prejudice and discrimination experienced by African Americans, Asian Americans, Latina and Latino Americans, and American Indians.

57. The researchers included this scale, they said, because "Negroes are a large and severely oppressed group and since imagery of 'the Negro' has become so elaborated in American cultural mythology" (106). The research in this area was a forerunner of more recent work differentiating "modern racism" from "traditional racism," a still urgent theoretical and empirical task. See, for example, Robert M. Entman and Andrew Rojecki, *The Black Image in the White Mind: Media and Race in America* (Chicago: University of Chicago Press, 2000), 1–59, as well as Cornel West, "A Genealogy of Modern Racism," in *Race Critical Theories: Text and Context*, ed. Philomena Essed and David Theo Goldberg (Malden, Mass.: Blackwell, 2002), 90–112.

58. The M scale sought to identify antiwoman feelings by asking respondents, men and women alike, whether women "should be returned to their proper place in the home as soon as the war ends" (107).

59. The genuine patriot is "free of rigid conformism, outgroup rejection, and imperialistic striving for power" (108).

60. Anti-Semitism, for example, had been found to correlate with "opposition to labor unions and racial equality"—and to membership in college sororities (104).

61. Also discarded was a tantalizing question about the hostility of authoritarian personalities to avant-garde art, which Adorno notes was thrown out because familiarity with such art was limited to only a sliver of the population. Adorno, "Scientific," 234.

62. For some administrations, the scale was cut to five items, eliminating all four about Jews and one of three about blacks. This was done both to make the form easier to complete and to make sure that the mention of Jews in the survey would not set off

alarms in the respondents (125). However, the researchers later came to believe the five-question survey did not offer adequate possibilities for cross correlations (133).

63. As Jay notes, prejudiced Europeans seemed to consider both blacks and Jews hypersexual, while the prejudiced veterans in Chicago in Bettelheim and Janowitz's sample tended to consider blacks hypersexual but did not associate hypersexuality with Jews. Jay, *The Dialectical Imagination*, 236, and Bettelheim and Janowitz, *Dynamics of Prejudice*, 30.

64. Rabinbach, "'Why Were the Jews Sacrificed?,'" 133. Adorno later recalled that his work with Horkheimer on "Elements of Anti-Semitism" "was determinative for my participation in the investigations carried out later" that resulted in *The Authoritarian Personality*. "Scientific," 230.

65. See note 2. Franz Fanon trenchantly connected anti-Semitism with racism in *Black Skin, White Masks*, written within a few years of *The Authoritarian Personality*. From a tellingly different location, he took up several of the same issues raised by that book as well by the Horkheimer–Adorno critique of Enlightenment. Fanon, *Black Skin, White Masks*, trans. Charles Lam Markmann (New York: Grove Press, 1967), 109–40.

66. Adorno, "Scientific," 231. While people who study the Frankfurt School tend to view *The Authoritarian Personality* in terms of the overall project of critical theory, and while there are moments in the book that support that view, even progressive social scientists can be forgiven for missing the underlying critique of capitalism. For an example of a sympathetic account of the development of the F scale that nevertheless seems blind to the book's radical social critique and includes a devastating critique of its neoconservative critics (who complained that it ignored "left-wing authoritarianism"), see David G. Winter, *Personality: Analysis and Interpretation of Lives* (Boston: McGraw-Hill, 1996), 213–51; see also Brown, *Social Psychology*, 477–546. Among the most important contemporary work on authoritarianism has been Bob Altemeyer's development of the right-wing authoritarianism (RWA) scale and his application of the main post–Cold War version of the F scale, the dogmatism scale (D scale, or DOG), for liberal political purposes. Altemeyer, "Dogmatic Behavior among Students: Testing a New Measure of Dogmatism," *Journal of Social Psychology* 142, no. 6 (2002): 713–21. Like Winter, Altemeyer shows how neoconservative claims about the existence of "left-wing authoritarianism" were in general empirically unsupportable. Altemeyer has serious methodological questions about the Berkeley studies that he seeks to resolve, and he has problems with their reliance on psychoanalysis—all in the name of reconstructing the project. See, for example, his *Enemies of Freedom: Understanding Right-Wing Authoritarianism* (San Francisco: Jossey-Bass, 1988). Yet for him, as for Winter, the radicalism underlying the critique of authoritarianism, its relation to Marxist analysis, is nowhere in sight. And for neither of them is racism against blacks a major issue in this context.

67. Wiggershaus, *Frankfurt School*, 422. Wiggershaus is particularly good at comparing the different political projects and conclusions of *The Authoritarian Personality* and *Dynamics of Prejudice*. While the former aims at the reduction of those social-psychological tendencies that function as the "subjective mediation of the objective social system" of capitalist mass production in order to make possible the realization

of social humanity, the latter endorses socialization to the existent as a tool for reducing prejudice. "The authors of the Chicago study did not share the Berkeley group's critical views of society, and . . . they regarded the ability to take part in the American way of life as a sign of a well-developed personality, while for the authors of the Berkeley study this was a sign of conforming to a society which was full of failures and injustices and therefore a breeding-ground for prejudice." *Frankfurt School*, 427; Adorno et al., *Authoritarian Personality*; and Bettelheim and Janowitz, *Dynamics of Prejudice*. For more on the utopian dimension of "Elements of Anti-Semitism," see Susan Buck-Morss, *The Origin of Negative Dialectics: Theodor W. Adorno, Walter Benjamin, and the Frankfurt Institute* (New York: Free Press, 1977), 179. Her argument illuminates the political project—and silences—of *The Authoritarian Personality*.

68. Horkheimer and Adorno, "Elements of Anti-Semitism," in *Dialectic of Enlightenment*, 169.

69. Quoted in Wiggershaus, *Frankfurt School*, 429. See also, for example, Theodor W. Adorno, "Sociology and Psychology," *New Left Review* 46 (November–December 1967): 67–80 and 47 (January–February 1968): 79–97.

70. Quoted in Wiggershaus, *Frankfurt School*, 429.

71. And this especially need not be true for practices that, like *The Authoritarian Personality* research, seek to promote emancipatory action. Lucius T. Outlaw Jr., "Life-Worlds, Modernity, and Philosophical Praxis: Race, Ethnicity, and Critical Social Theory," in *On Race and Philosophy* (New York: Routledge, 1996), 159–82.

72. Jacqueline D. Martinez, for example, discusses the relations between representations and self-representations in *Phenomenology of Chicana Experience and Identity: Communication and Transformation in Praxis* (Lanham, Md.: Rowman & Littlefield, 2000).

73. Herbert Marcuse, *An Essay on Liberation* (Boston: Beacon Press, 1969); *Counterrevolution and Revolt* (Boston: Beacon Press, 1972); and "The Affirmative Character of Culture," in *Negations: Essays in Critical Theory*, trans. Jeremy J. Shapiro (Boston: Beacon Press, 1968), 88–133.

74. Dyer, *White*, 7.

75. Dyer, *White*, 10.

76. Theodor Adorno and Hanns Eisler, *Composing for the Films* (London: Athlone, 1994).

77. Mowitt's analysis concentrates on what he calls the "percussive field," performance embodying a hybrid of determinations, which can be conceptualized in terms of a "musicological division, a sociological division, and, for lack of a better term, a psychoanalytical psychological division." *Percussion*, 4.

78. Mowitt, *Percussion*, 34–41.

79. Mowitt, *Percussion*, 36.

80. Horkheimer and Adorno, "Elements of Anti-Semitism," 172.

8

Vergangenheitsbewältigung in the United States: On the Politics of the Memory of Slavery

Thomas McCarthy

> The settlement of the North American continent was . . . a consequence not of any higher claim in a democratic or international sense, but rather of a consciousness of what is right which had its sole roots in the conviction of the superiority and thus of the right of the white race.
>
> —Adolf Hitler, 1932[1]

It seems that wherever one turns these days, questions of how to deal with difficult pasts have risen to the top of national and international agendas.[2] Think, for instance, of the recent transitions from authoritarian to democratic regimes in Latin America, South Africa, eastern Europe, and elsewhere; of the international tribunals established to examine human rights abuses in Serbia and Rwanda; of the redress claims of indigenous peoples in Australia, Mexico, Canada, and elsewhere; or of the reparations recently paid by Swiss banks, European insurance companies, and German corporations for harms inflicted during the National Socialist period. Redressing past wrongs has increasingly come to be seen as essential to establishing present conditions of justice in societies scarred by the continuing effects of those wrongs.

The general premise of this chapter is that the United States has not yet adequately dealt with the many forms of racial injustice endemic to its national past. And the expectation animating it is that our thinking about this failure, its consequences, and possible remedies for it can be sharpened by drawing on the German case, particularly Germany's renewed efforts in the 1980s and 1990s to face the painful truth of the National Socialist past of the 1930s and 1940s. In that situation, the forum in which public memory was exercised and consciousness raised was a debate among historians—a *Historikerstreit*—that spilled over into public awareness. That peculiar circumstance allowed the

links between changing public memory and changing political culture and collective identity to appear in sharp relief. One key issue in that debate concerned the role that anti-Semitism, as a racialized mode of perception and interaction, played in the Holocaust. Others concerned the collective liability of
present-day Germans for state-sanctioned and state-implemented atrocities in
the past, the cultural and political costs of suppressing painful memories and
refusing to mourn, the relation of professional to popular history and of both
to public sites and rituals of commemoration, and the forms of patriotism and
collective identity suitable to a democratic society with an oppressive past. In
these and other respects, the German historians' debate may throw some additional light on our own tortured attempts to come to terms with a past of racial
injustice.[3]

I shall focus here on only one of the major constellations of racial injustice
that disfigure our past and present, the one associated with racial slavery and
its aftermath. The "logics" and "dynamics" of the constellations associated
with the near extermination of Native Americans; the forceful subjection of
the inhabitants of territories conquered from Mexico; the involuntary incorporation of native Hawaiians, Puerto Ricans, and Alaskan Eskimos; and the
exclusion or oppression of various groups of immigrants are sufficiently different to warrant separate treatments. Moreover, it is the black/white divide
that has most deeply marked the topography of American racial politics from
before the Civil War to the present day. The first section will focus on the recent debates in Germany concerning the role that publicly working through
the past can play in reshaping national culture and identity. The second section will use insights gleaned from that discussion to review our own failure
to come to terms with a past in black and white. I will conclude, in the third
part, with some thoughts on how public memory might figure in debates
about policies that address the legacy of slavery and segregation.

I

From the close of World War II to the present, Germany has been engaged in
an ongoing effort to come to terms with its Nazi past—in shifting circumstances and with varying aims, approaches, and results.[4] Immediately after
the war, a defeated and divided Germany had various measures relating to its
recent past imposed on it by the victorious allies—war crimes trials, denazi-
fication procedures, reeducation processes, and the like. From 1949 through
the early 1960s, however, dealing with the past was largely though not completely suspended, as energies were marshaled in the service of *Wiederauf-
bau*, or rebuilding. During that period, a general turning away from the Nazi

period was supported by the dominant view, in public life and in the schools, that the twelve years of National Socialism were an aberration in German history foisted on the people by Hitler and his henchmen. Reparations were made to Israel, the "economic miracle" proceeded apace under Adenauer and Erhard, and the Nazi affiliations of major public figures were concealed behind a wall of silence. A number of German intellectuals who grew to young adulthood under National Socialism and came to maturity after the war protested this curtailment of critical investigation into the past in the late 1950s but with limited effect until, in the second half of the 1960s, student radicalism and the accession of the Social Democrats to power tipped the balance in favor of a determined effort to come to terms with the past. As a result and aided by new access to Nazi documents, in the 1970s there began a steady stream of scholarly studies that left little room for doubting or denying the character and extent of Nazi crimes, the complicity of various German elites, the widespread support among large segments of the population, or the roots of Nazism in German history and culture. But in the 1980s, after the Christian Democrats returned to power under Helmut Kohl, conservative intellectuals were encouraged to take advantage of the new political climate to reclaim political-cultural dominance from the left opposition. This was the setting for the well-known *Historikerstreit*, or historians' debate, of the mid-1980s, which I shall be considering here.[5]

Ernst Nolte, Michael Stürmer, Andreas Hillgruber, and other professional historians undertook to reinterpret the events of the Nazi period in ways that reduced their singularity and enormity—for instance, by comparing the Final Solution to other mass atrocities of the twentieth century, from the massacres of the Armenians by the Turks to the Stalinist purges of the 1930s. Indeed, the Bolshevik Revolution and its aftermath also served as the major explanatory factor in their account of the recent German past: Hitler and Nazism were a response to the threat of Bolshevism from the East. In addition to "normalizing" and "historicizing" the Holocaust in these ways, historical work from this quarter also promoted a shift in perspective from solidarity with the victims of Nazism to solidarity with the valiant German troops fighting on the eastern front and with ordinary Germans suffering through the war's grim end. There was, of course, a political-cultural point to all this: it was time for Germany to leave behind its Nazi past, turn toward the future, and assume its rightful place among the leading nations of the world. It was worse than an intellectual error to view a proud German history solely through the distorting lens of a twelve-year aberration; it was a political failing as well, for it impeded formation of the strong national identity and confident national purpose needed for effective action in rapidly changing European and global settings. By that time, most of the country's inhabitants had been born after the war or had been too young during the Nazi period to bear any individual responsibility for it. Dwelling on a past that was not theirs served no better purpose than public self-flagellation and blocked the normal development of patriotic identification with the fortunes of the nation.

With such arguments, and in concert with their political allies, the conservative historians were putting revisionist history to public use in the interests of reshaping public memory—and thus German self-understanding—and of relieving public conscience so as to revitalize German patriotism. And it was precisely to this political-cultural challenge that Jürgen Habermas, Hans Mommson, and other German left-liberal intellectuals responded in the *Historikerstreit*.[6] I want now to consider briefly their responses concerning the public use of history and to do so from the interested standpoint of our own difficulties in coming to terms with the past.

The overriding political-cultural issue behind the historians' dispute might be put as follows: what should be the attitude of present-day Germans toward a Nazi past in which most of them were not directly implicated? Often enough, the collective past is a burden on the present, and the stronger the memories of it, the greater the burden. If the past in question involves terrible crimes for which amends can never really be made, the problems for collective identity and collective action can be immense. With worries of this sort in mind, many Germans felt in the mid-1980s that forty years of dealing with the Nazi past was enough and that it was time for Germany to move on—to reestablish continuities with the many glorious aspects of its history and traditions, to foster a more positive self-understanding, and to play a more self-confident and self-interested role in international affairs than its postwar pariah status had permitted. Those who argued against this—successfully in the end—noted that the process of publicly facing the past had gotten fully under way only in the late 1960s and was already throttled in the early 1980s by the *Tendenzwende*, or change of direction, set in motion when the Christian Democrats regained power under Kohl. And the character of that change—particularly the heavy-handed attempts to reverse the political-cultural accomplishments of the 1970s and to renew German patriotism, encapsulated by the infamous events at Bitburg in 1985—made it clear that Germany had not yet effectively worked through its past but was rather in the process of trying to repress it.[7] The questionable work of the conservative historians enlisted in these efforts only proved the point: professional history was being misused to improve Germany's weak self-image by touching up the ugly picture of its recent past.

There were, of course, historiographic criticisms of that work by other historians, but the line of criticism I want to focus on stressed rather the political implications of this effort to leave the painful past behind. Jürgen Habermas, in particular, advanced the argument that German national identity was inseparable from its historical consciousness and that any major shifts in German public memory would leave their mark on German self-understanding, with practical-political consequences. If those shifts were in the direction of denying and repressing the past instead of confronting and dealing with it, they would likely lead to forms of "acting out" rather than "working through," symptoms of which could already be discerned in German public life, most notably in various expressions of a mounting xenophobia. For what was at issue here was not a temporary aberration but a catastrophe with deep roots in German history and culture. Historians of the Holocaust had, for instance, pointed to a virulent strain of popular anti-Semitism as a contributing factor, a diagnosis later reinforced and sharpened in Daniel Goldhagen's *Hitler's Willing Executioners*.[8] Long-standing, widespread, and deeply rooted views of German racial superiority and Jewish racial inferiority had shaped a popular mind-set that was, Goldhagen argued, a necessary if not sufficient condition for the attempted Judeocide. Even those born later, who bore no individual moral guilt in that connection, had a continuing responsibility to work up, on, and through such elements of German political culture in an effort to break with the past. Failure to do so, Habermas argued, would come back to haunt German public life, for allowing the motivational force of such beliefs and attitudes to persist would only heighten the risk of repeated outbreaks of racially imbued thinking and acting, as already evinced in the growing conflicts over asylum and immigration. It would also amount to a renunciation of Germany's collective obligation to make amends for the past and a show of disrespect for its many victims.

On this point, referring to Walter Benjamin's idea of reversing the usual triumphal identification with history's winners for an anamnestic solidarity with its victims, Habermas writes, "There is the obligation incumbent upon us in Germany . . . to keep alive, without distortion, and not only in an intellectual form, the memory of the sufferings of those who were murdered by German hands. . . . If we were to brush aside this Benjaminian legacy, our fellow Jewish citizens and the sons, daughters, and grandchildren of all those who were murdered would feel themselves unable to breathe in our country."[9] Public remembrances and commemorations of the suffering of victims—through artistic as well as historical representations, in public rituals and public places, in school curricula and mass media—play crucial roles in transforming traditions and in determining what will or will not be passed on to future generations. Whether past evils are kept present in public consciousness, whether their victims are still mourned, Habermas continues, are central elements of who "we" (Germans) are and who "we" want to be. For recognizing past evil as integral to German history, as issuing "from the very midst of our collective life"—rather than as marginal or accidental to it—"cannot but have a powerful impact on our self-understanding . . . and shake any naive trust in our own traditions."[10] It is, in fact, an essential ingredient in any genuine effort to re-form national identity in full awareness of the horrors that issued from its previous formation. The unity of this "we" is, to be sure, by no means given: it is something that has to be continually shaped and reshaped in the public sphere. For in the politics of public memory there is usually a polyphony of voices, emanating from a diversity of "subject positions": the voices of victims and perpetrators; of resisters and collaborators; of those directly involved and those who were born later; of different regions and cultures, races and classes, political ideologies, and religious convictions; and so forth.[11] In a democratic context, this means that representations of the past may be publicly contested from perspectives that are linked to conflicting understandings of the present and orientations toward the future. And in the resultant dialectic of past, present, and future, debates over what happened and why interpenetrate with differences of interest and concern, conviction and attitude, and experience and hope among the various participants.[12] This is so in the German debates and, as we shall see, even more so in the American—where the immense presence of the descendants of slaves in the body politic gives the idea of solidarity with the victims of history a different political edge than it has in Germany and where southern views of slavery, the Civil War, Reconstruction, and their aftermath managed to gain a hegemony unlike anything to be found in the defeated Germany.

Another issue in the *Historikerstreit* was the extent to which historical scholarship can and should inform the politics of memory in the public sphere by, among other things, introducing an element of objectivity into what might otherwise become simply a matter of power. To be sure, the ideas of "objectivity" in question were, for the most part, "postdeconstructive" rather than foundationalist.[13] It was generally agreed that narratives and interpretations are not simply dictated by facts; that their construction is always informed by the historians' questions, interests, standpoints, temporal positions, and the like; and that there is no absolute divide between facts and interpretations but rather a continuous spectrum. However, the latitude for reasonable disagreement is palpably different at different points in the spectrum. As one moves in the "factual" direction, the constraints imposed by the evidence—documents, eyewitness reports, quantitative data, and so forth—significantly narrow the range of reasonable disagreement. The critical use of such sources by the community of historical scholars results in the elimination of many proposed interpretations, as the factual claims and presuppositions germane to them are submitted to critical scrutiny, as happened, for example, with the "Auschwitz lie" and the "Lost Cause" view of the Civil War. For though historical judgment is unavoidable, it is exercised in critical dialogue with a community of historians that can and often does achieve something approaching unanimity with regard to how the available sources bear on the plausibility of this or that interpretation.[14] And, as Saul Friedlander, Carlo Ginzburg, Jürgen Habermas, and others have argued concerning the historians' debate over the Holocaust, if nonfoundationalist practices of objectivity and truth were not possible, there would be no lies, and might would make right, from which there could be no appeal to the evidence of historical inquiry.

The question of objectivity raises moral and ethical as well as epistemic issues; representations of the past can be faulted not only for their lies, distortions, or half-truths but also for the unfairness they show and injustice they do to the victims of history. This can be seen, for instance, in the use, misuse, or nonuse a historian makes of the victims' own testimonies and narratives, in how she or he "negotiates" the relationships among the competing "micronarratives" of perpetrators, victims, and onlookers and between them and her or his own "macronarrative."[15] And the results of those negotiations have to be submitted to the scholarly community at large, where they will be renegotiated in the light of other judgments of fairness and ethical-political senses of solidarity. This becomes especially pressing when the descendants of victims live among "us" and experience disrespect for past suffering as a failure of solidarity in the present. As historical scholarship intersects with ethical-political debates about who "we" are and want to be as a people, about what is really in the common good and general interest, questions of doing justice to the victims of the past interpenetrate with questions of inclusion and exclusion in the present. Pablo De Greiff has put this point as follows: "we have an obligation to remember what our fellow citizens cannot be expected to forget," in the normative sense of what we cannot reasonably expect them to forget.[16]

What are we to make politically of these efforts to come to terms with the past? It is impossible to weigh their effects on West German political culture with any precision. There is no doubt in anyone's mind that the changes have been considerable. But how much of that is due to the external imposition of a democratic constitutional order and international pressure on its internal affairs, how much to the German "economic miracle" and widespread prosperity, and how much to countless other factors not directly connected with the *Aufarbeitung der Vergangenheit*, as Adorno called it, is difficult to say. On the other hand, we do have two strong comparative indicators of the political-cultural importance of publicly dealing with the Nazi past: Austria and East Germany. In Austria, which after the war represented itself as the passive victim of German aggression, there was never more than superficial gestures in that direction. And the results have been clear for all to see. Though it too is democratic and prosperous, its politics is still haunted by specters of its Nazi past. At the latest, since the end of the 1980s, when Kurt Waldheim was elected president after it was disclosed that he had lied about his wartime past (he had joined the German army in 1938 and later served with units that were involved in war crimes in Yugoslavia and Greece), and in spite of the anti-Semitic overtones of his campaign, the return of the repressed has been un-mistakable. Under Jörg Haider, the Austrian Freedom Party rapidly rose to prominence in the 1990s, regularly garnering about one-quarter of the popu-lar vote and eventually joining in a ruling coalition with the conservative Aus-trian People's Party. That it could do so on the basis of an antiforeigner plat-form and accompanied by an only partly veiled anti-Semitic rhetoric elicited shocks of recognition in the rest of Europe. By contrast, West Germany's neonationalist and xenophobic Republican Party, under Franz Schönhuber, enjoyed a comparatively brief rise at the end of the 1980s and to only a frac-tion of the height.

Yet closer to home, the fall of the Berlin Wall in 1989 and the hasty unifi-cation of East and West Germany in 1990 provide another comparative per-spective. For unlike the Federal Republic of Germany, the German Demo-cratic Republic dealt only superficially with its Nazi past. The official legitimation of the postwar communist regime as the triumph and rule of an-tifascist forces made that unnecessary. And after unification, it was the Stal-inist and post-Stalinist past that occupied public attention. But here, too, the return of the repressed was unmistakable. The antiforeigner violence that ex-ploded in the early 1990s and the generally xenophobic character of East Ger-man political culture made it clear that they had never worked through their Nazi past. It is, of course, true that after 1990 the process of reshaping an en-larged national identity for Germany as a whole was accompanied by various symptoms of political-cultural backsliding, including surges of neonational-ism and xenophobia and troubling appearances of anti-Semitism. But the worst of that came in the early 1990s, when the Christian Democrats ex-ploited the conflict potential generated by the vastly altered and deeply asym-metrical political situation to put the issues of asylum, immigration, and "guest workers" at the top of the public agenda; and even then, it was much worse in the East than in the West. In the West, the spontaneous popular protests against antiforeigner violence, the rising opposition to nativist poli-tics, and the continuing hold on the public mind of a civic nationalism defined by the liberal and democratic principles of the Basic Law made clear how great the discontinuities with the past had become. This is not to say that Ger-many has fully "mastered" its Nazi past; there is ample indication that this is certainly not the case. It is only to say that the politics of memory practiced there since the 1960s has had a profound effect on its political culture and na-tional identity.

II

Using the process of *Vergangenheitsbewältigung* in postwar Germany to gain perspective on the politics of the memory of slavery in the United States might seem, on the face of it, to be a stretch. After all, it has been nearly a century and a half since the end of slavery, and there have already been several rounds of intense public debate concerning it, in varying political circumstances, from post–Civil War Reconstruction to the post–World War II civil rights movement. Yet, as historians of professional and public history have made clear, the politics of memory on this subject went badly from the time that four million, mostly penniless, propertyless, jobless, and illiterate former slaves were set adrift in the post–Civil War South. After a brief, fiercely contested period of Reconstruction ending in 1877, the price paid for reunion was the reestablishment of white supremacy in the states of the former Confederacy.[17] As it has sometimes been put, the South lost the war but won the peace. And part of winning the peace was a reversal of the usual rule that victors in war get to write history: the professional and public history of slavery, the Civil War, and Reconstruction were dominated by prosouthern, antiblack perspectives until after World War II. Only since the rise of the postwar civil rights movement has that hegemony been overturned among professional historians, and the matter is still unresolved in public historical consciousness.

One might suppose that with the founding of the American Historical Association in 1884, racist historiography would have waned as professional historians began to replace their amateur predecessors. But prior to World War I, the "scientific" history of race in America was based largely on "scientific" (biological or anthropological) racism, and historiographic "impartiality" took the form of avoiding "partiality" against the antebellum South in the interest of sectional reconciliation.[18] Especially after the generation of historians who had living memories of the war and Reconstruction was displaced by generations who didn't, the aim of building a national community of professional historians, free of sectional conflict, motivated the negotiation of a consensual version of slavery and its aftermath. And abetted by the pervasive racism of the period—in the North and West as well as the South and across the boundaries of social class and political party—professional historians did in fact manage to achieve a high degree of historiographic agreement along racist and nationalist lines. This included a romanticized version of antebellum plantation life with softened images of slavery, a depiction of abolitionists and Radical Republicans as extremist agitators, and an account of the outrages of Reconstruction, replete with southern white "scalawags," grasping northern "carpetbaggers," and impudent black freedmen—that is, just the sorts of views that were disseminated to the nation at large in Thomas Dixon's fictional *The Clansman* (1907); D. W. Griffith's film version of it, *The Birth of a Nation* (1915); Claude G. Bowers's popular history of Reconstruction, *The Tragic Era* (1928); and countless other widely received portrayals. In this process of historiographic convergence, "there was considerably more give on the northern side, more take on the southern." One reason for this was "the near unanimous racism of northern historians" in this period, fostered by the rise not only of "scientific" racism and social Darwinism but also of American expansionism, Anglo-Saxonism, and consciousness of the white man's "civilizing mission."[19] Another was the large number of southern historians working in the North and the virtual absence of northern historians employed in the South.[20] Thus, there were "no southern centers of pro-northern historiography to compare with [William A.] Dunning's Reconstruction seminar at Columbia, which attracted scores of southern students, who under Dunning's direction turned out a stream of studies" that dominated Reconstruction historiography for decades.[21] And southern historians employed in the South worked under very strong constraints to hold to the received version of slavery and its aftermath. Black historians dissented, to be sure, but their work was marginalized in the profession by the white mainstream—John Hope Franklin was the first black historian to receive a regular appointment at a white institution, in 1956—and was consigned to nonmainstream venues, particularly the *Journal of Negro History*, founded in 1916.[22]

In the interwar period, especially in the 1930s, this ruling consensus, while remaining dominant, came under increasingly sharp attacks from different corners of the rapidly expanding ideological spectrum—not only from racial egalitarians, black and white, but also from northern and southern liberals and from Marxists and other left intellectuals.[23] There were a number of influences at work here: the new antiracist anthropology that challenged scientific racism, the repellent harshness of southern racism as epitomized in the numerous lynchings, the critical interpretive frameworks provided by left political and social thought, and the rise of a new generation of dissident historians, North and South. But despite this breakdown in consensus, no alternative synthesis appeared until after World War II. Thus, the overtly racist views of slavery propounded in the extremely influential work of Ulrich B. Phillips had no effective competitors and was still being incorporated into best-selling textbooks, such as that coauthored by Samuel Eliot Morison and Henry Steel Commager in 1930, with numerous subsequent editions.[24] Similarly, the dominant view of Reconstruction propounded by Dunning and his students—who represented it as a regime of humiliation imposed on the prostrate South by vindictive radicals and valiantly resisted by the Knights of the Ku Klux Klan—came under attack but was not displaced and entered into public consciousness through incorporation into popular fiction, film, and history. And again, the views of black historians, some of whom were now Harvard-trained professionals, were disregarded by most orthodox historians of the South, including the views advanced by W. E. B. DuBois in his monumental *Black Reconstruction* (1935).[25] Despite the continuing dominance of the racist orthodoxy, however, the underlying consensus among historians gave way in the interwar years to a conflict of interpretations.

The new antiracist synthesis toward which dissident historians had begun pointing in the 1930s finally took shape and achieved dominance after World War II. The horrors perpetrated by the Nazis under the banner of racial superiority and inferiority, the decline of scientific racism and social Darwinism, the worldwide breakup of colonial empires, the exigencies of international competition during the Cold War, and the rise of the civil rights movement gave wind to the writings of younger, heterodox historians who were formed in the interwar years.[26] Works by historians of that generation, North and South, who were committed to racial equality began to appear in the 1950s and by the close of the 1960s had completely transformed the historiography of slavery, the Civil War, Reconstruction, and post-Reconstruction.

The politics of the public memory of slavery and its aftermath gained momentum in the 1880s and 1890s, driven by many of the same forces that drove historical scholarship and in much the same direction. The public memory of the Civil War was particularly contested, for the meaning conferred on this great conflict in the nation's past was perceived to be closely connected to competing visions of the nation's future. In the end, "race" lost out to "reunion."[27] The demands of sectional reconciliation were met by figuring the war as a fight between valorous brothers while leaving the slavery and emancipation that were its cause and outcome in the shadows. This configuration also presented fewer obstacles to the reestablishment of white supremacy in the South, which generally met with less and less resistance as racism intensified in all regions of the country and the Republicans, in order to hold on to their northern white constituency, increasingly distanced themselves from the politics of racial equality. By the time of the fiftieth anniversary of the battle of Gettysburg in 1913, the central public commemoration could be staged as a "Great Reunion" among thousands of white veterans from both armies, with scarcely a mention of the Emancipation Proclamation, whose fiftieth anniversary also fell in that year. As the Baltimore *Afro-American Ledger* summed up the situation at that time, "Today the South is in the saddle, and with the single exception of slavery, everything it fought for during the days of the Civil War, it has gained by repression of the Negro within its borders. And the North has quietly allowed it to have its own way."[28]The last line proved to be an underestimation of the situation. That same year, the newly inaugurated Woodrow Wilson, in collaboration with the newly elected south-

ern Democrat–dominated House and Senate, initiated a policy of racial segregation in federal government agencies, a policy that eventually expanded,
especially under the New Deal, to include most federally sponsored programs
in employment, training, and housing, among others, as well as in federal
prisons and, as previously, in the armed services.[29] That is to say, from that
point until the 1950s or 1960s, federal agencies were not only a prime locus
of racial segregation but also enforcers of the "separate but equal" dispensa-
tion and propagators of it throughout the land. And, as W. E. B. DuBois noted
in 1935, a segregated society required a segregated historical memory: there
was a "searing of the memory" in America by white supremacist historiography and a public consciousness that had "obliterated" the black experience
and the meaning of emancipation.[30]

Given the enormous shifts in the historiography of slavery and its aftermath since the 1960s, one might suppose, especially in the wake of the civil
rights movement, the same to be true of public memory. And there have, to
be sure, also been important changes in the latter; but those who study popular uses of history have repeatedly noted a significant gap between academic
and public historical consciousness of these matters. "Generally Americans
believe that slavery was a Southern phenomenon, date it from the antebellum
period, and do not think of it as central to the American story." They are generally ignorant of the fact that "by the time of the Revolution it had become
a significant economic and social institution in every one of the thirteen
colonies and would remain so in every region of the new nation well into the
nineteenth century."[31] Moreover, many think of legally institutionalized racial
oppression as ending with emancipation and know rather little about racial relations in the post-Reconstruction South, and most are quite ignorant of institutionalized racism in the rest of the country—for instance, of the roles it
played in the formation of the American working class in the nineteenth century, in structuring immigration policy and citizenship law throughout our
history, and in the policies and programs of the federal government in the
twentieth century.[32] With the German discussions in mind, one might be
tempted to say that though our *Historikerstreit* concerning slavery and its aftermath effectively ended, at least in regard to fundamentals, in the 1960s and
1970s the process of public *Vergangenheitsbewältigung* has only just begun.[33]

A number of different reasons are offered for the lag in public historical
consciousness. To begin with, there is a clear popular preference for history
that confirms rather than confronts positive portrayals of the nation's past.
Thus, in public memory, what Nathan Irwin Huggins called the "master narrative" of American history remains largely unshaken: "a national history
teleologically bound to the Founders' ideals rather than their reality," an
"inexorable development of free institutions and the expansion of political

liberty" in which racial slavery and oppression are treated as regional "aberrations—historical accidents to be corrected in the progressive upward reach of the nation's destiny."[34] And then there is the appalling state of history instruction in the schools: "much of the best and latest scholarship never reaches high-school students because most high-school history courses are taught by teachers with inadequate training in history. . . . In Louisiana, 88 percent of the students who take history in high school are taught by teachers who have not even a college minor in history. In Minnesota, the proportion is 83 percent, in West Virginia 82 percent, in Oklahoma 81 percent, in Pennsylvania, 73 percent, in Kansas 72 percent." Similarly, in Maryland, Arizona, South Dakota, and Mississippi, the percentages are 70 percent or greater.[35] Nor is this failure generally remedied at the postsecondary level: U.S. history courses are not required, even for liberal arts degrees, in more than four-fifths of our college and universities. But the most frequently mentioned reason for the gap is the continuing volatility of race relations: talk about racial injustice in the past is typically experienced, by both blacks and whites, as being also about the present and is reacted to accordingly. This is not only the case in the South, though the heightened activism of southern heritage groups has exacerbated the difficulties there;[36] it holds for whites across the country and for blacks as well.[37] In short, relations to the passions and interests of the present are integral to the politics of the memory of racial injustice and have to be addressed as such.

Like Germany and so many other countries, the United States has a past that is still present, that refuses to pass away. And it is just the haunting presence of the past that the politics of public memory seeks to address. This type of cultural politics is, of course, not new. It is practiced every day by public historians, museum curators, artists, writers, journalists, and others in mass communication; it is a familiar element of local and national politics; and it has historically resulted in various forms of institutionalized memory. I am attempting here only to delineate more sharply and underline more emphatically its irreplaceable role in American society. Until legal, institutional, normal, everyday racism is publicly and widely understood to have been integral to U.S. history and identity as a nation, it will, I am suggesting, continue to encounter major obstacles to developing the degree of transracial political solidarity required for democratic solutions to the forms of racial injustice that are its continuing legacy. Without a developed awareness of the sources and causes of racialized practices and attitudes in the United States, Americans will, I suspect, continue to find it extremely difficult even to carry on reasonable public discussions of racially inflected problems, let alone arrive at just and feasible solutions to them. As Nathan Irwin Huggins has put it, whites and blacks are "joined at the hip," they have a "common story" and "share the same fate"; that is, they belong to the "same community" and cannot work out their futures independently of one another.[38]

But the United States has, of course, historically been a land of immigration, and that complicates the politics of memory considerably. The diversity of subject positions in our society not only is marked by the differences of class, age, gender, and so forth found in any society and by black/white racial differences and North/South sectional differences. It also includes positions connected with the conquest, settlement, and expansion of America and with the policies and practices of U.S. immigration. What does the politics of memory mean, for instance, to the large numbers of recent immigrants whose cultural memories take them back to other worlds? I cannot even begin to sort out these immense complications here, but I do want to argue that the responsibility to come to terms with the past of slavery and segregation is borne by the political community as a whole regardless of ancestry. This is so not only because the horrors perpetrated were generally state sanctioned and frequently state implemented (that is, were corporate evils for which there is corporate responsibility) or only because naturalized citizens who expect to share in the inherited benefits of a continuing enterprise must also share in its inherited liabilities but also because immigrant groups, whatever their prior background, unavoidably become "joined at the hip" to blacks and whites, become members of the same community of fate. The black/white polarity has fixed the geography of the color-coded world to which successive waves of immigrants have had to adapt; there is no comprehending the bizarre ethnoracial categories into which Americans have been and still are forced, apart from that polarization and its effective history. This is not at all to deny that Americans of diverse origins have their own histories to relate and their own politics of memory to pursue. It is merely to point out that the history of slavery and its aftermath has formed a template for those histories, that they have been shaped by it, and that their fates have been inextricably entangled in the racialized politics that is its legacy.

This broad and deep diversity of subject positions is sure to be reflected in the democratic politics of public memory—in rival narratives, conflicts of interpretation, and other forms of cultural-political contestation. There is no need for unanimity here for one substantive version of the American past to which all parties subscribe, but if there is to be public communication across differences, citizens do have to see themselves as members of the same political project, defined in large part by overlapping interpretations of constitutional rights, principles, and values. This is not a matter of returning to pure origins or foundations; there can be no reasonable doubt that our foundations were fractured from the start. But it is also not a matter of simply condemning them or burying them forever under heaps of criticism. It was, after all, the same motley of religious and philosophical ideas that was used to justify both slavery and abolition, both segregation and its dismantling. The politics of memory has to identify those deep tensions and ambivalences in our political-cultural heritage and trace the ways in which ideas implicated in injustice could, on critical reinterpretation, serve as resources for attacking it. It has to comprehend how black Americans struggling for freedom and equality were able to invoke putatively universal rights and principles and argue that they were being betrayed—how, in Judith's Butler's formulation, they could "seize the language of the universal and set into motion a 'performative contradiction,' claiming to be covered by it and thereby exposing the contradictory character" of hegemonic formulations.[39]

Successive waves of immigrants have also been able to tap into that political-cultural heritage to gain a place for themselves in American society, but because of the polarized force field of racial relations pervading it, they did so not only by tapping into the critical potential of universalistic ideals but also by making strategic use of their dominant, exclusionary interpretations.[40] An inclusionary politics of memory would today have to be conceived as a multiracial, multiethnic, multicultural dialogue aiming not at unanimity but at mutual comprehension, mutual recognition, and mutual respect. Anglo-assimilationism is in its death throes; the idea of a mosaic of self-enclosed subcultures is a nonstarter; what is left to us, it seems, are versions of an interactive and accommodative diversity of forms of life, with an overarching democratic political culture that leaves room for ongoing contestation, critique, and reinterpretation of its basic principles and values.[41] What has never been the case but must be the case, if we are ever to get beyond the racialized politics of our public sphere, is that blacks participate as equal partners in public life and public discourse. It is obvious that no one can speak for them in a public dialogue of this sort. But if they are to be included as equals, much will have to change in the massively unequal conditions of life and politics that have historically muted their voices.[42] So we seem to be caught again in a familiar circle.

In the final section, I want to take a brief look at one way a politics of public memory might help us break out of that circle. Consistent with the focus of this chapter, I shall be stressing the importance of historical enlightenment. To forestall possible misunderstandings: I am not claiming that the politics of memory exhausts the politics of race. The furthest thing from my mind is to deny the importance of social-structural factors such as the protection of group interests in the maintenance of social dominance. Nor do I harbor the slightest doubt that psychodynamic and sociopsychological factors are especially virulent in this domain. Nor, as I hope my discussions of the dialectic of past, present, and future in sections I and II make clear, do I think that the past can be separated off, either in theory or in practice, from the present and future. As I trust will become clearer in the course of section III, my selective focus here on historical consciousness is for analytical purposes only.[43]

III

Politics in America has been racialized from the start, and even after the successes of the civil rights movement, race remains "our nation's most difficult subject."[44] On the one hand, there has been an extensive liberalization of white attitudes toward racial equality since the 1950s. The great majority of whites are now opposed in principle to segregation and discrimination against blacks and in favor of integration, equal opportunity, and freedom of choice in employment, schooling, housing, and the like. On the other hand, when it comes to government policies and programs meant to implement these principles, agreement breaks down. So, to begin with, we have to try to grasp the nature and sources of this discrepancy. There is substantial empirical evidence indicating that among the most important sources of disagreement on such matters is the degree of "racial resentment": the greater the resentment whites feel toward blacks, the greater the likelihood they will be opposed to racially inflected remedial measures and inversely for greater solidarity.[45] Since the 1950s, biological racism seems to have increasingly given way to a kind of ethical racism expressed in psychological and cultural stereotypes.[46] The view that blacks suffer disproportionately from character defects of various sorts seems to be quite widespread among whites.[47] And this fits with the equally widespread view that black socioeconomic disadvantages are largely the result of their possessing too little of the crucial economic-individualistic virtues—motivation, self-discipline, hard work, and the like—that enabled Irish, German, Italian, Jewish, and other minorities to overcome prejudice and work their ways up. On this view, too many blacks prefer to depend on government handouts rather than trying to make it on their own, thus adding to the list of missing virtues "independence" and "self-reliance." There is, of course, a great deal of variation in opinion among whites on these matters, with a significant proportion rejecting this line of reasoning and the stereotypes on which it depends altogether. And even within the majority that accepts them, there are wide variations in the strength with which they are held and, presumably, their susceptibility to influence by evidence, argument, and experience. But there is no doubt that, overall, what George M. Frederickson called "the black image in the white mind" is still a major determinant of views on racial policies.

Two other important variables are whether discrimination is believed to be a thing of the past and whether the history of slavery and segregation is taken to be a major cause of the inequalities African Americans suffer under at present. Most blacks answer no to the first and yes to the second and in fact prominently cite these factors in justifying policies aimed at remedying racial inequalities, whereas most, though by no means all, whites do the opposite.[48] And that difference is consequential: the beliefs that racial discrimination has been eliminated, that "the playing field is now level," but that blacks, because of weaknesses of character, persist in seeking handouts and that they thereby claim and receive unfair advantages over whites are further ingredients in the racial resentment syndrome that is the best single predictor of views on racial policies. There are other elements, some so improbable that one hesitates to mention them, but at the same time so often noted that one can't simply ignore them. Orlando Patterson reports them as "misperceptions": "Only 31 percent of Euro-Americans believe that Afro-Americans have less opportunity to live a middle-class life than they do, compared with 71 percent of Afro-Americans [who believe this]. Most extraordinary of all, 58 percent of Euro-Americans think that the average Afro-American is as well off or better off than Euro-Americans in their income and housing condition."[49]

Even these sketchy remarks may be sufficient to locate one important contribution a politics of the memory of slavery and segregation might make to the larger politics of race in our society. Persistent racial injustices cannot be addressed by government action without significant support from whites. Opponents of such action are able to tap into and simultaneously add to a large reservoir of racial resentment by representing proposed policies as violations of the basic principles and values of American individualism and thus as promoting undeserved and unfair advantages for blacks at the expense of whites. In the give-and-take of a democratic public sphere, it is typically the case that complex issues can and will be interpreted, contextualized, and framed (or "spun") in different and competing ways. And there is a lot at stake in which frame predominates in public discourse, for that determines the definition of the problem, decides what is central and marginal to it, and circumscribes its justified and feasible resolutions. In the case at hand, effectively recontextualizing the racial issues of today as the latest chapter in the continuing story of slavery and its aftermath is, I want to suggest, an important means of countering attempts to tap into the reservoir of racial resentment and of diminishing that reservoir itself. The greater the public familiarity with and knowledge of that history, the greater are the chances of effectively interpreting current problems as belonging to its accumulated effects and thus of publicly framing them as moral issues or issues of justice.[50]

Consider only one example: the yawning wealth gap between white and black households, usually estimated to be about six to one.[51] I am suggesting that it could well have a significant effect on the public's understanding of that gap to know that much of it is due to differences in the respective rates of home ownership, which is the major form of savings in the working middle class, and that government housing programs from the 1930s to the 1950s overtly and almost totally excluded blacks from participation.[52] Until 1948, the Federal Housing Association's (FHA's) *Underwriting Manual* explicitly identified blacks as unreliable and undesirable buyers. And it also included a model racial covenant, that is, a contractual clause preventing resale to blacks. Of the nearly three million housing units that received FHA insurance from 1935 to 1950, less than 1 percent, or about 25,000 units, was for black occupancy. More generally, of nine million new private dwelling units constructed in that period, less than 1 percent was open to purchase by nonwhite Americans. And that was a crucial period in the massive migration of blacks from country to city and South to North: "In 1940, 77 percent of black Americans still lived in the South—49 percent in the rural South. . . . Between 1910 and 1970, six and a half million black Americans moved from the South to the North; five million of them moved after 1940, during the time of the mechanization of cotton farming. In 1970, when the migration ended, black America was only half Southern, and less than a quarter rural: 'urban' had become a euphemism for 'black.'"[53] A major result of government policies during this period—in conjunction, of course, with the discriminatory practices of mortgage loan departments, real estate agencies, and neighborhood "improvement" associations, among others, as well as with the massive white flight to suburbia—was a pattern of urbanization that left black Americans the most residentially segregated minority in the country, a condition that has persisted, along with many of its causes, down to the present day.[54] And residential segregation is, of course, a major factor in reproducing other inequalities, as it has a direct impact on employment opportunities, the quality of education and other public services, the availability of home and business loans, and electoral power, among other things.

Understanding the black/white wealth gap in this way, as a cumulative effect of the history of racial injustice—and one could tell similar stories about the origins of other existing inequalities—is likely to make a difference, I am suggesting, in the judgments of many whites as to whether proposed measures are "deserved compensations" for discrimination or "unfair advantages." For a politics of memory to be politically successful, it is not necessary to convince everyone. It is surely the case that in some segments of the population, racial resentment is rooted in deep-seated prejudices that are largely impervious to rays of light from the cultural-political public sphere.[55]

But this is by no means true of all segments, particularly not of those strongly committed to the idea of racial equality. However, even the latter normally have to be convinced that any particular racial policy is in truth a fair and proportionate remedy for the effects of clear and persistent discrimination. And it is often difficult to see how that could happen without a serious upgrading of public memory to provide the necessary background for public justifications of a historical sort. From this perspective, then, there is a political need for historical enlightenment.[56]

In the absence of widespread public familiarity with the causal background to contemporary racial problems, the political-cultural resources for resisting racist reframings of them are seriously impoverished. The thinness, spottiness, and frequent incorrectness of public historical consciousness of the story of race in America makes the cultural-political struggle to contextualize such issues historically always an uphill struggle and often an impossibly steep one. But even if this diagnosis is correct and part of the cure lies in broadening and deepening the public memory of slavery and segregation, how could that possibly be accomplished? The answer I am proposing, in its most abstract formulation, is through a politics of memory. Even in that abstract form, it has the virtue of directing attention to some underdiscussed political-cultural issues and underdeveloped cultural-political strategies. Moreover, as we can learn from our own history and from efforts to come to terms with the past in other parts of the world, there are already a plethora of tested models for filling in that formula and no obvious limits to imagining others. Given the peculiar gap between academic historical scholarship and public historical consciousness that marks our own situation, the politics of education has to be an important part of the politics of public memory in the United States.[57] In too many areas, conservative groups with racist ideologies have been much more active and effective in local school politics than their antiracist counterparts, all the more so as the very high degree of segregation in the schools effectively excludes or diminishes the voices of blacks in predominantly white districts. Unless antiracist whites in such districts take it on themselves to organize and struggle for curriculum reform, not much is likely to change at that level. And at the state level, the disgraceful minimization of degree requirements for high school history teachers—not to mention the common practice of farming out history courses to athletic coaches—is likely to be changed only by organized political pressure for strengthening state certification requirements. Beyond school politics, there is the larger field of public education centered around museums, exhibitions, performances, historical sites, holidays, celebrations, commemorations, and other public rituals. Social actors pursuing a politics of memory could certainly make a big difference there, for instance, by organizing a national campaign for a national museum of slavery. Broad social movements and the voluntary associations that subtend and spring up from them also typically generate flows of aesthetic activities that give multiform expression to their memories, perceptions, and concerns.[58] In mass-mediated societies such as the United States, this dimension of cultural politics is particularly important. To be sure, black Americans have long engaged in these forms of the politics of memory, but usually without the requisite level of support among whites.

Much of this may go without saying, and I have no intention of trying to list here all the forms of cultural politics peculiar to the field on which the politics of public memory is contested. But in closing, I would like only to mention another possible vehicle of public memory: reparations claims. In my view, one of the strongest arguments in favor of going ahead with the class-action lawsuits now being prepared is that, in present circumstances, this could prove to be the most effective means of igniting a "national conversation on race." On the other hand, there are a number of weighty arguments against taking this path—including the hostile reaction it is likely to elicit in broad segments of the population—that also have to be seriously considered. But I shall not attempt that here.[59]

Among white Americans, the political will to deal with the catastrophic situation of the urban "underclass," particularly the millions of "truly disadvantaged" blacks living in inner-city ghettos, is evidently too weak to resist the politics of racial resentment waged so effectively in recent decades.[60] To strengthen that will, it seems, we have to diminish the reservoir of racial resentment and make it more difficult to draw on it in framing issues of racial policy. I have tried to argue that a politics of the public memory of slavery and segregation could be one way of doing so. In present circumstances, it enjoys the advantage of having academic historical scholarship on its side. It suffers the disadvantage of having our political-cultural elites largely opposed to it or, at best, insufficiently interested in it. But that has been the starting point of most social movements. If enough people were to think it important enough, it could become a significant force for change. In any case, as with *Vergangenheitsbewältigung* in Germany, it may well be the only way that the descendants of the victims will be able to breathe freely in our country.

NOTES

For comments on earlier drafts of this chapter, I want to thank Derrick Darby, Dilip Gaonkar, Robert Gooding-Williams, and Jürgen Habermas.

1. Cited in Charles Mills, *The Racial Contract* (Ithaca, N.Y.: Cornell University Press, 1997), 106. Mills draws comparisons between the Nazi extermination of the

Jews, the "American Holocaust" visited on indigenous populations, and the "slow-motion Holocaust" of African slavery in respect of the millions who died horrific deaths in each, the systematic nature of the violence visited on them, and the racist ideologies that served to justify it. I shall be using "race," without quotation marks, to designate concatenations of social meanings, practices, identities, institutions, and the like that are internally connected with racial categorizations. It goes without saying that they are no less real for not corresponding to biologically fixed natures.

2. See Ruti G. Teitel, *Transitional Justice* (Oxford: Oxford University Press, 2000); Priscilla Hayner, *Unspeakable Truths* (London: Routledge, 2000); Martha Minow, *Between Vengeance and Forgiveness* (Boston: Beacon Press, 1998); and Elazar Barkan, *The Guilt of Nations* (Baltimore: The Johns Hopkins University Press, 2000).

3. There is another feature of German efforts to come to terms with the past that is relevant to our situation: the reparations paid to Jews since the end of the war and, more recently, to forced and slave laborers of diverse ethnic backgrounds. There has been a recent resurgence of interest here in the question of reparations for slavery and segregation; the Reparations Coordinating Committee, led by Charles Ogletree of Harvard Law School and Randall Robinson of TransAfrica, is preparing class-action lawsuits for that purpose. I discuss the morality of reparations for slavery in "Coming to Terms with the Past, Part II," *Political Theory* 32, no. 5 (October 2004), and the politics thereof in "Repairing Past Injustice," in *Reparations for African-Americans*, ed. Howard McGary (in press).

4. See Richard J. Evans, *In Hitler's Shadow* (New York: Pantheon Books, 1989), for a sketch of these shifts and a good account of the historians' debate of the 1980s. I shall be concerned here with the West German story; the East German story was quite distinct until their separate trajectories began to merge after reunification.

5. Many of the relevant documents, in English translation, are collected in *Forever in the Shadow of Hitler*, trans. J. Knowlton and T. Cates (Atlantic Highlands, N.J.: Humanities Press, 1993), and *Reworking the Past*, ed. Peter Baldwin (Boston: Beacon Press, 1990).

6. In addition to the collections mentioned in the preceding note, see the helpful discussions by Evans, *In Hitler's Shadow*, and Charles S. Maier, *The Unmasterable Past* (Cambridge, Mass.: Harvard University Press, 1988). A number of Habermas's contributions to the debate have appeared in English translation in a collection of his essays, *The New Conservatism*, trans. S. Weber Nicholsen (Cambridge, Mass.: MIT Press, 1989).

7. The Bitburg incident involved a Kohl-staged memorial ceremony at a German military cemetery during which then-President Reagan laid a wreath to honor the dead, among whom were a number of Waffen-SS troops. See Geoffrey Hartmann, ed., *Bitburg in Moral and Political Perspective* (Bloomington: Indiana University Press, 1986). Not long thereafter, Kohl appeared at a congress of German expelees from Silesia (in present-day Poland) and voiced his support for the German state boundaries of 1937, which included about one-third of Poland.

8. Daniel Goldhagen, *Hitler's Willing Executioners* (New York: Alfred A. Knopf, 1996). See also Habermas's speech on the occasion of the awarding of the German Democracy Prize to Goldhagen in 1997, "On the Public Use of History," in Haber-

mas, *The Postnational Constellation*, trans. Max Pensky (Cambridge, Mass.: MIT Press, 2001), 26–37.

9. This passage appears in an earlier (1987) article with the same English title as Habermas's address at the award ceremony for Goldhagen (see n. 8), "On the Public Use of History," in *The New Conservatism*, 229–40, at 233. It hardly needs mentioning that with the appropriate substitutions of "American" for "German" and "African American" for "Jewish," this sentiment might be directed toward our situation as well—but with at least three very important differences. First, today, German Jews number in the tens of thousands, while African Americans number in the tens of millions, so shaping an American "we" inclusive of the descendants of the previously excluded is a task of a significantly different order than forming an inclusive German "we." Second, like most Europeans, Germans tend to think of themselves as belonging to an ethnocultural nation, whereas the American people—at least since the decline of Anglo-Saxonism—generally understands itself to be multiethnic and, increasingly, multicultural. Finally, the United States fought a civil war over slavery.

10. J. Habermas, "On the Public Use of History," in *The Postnational Constellation*, 45–46.

11. On the notion of a "subject position," see Dominick LaCapra, "Representing the Holocaust: Reflections on the Historians Debate," in *Probing the Limits of Representation*, ed. Saul Friedlander (Cambridge, Mass.: Harvard University Press, 1992), 108–27.

12. Carlos Thiebault elaborates this dialectic in the democratic politics of memory in "Naming Evil," in *Razones de la Justicia*, ed. Maria Herrera and Pablo De Greiff (in press).

13. LaCapra uses this term in "Representing the Holocaust," 111.

14. This is a point argued by Martin Jay in "Of Plots, Witnesses, and Judgments," in Friedlander, *Probing the Limits of Representation*, 97–107.

15. This is the terminology of Martin Jay in the paper cited in the previous note.

16. Pablo De Greiff, "The Duty to Remember," forthcoming in Herrera and De Greiff, *Razones de la Justicia*.

17. See Eric Foner, *A Short History of Reconstruction* (New York: Harper and Row, 1990), and David W. Blight, *Race and Reunion* (Cambridge, Mass.: Harvard University Press, 2001).

18. See Peter Novick, *That Noble Dream* (Cambridge: Cambridge University Press, 1988), chap. 3, "Consensus and Legitimation." The remarks on historiography that follow draw on Novick's account.

19. Novick, *That Noble Dream*, 76.

20. Novick lists some of the former in *That Noble Dream*, 77–78, including Woodrow Wilson, who was born in Virginia in 1856 and grew to adulthood during Reconstruction.

21. Novick, *That Noble Dream*, 78.

22. One exception to this rule was an article by W. E. B. DuBois, "Reconstruction and Its Benefits," *American Historical Review* 15 (1910): 781–99.

23. See Novick, *That Noble Dream*, chap. 8, "Divergence and Dissent."

24. S. E. Morison and H. S. Commager, *The Growth of the American Republic* (New York, 1930). Novick cites the following passage (229): "Sambo, whose wrongs moved the abolitionists to wrath and tears . . . suffered less than any other class in the South from its 'peculiar institution.'. . . There was much to be said for slavery as a transitional status between barbarism and civilization." On p. 350, n. 46, he reports that in the 1950s, "Protests by Negro students and others at the City College of New York were ultimately successful in ending the use of [this text] in classes because of its racist characterizations of Negroes."

25. W. E. B. DuBois, *Black Reconstruction in America, 1860–1880* (New York: Atheneum, 1935; reprinted with an introduction by David Levering Lewis in 1992). In the concluding chapter of that work, "The Propaganda of History," DuBois provided an impassioned overview of post-Reconstruction historiography, including then-current textbooks: "This chapter, therefore, which in logic should be a survey of books and sources, becomes of sheer necessity an arraignment of American historians and an indictment of their ideals" (725). The story of slavery, the Civil War, Reconstruction, and post-Reconstruction they present "may be inspiring, but it is certainly not the truth. And beyond that it is dangerous" (723).

26. See Novick, *That Noble Dream*, 348–60.

27. See Blight, *Race and Reunion*.

28. July 5, 1913. Cited in David Blight, "Quarrel Forgotten or a Revolution Remembered?" in *Union and Emancipation*, ed. D. Blight and B. Simpson (Kent, Ohio: Kent State University Press, 1997), 175.

29. See Desmond King, *Separate and Unequal: Black Americans and the US Federal Government* (Oxford: Oxford University Press, 1995).

30. The phrases in quotes come from the last chapter of DuBois, *Black Reconstruction in America*, 725 and 723.

31. James Oliver Horton, "Presenting Slavery: The Perils of Telling America's Racial Story," *The Public Historian* 21 (1999): 21. He refers, for instance, to the fitting out of slave ships in New England and the financing of the slave trade by New York and Pennsylvania merchants.

32. See, for instance, David R. Roediger, *The Wages of Whiteness: Race and the Making of the American Working Class* (London: Verso, 1999); Matthew Frye Jacobson, *Whiteness of a Different Color: European Immigrants and the Alchemy of Race* (Cambridge, Mass.: Harvard University Press, 1998); Rogers M. Smith, *Civic Ideals: Conflicting Visions of Citizenship in U.S. History* (New Haven, Conn.: Yale University Press, 1997); and King, *Separate and Unequal*.

33. This is not to deny the continuing disagreements among professional historians of race that Novick recounts in *That Noble Dream*, 469–91; it is only to say that the white supremacist historiography that was hegemonic from the end of Reconstruction through World War II is no longer a viable option.

34. Nathan Irwin Huggins, *Black Odyssey* (New York: Vintage Books, 1990), xii.

35. Horton, "Presenting Slavery," 23. Jonathan Zimmerman summed up the situation in an op-ed piece for the *New York Times*, July 11, 2001: "Across the country, about 54 percent of history students in grades 7 to 12 are taught by teachers who have neither a major nor a minor in history" (A21).

36. The ongoing controversies about the public use of the Confederate flag are obvious indications of this. There are many others. Horton relates that when John Latschar, park superintendent at Gettysburg National Battlefield, suggested in a public lecture that the Civil War may have been fought over slavery, "the Southern Heritage Coalition condemned his words, and 1,100 postcards calling for his immediate removal flooded the Office of the Secretary of the Interior" (26).

37. Horton notes the numerous reports from interpreters at historical sites of negative reactions by white visitors to presentations of slavery—even at plantation sites (27–28). He also notes negative reactions by blacks to such presentations, which they often experience as painful and disturbing (29–30). The wisdom of preserving the memory of slavery has long been debated among black intellectuals, by Alexander Crummell and Frederick Douglass, for instance, as well as by Booker T. Washington and W. E. B. DuBois.

38. Huggins, *Black Odyssey*, xliv. In using the terms "solidarity" and "community," I am not signaling a communitarian line on political integration. Rather, I am referring broadly to the "political imaginary" that defines individuals' and groups' sense of belonging to a larger political community; and I am arguing that only insofar as whites and blacks imagine themselves to be integral parts of the same political community will the task of taking collective action on common goals related to the legacy of slavery be amenable to democratic resolutions.

39. Judith Butler, *Excitable Speech* (New York: Routledge, 1997), 89. See also Patricia J. Williams, "Alchemical Notes: Reconstructing Ideals from Deconstructed Rights," in *Critical Race Theory*, ed. R. Delgado and J. Stefancic (Philadelphia: Temple University Press, 2000), 80–90.

40. As Dilip Gaonkar has remarked in conversation, this tension presents peculiar problems for those contemporary "model minorities" who, unlike earlier European immigrants, get reracialized not as white but as "Asian American," thus marking another dimension of the American racial topography. The price of their higher standing in some spheres (such as education and employment) is their marginalization in others (such as politics and culture). For such minorities, understanding America's racialized past would seem to be particularly important to comprehending and transforming their own situation. See, for instance, Claire Jean Kim, *Bitter Fruit: The Politics of Black-Korean Conflict in New York City* (New Haven, Conn.: Yale University Press, 2000).

41. See Habermas, "Struggles for Recognition in the Democratic Constitutional State," in *Multiculturalism*, ed. Charles Taylor and Nancy Gutman (Princeton, N.J.: Princeton University Press, 1994), 107–41, and Robert Gooding-Williams, "Race, Multiculturalism, and Democracy," *Constellations* 5 (1998): 18–41.

42. On the nature and sources of "deliberative inequalities," see James Bohman, *Public Deliberation* (Cambridge, Mass.: MIT Press, 1996), chap. 3, and James Bohman, "Deliberative Democracy and Effective Social Freedom: Capabilities, Resources, and Opportunities," in *Deliberative Democracy*, ed. J. Bohman and W. Rehg (Cambridge, Mass.: MIT Press, 1997), 321–48.

43. See notes 45, 48, and 56.

44. Donald R. Kinder and Lynn M. Sanders, *Divided by Color* (Chicago: University of Chicago Press, 1996), 11. I draw on empirical material provided by Kinder and

Sanders in the analysis of racial politics that follows. For a broader survey of views on the role of race in American politics, see the collection by D. O. Sears, J. Sidanius, and L. Bobo, eds., *Racialized Politics: The Debate about Racism in America* (Chicago: University of Chicago Press, 2000).

45. As stated by Kinder and Sanders in *Divided by Color*, "On equal opportunity in employment, school desegregation, federal assistance, affirmative action at work, and quotas in college admissions, racially resentful whites line up on one side of the issue, and racially sympathetic whites line up on the other. Racial resentment is not the only thing that matters, but by a fair margin racial resentment is the most important" (124). For an alternative view that places perceived group positions and interests at the center of the politics of race, see Lawrence Bobo, "Racial Beliefs about Affirmative Action: Assessing the Effects of Interests, Group Threat, Ideology, and Racism," in Sears et al., *Racialized Politics*, 137–64. For another version of the social-structural approach that stresses the role of race in social stratification hierarchies, see Jim Sidanius and Felicia Pratto, *Social Dominance: An Intergroup Theory of Social Hierarchy and Oppression* (New York: Cambridge University Press, 1999). Admittedly, to the extent that the politics of race is driven by the protection of group interests or the maintenance of social dominance, it would be less susceptible to amelioration by a politics of memory; beliefs in racial superiority/inferiority would be secondary factors—ideological justifications for existing inequalities in the distribution of material and symbolic resources—whereas the line I pursue gives some independent force to such beliefs. It seems probable that all these factors and more are at work in our racialized politics and that effective political action in this domain will have to deal with all of them. How much weight should be given to each and in which circumstances is not likely an issue capable of definitive empirical resolution. In any event, in the present context I am content to leave indeterminate the extent to which our racialized politics can be improved by a politics of memory, though the argument would lose its point if that extent were not considerable. My characterization of these opposing positions is indebted to Derrick Darby's discussion in "Can Rights Combat Racial Oppression?" (unpublished).

46. Not completely, of course, as the hubbub around *The Bell Curve* by Richard J. Herrnstein and Charles Murphy (New York: Free Press, 1994) indicates. Kinder and Sanders report a study in which about 75 percent of whites rejected the proposition that blacks come from a biologically inferior race, against about 10 percent who agreed with it (326 n. 60). To be sure, biological racism also typically includes psychological and cultural stereotypes, but unlike ethical racism, it takes them to be biologically rooted and thus largely unalterable.

47. See Kinder and Sanders, *Divided by Color*, chap. 5, and the survey results summed up in the table on p. 107.

48. Kinder and Sanders, *Divided by Color*. A similar divide is reported by Sears et al. in *Racialized Politics*, 9–16, drawing on the extensive survey analyses of Howard Schuman et al. in *Racial Attitudes in America: Trends and Interpretations*, rev. ed. (Cambridge, Mass.: Harvard University Press, 1997). As I shall explain later in this chapter the view that discrimination has been largely overcome and that persistent inequalities are due not to white racism but to black culture and character figures im-

portantly in the lower level of white support for government programs meant to address them. This means, of course, that the politics of memory, however necessary it may be to gaining enduring majority support for race-targeted reforms, is by no means sufficient. Politically contested interpretations of the present and of its relation to the past are very important factors in the politics of race, and a more complete discussion would have to take them into account; but here I address the latter only briefly and the former not at all. So I do not claim to be offering a complete picture, nor do I suppose that past and present can be kept apart either in theory or in practice. I am merely focusing analytically on the past so that I can develop the neglected dimension of public memory. I am grateful to Derrick Darby for pressing this point.

49. Orlando Patterson, *The Ordeal of Integration* (Washington, D.C.: Civitas, 1997), 57.

50. The importance of preexisting cultural beliefs in enabling and constraining the definition of problems, their causes, and their solutions is stressed by social mobilization theorists who use a frame approach. See, for instance, David A. Snow and Robert D. Benford, "Ideology, Frame Resonance, and Participant Mobilization," *International Social Movement Research* 1 (1988): 197–217.

51. See, for instance, Melvin L. Oliver and Thomas M. Shapiro, *Black Wealth/White Wealth* (New York: Routledge, 1995).

52. King, *Separate and Unequal*, chap. 6.

53. Nicholas Lehmann, *The Promised Land* (New York: Vintage, 1992), 6.

54. See Douglas Massey and Nancy Denton, *American Apartheid: Segregation and the Making of the Underclass* (Cambridge, Mass.: Harvard University Press, 1993).

55. The social-psychological approach to racial resentment of Kinder and Sanders does in fact stress its affective as well as its cognitive side, and it does recognize the sometimes considerable independence of affects from beliefs. In particular, negative feelings toward blacks sometimes operate covertly in relation to stated beliefs and sometimes even unconsciously in relation to conscious awareness of prejudice.

56. Robert Gooding-Williams has objected in conversation that in focusing on ignorance and false belief, my argument gives too much weight to the cognitive dimensions of racism. That is indeed my admittedly one-sided emphasis here—though the politics of memory, as I understand it, does include public rites, representations, and activities of many different sorts, all of which have their affective sides. But my choice of argumentative emphasis should not be construed as theoretically calling into question the importance either of perceived interests or of deeply entrenched prejudices and other less "cognitive" factors. I want to argue only that historical consciousness and historical enlightenment also have an important role to play in the politics of race.

57. In "Race, Multiculturalism, and Democracy," Robert Gooding-Williams stresses the importance of "race-conscious multicultural education" in fostering the capacity for democratic deliberation in a society like ours.

58. See, for instance, the discussion of the "tools of memory making" in South Africa in S. Nuttall and C. Coetzee, eds., *Negotiating the Past* (Cape Town: Oxford University Press, 1998).

59. I do so in the two essays mentioned in note 3.

60. This has led a number of theorists and activists to advocate class-based rather than race-based policies to deal with urban poverty. But public support for such policies is also affected by their racial subtext and the willingness of political opponents to exploit it. So it is difficult to see how an effective political response to urban poverty could be mounted and sustained while ignoring the operations of racial resentment. Reparations payments to fund a "Marshall Plan" for urban ghettos are increasingly mentioned as another possible line of attack.

9

Resistance to Memory: The Uses and Abuses of Public Forgetting

Andreas Huyssen

In contemporary culture, obsessed as it is with memory and trauma, forgetting has a consistently bad press. It is described as the failure of memory: clinically as dysfunction, socially as distortion, academically as a form of original sin, experientially as the lamentable by-product of aging. This negative take on forgetting is of course neither surprising nor particularly new.

We may have a phenomenology of memory, but we certainly do not have a phenomenology of forgetting. The neglect of forgetting can be documented in philosophy from Plato to Kant, from Descartes to Heidegger, Derrida, and Umberto Eco, who once denied on semiotic grounds that there could be something like an art of forgetting analogous to the art of memory.[1] Forgetting is simply no topic for metaphysicians, antimetaphysicians, or semioticians, whereas memory clearly is. The poets, in turn, from Homer to Goethe, have warned us against the dangers of lotophagy and self-forgetfulness in the present, and whole cultural movements such as the Renaissance or romanticism have made memory a central project. And even the movies have made the presence of memory the criterion for distinguishing a human from a cyborg (*Blade Runner*), or they represent forgetting as a murderous CIA experiment gone awry (*The Bourne Identity*). But when it comes to theorizing forgetting, it appears at best as an unavoidable supplement of memory, a deficiency, a lack to be filled, rather than as the multiple-layered phenomenon that serves as memory's very condition of possibility.

Issues of memory and temporality have of course been central to the work of Adorno and Benjamin. Adorno's much-quoted and often-abused statement about the writing of poetry after Auschwitz being barbaric has played a central role in the debates about the limits of representation and about the aesthetics and ethics of how to remember the Holocaust. Less well known but equally influential has been his thesis that all reification is a forgetting, a thesis that sees the forgetting of labor in the production of commodities as the very ground for commodity fetishism and its insidious effects on structures of subjectivity in modern culture. This argument issuing from Marx and political economy has found popular appeal in the notion that consumer fetishism equals oblivion, and it has shaped the generally negative and critical take on issues of nostalgia in contemporary consumer culture. In the process, however, the grounding of the argument in an ethos of production was itself forgotten. Nevertheless, the very rise of a publicly and politically effective memorial culture across the globe in the 1990s does not sit easy with Adorno's claim—not unless one were oneself to embrace Adorno's rhetoric of exaggeration and say that capitalism now exploits and markets even that which is needed to resist forgetfulness, namely, memory itself. Clearly, there is some truth in the notion of memory exploitation, but it does not exhaust the multiple effects of late twentieth-century memorial culture. Adorno's view of the identity of commodity and forgetting would not even permit us to analyze the complexities of public memory debates, an analysis that must include both the disabling and the enabling dimension of memory politics and memory markets.

If anything, Benjamin has been even more influential in contemporary memory debates. His call to brush history against the grain, his distinction between *Erinnerung* and *Gedächtnis*, his understanding of memory's power to disturb and to disrupt, his critique of all progressive linear modes of historiography, his eye for the constitutive linkage between culture and violence, and his speaking out for the dispossessed of all times have become staple and citation in much transnational work on the politics of memory. But both Adorno and Benjamin, engaged in a life-and-death struggle against the fascist politics of forgetting, were for understandable historical reasons unable or unwilling to focus on potentially generative aspects of forgetting. In different ways, the demand for memory held sway in their fundamental concern with temporality, and this may at least partially explain their continuing influence and presence in contemporary thought. Their work thus needs to be seen as part of a long and complex history of forgetfulness regarding forgetting in European thought and literature. At the same time, Adorno's and Benjamin's exploration of temporality itself as a changing historical phenomenon that responds to political and cultural pressures must be remembered as we try to grasp the memorial culture of our day with its slowly changing sense of time and space.

That long history of forgetfulness regarding forgetting has been magisterially described in Harald Weinrich's recent book *Lethe: Kunst und Kritik des Vergessens* (1997).[2] Weinrich posits an "ars oblivionis" in analogy to Frances

Yates's *Art of Memory*.[3] But as the subtitle indicates, an "ars oblivionis" cannot be had without a simultaneous critique of forgetting. This difference in status between memory and forgetting is further emphasized in Paul Ricoeur's observation that we speak of a duty to remember but never of a duty to forget.[4] People would probably be scandalized by the suggestion that just as there is an ethics of memory work, there could also be an ethics rather than only a pathology of forgetting. Memory, at any rate, seems to require effort and work; forgetting, on the other hand, just happens.

This binary structure remains deeply entrenched. Thus, even when historians such as Charles Maier lament a surfeit of memory in contemporary culture, they will not go so far as to advocate forgetting.[5] Nor will our professional memorians make enough of the paradox that phenomenologically and psychoanalytically forgetting actually creates memory. Nor will they celebrate creative forgetting as Nietzsche once did when he acknowledged that memory without forgetting is a pathological affliction. Nietzsche spoke of the hypertrophy of history, just as we might speak today of a hypertrophy of memory.[6] However, the opprobrium remains reserved for forgetting, never for memory. There may be too much memory, but it's too much of a good thing. In the meantime, forgetting continues to hover under a cloud of moral suspicion, avoidable failure, undesirable regression, and critical neglect. Memory, on the other hand, is considered crucial for the social and cultural cohesiveness of a society. Identities of any kind depend on it. A society without memory is anathema.

The moral demand to remember therefore has been articulated in religious, cultural, and political contexts, but nobody apart from Nietzsche has ever made a general case for an ethics of forgetting. Neither will I do so here, but clearly we need to move beyond the "commonsense" binary that pits memory against forgetting as irreconcilable opposites.[7] We must also get beyond simply restating the paradox that forgetting is constitutive of memory. For to acknowledge this paradox is too easily reconcilable with the continued privileging of memory over forgetting. Case in point: Heidegger's *Sein und Zeit*. In a little-noticed aside, Heidegger recognizes that memory is possible only on the ground of forgetting and not vice versa while at the same time arguing that the power of forgetting (*die Macht des Vergessens*) is destructive and inauthentic while only *Erinnerung* has authenticity.[8] In other words, something inauthentic and destructive is at the very foundation of that which is most highly valued by the philosopher: *Erinnerung*. There may be some real wisdom in Heidegger's marginal remark. His overall argument, however, which reappears in Adorno in its Marxist incarnation (the forgetting of production as the ground for commodity fetishism), prevents us from exploring specific cases in which forgetting might have that legitimacy consistently denied it in political thought, philosophy, and literature. We need only remind ourselves of the pathology of total memory, as Borges describes it so brilliantly in his story *Funés, el memorioso*, to acknowledge that forgetting, in its mix with memory, is crucial to both conflict and resolution in the narratives that make up our public and intimate lives. Forgetting not only makes life livable but is the basis for the miracles and epiphanies of memory itself.

Weinrich and Ricoeur, in their attempt to theorize forgetting, tell an old story, but forgetting in our post-twentieth-century world does carry a very specific burden. Both authors respond to the pressures of our times by giving the memory of the Shoah a key role in their works. Weinrich's penultimate chapter treats texts by Eli Wiesel, Primo Levi, and Jorge Semprun; Ricoeur, troubled as he is by the simultaneous surfeit of memory and excess of forgetting in contemporary media culture, foregrounds this public preoccupation as a major impetus for the writing of *La mémoire, l'histoire, l'oubli*. But in the end, the phenomenology of forgetting that Ricoeur offers is still only a short concluding chapter in a book dedicated to history and memory, but it stands as an important quest to differentiate between forms of forgetting as they play out in the political and public spheres.

I

I would therefore like to take up the challenge posed by the all-too-brief chapter on forgetting in Ricoeur's book. My purpose, too, is to go beyond the simplistic opposition of remembrance and oblivion by differentiating between forms of forgetting as they play out in the political and public sphere. Forgetting needs to be placed in a field of terms and phenomena such as silence, disarticulation, evasion, effacement, erosion, and repression—all of which reveal a spectrum of strategies as complex as that of memory itself. Ricoeur suggests some basic distinctions: first, forgetting as *mémoire empêchée* (blocked memory), which is related primarily to the Freudian unconscious and the repetition compulsion; second, forgetting as *mémoire manipulée* (manipulated memory), which is inherently related to narrativity in the sense that any narrative is selective and will imply, passively or actively, a certain forgetting of how a story could have been told differently; and, third, *l'oubli commandé* (the command to forget) or institutional forgetting, which pertains in the case of amnesty. I do find Ricoeur's attempt to define modes of forgetting constructive but would like to complicate his second and third mode by inserting them into specific historical contexts.

Much of my own past work on memory has been concerned with the politics of public memory, a topic that has been central to Germans of my generation since the 1960s. As a literary and cultural critic I was always interested in the politics of memory in relation to what Jan Assmann has called cultural memory: the memory embodied in artifacts such as fiction, drama, and film but also monuments, sculpture, painting, and architecture.[9] At the same time, I have never analyzed such cultural objects in isolation. I have always emphasized their constitutive role for the transformation of public memory itself. Through symptomatic readings of cultural memory in this sense, my aim has been to trace the ways in which the post-Shoah world has dealt with that catastrophe, separate and apart from politicians' speeches, parliamentary debates, government measures of restitution or reparation, trials, and prosecutions.

Given the wealth of Holocaust representations over the decades, I have become increasingly skeptical about demands that on principle posit an aesthetics and an ethics of nonrepresentability, often by drawing on a misreading of Adorno's post-1945 statement about poetry after Auschwitz.[10] When not acknowledging that the limits of representation becomes itself an ideology, we are locked into a last-ditch defense of modernist purity against the onslaught of new and old forms of representation, and ethics is in danger of being turned into moralizing against any form of representation that does not meet the assumed standard. The result is a Holocaust formalism that all too often draws on the old distinction between art and mass media, high and low culture. To the cultural historian, it is therefore preferable to analyze how representations in different aesthetic and narrative modes and in different media have shaped processes of public memory and forgetting in different countries and cultures. Of course, representations of historical trauma do pose formidable theoretical and political challenges, but this should not prevent us from acknowledging the changing conditions of mediation and transmission that may require new forms, new genres, and new media for public memory to renew itself.

Without questioning the continued need for public memory of the Shoah, I want to discuss a politics of public forgetting different from the one we all know as simply repression or denial. I will make a historical case in favor of public forgetting—not in the abstract or in general, to be sure, but in relation to concrete situations in which a public forgetting proved to be constitutive of a politically desirable memory discourse. This is not a Nietzschean move privileging creative forgetting. In the second of his *Untimely Meditations*, Nietzsche favored a kind of superhistorical stance in an overblown attempt to argue for a radically new German culture in the spirit of classical Greece. By contrast, my argument for a politics of forgetting is historically specific, wholly contingent, and it makes its own politics explicit. Trying to legislate forgetting, as my examples will show, is as futile as attempting to legislate correct ways of remembering. My aim is rather to explore the complexities and effects of public forgetting that are lost both in the moralizing and in the epistemological accounts of the nexus between memory and forgetting.

I will take two recent debates in which memory and forgetting are engaged in a compulsive pas de deux: Argentina and the memory of the state terror and Germany and the memory of the *Luftkrieg*. The common denominator and context for both is of course the Holocaust. The political link between these two geographically and historically so disparate cases is that, in both, forgetting as well as memory has been crucial in the transition from dictatorship to democracy. Both feature a form of forgetting necessary to make cultural, legal, and symbolic claims for a national memory politics. Especially in the German case, I am tempted to speak of a politically progressive form of public forgetting while recognizing that a price has to be paid for any such instrumentalization of memory and forgetting in the public realm. Even politically desirable forms of forgetting will result in distortions and evasions. The price to be paid is comprehensiveness, accuracy, and complexity.

In Argentina, it was a political dimension of the past, namely, the killings by the armed urban guerrilla, of the early 1970s, that had to be "forgotten" (silenced, disarticulated) in order to allow a national consensus of memory to emerge around the victim figure of the *desaparecido*.[11] In Germany, by contrast, it was the experiential dimension of the carpet bombings of German cities in World War II that had to be forgotten in order to make the full acknowledgment of the Holocaust a central part of national history and self-understanding. My point here is that memory politics itself cannot do without forgetting. This is, after all, the meaning of Ricoeur's *oubli manipulé*, which results from the unavoidability of memory's mediation through narrative. But contrary to Ricoeur, who argues that *oubli manipulé* is the result of *mauvaise foi* and a *vouloir-ne-pas-savoir*, I argue that conscious and willed forgetting can be the product of a politics that ultimately benefits both the *vouloir-savoir* and the construction of a democratic public sphere. I aim to show that just as *oubli manipulé* does not have to be seen in exclusively negative light (depending on who it is who manipulates and for what purpose), *oubli commandé* (amnesty) may have effects precisely counter to the intentions of its advocates.

II

Argentina provides my first example for both propositions. Ever since the end of the military dictatorship in 1983, Argentina has been engaged in a political, juridical, and symbolic struggle not to forget the fate of the *desaparecidos*, the roughly 30,000 victims of the state terror perpetrated by the military dictatorship and its squads in the years 1976–1983. Forgetfulness was clearly attractive to a large part of Argentinean society after the fall of the regime in 1983. But the intense human rights struggle waged to acknowledge the criminality of the military regime proved to be largely successful. Legal convictions remained insufficient and were cut short by President Menem's amnesty law of 1990, a law recently challenged by Argentina's new president, Néstor Kirchner.

Memory of the dictatorship clearly was crucial for the success of Argentina's transition to democracy, and Argentina today, despite its economic woes, has arguably the most intense memory debates of any of the Latin American countries that were plagued by military campaigns of repression, torture, and murder in the Cold War decades after the 1960s—more intense than those in Brazil, Uruguay, Chile, and Guatemala. This "success" has certainly been a factor in keeping the military in the barracks during the economic and social free fall of Argentina since 2001. At the same time, the very success and effectiveness of memory politics depended on the form of forgetting that Ricoeur labeled *mémoire manipulée*. And it involved an *oubli commandé* that only served to strengthen the moral support for human rights activists.

A little more background may be required here. Ever since 1977, the public protests and weekly demonstrations of the mothers and grandmothers of the Plaza de Mayo in Buenos Aires have kept the terror of the Argentinian state against its own citizens in the public eye. International coverage of these protests, beginning with the soccer world championship of 1978, has provided a kind of security blanket at least for some of the protesters during the years of the dictatorship itself. Neither direct threats nor vilifications of the mothers as the "madwomen of the Plaza de Mayo" (*las locas*) were able to distract this group of courageous women from their goal of establishing what happened to the disappeared and who was responsible.

After Argentina's war with Britain over the Malvinas had gone awry and soon after civilian rule was reestablished in 1983, the Argentine National Commission on the Disappeared (CONADEP) published a major official collection of testimony titled *Nunca más* (Never again).[12] With the title providing an explicit and emphatic reference to Holocaust discourse, the volume documented in great detail the horrors of the dirty war waged by the military's paranoid campaign against "subversion" and for national purification. It had wide distribution and impact, and it provided the symbolic and empirical basis for the subsequent trial of the junta generals in 1985. Linked as the trial was to public hearings and extended media coverage, it became a central factor in reestablishing the state of law in Argentina. Taken together, *Nunca más* and the trial delegitimized the ex post facto justification of the coup contained in the theory of *los dos demonios*, the two demons, which had a certain purchase during the Alfonsin years right after 1983. The two devils were the terror squads of the radical right and the terror of the numerically rather insignificant leftist urban guerrillas, which never numbered more than 600 to 800 combatants in the whole country. Both were held to be equally responsible for triggering the military coup. This apologetic theory of the two demons, which retrospectively legitimized the coup, conveniently ignored the proven link between the death squads and the military and gave a free ride to fellow travelers and beneficiaries of the regime. But it was now slowly replaced by the emerging consensus that grave human rights violations had occurred, a notion that neither the Marxist left nor the radical right had ever taken seriously. After the military defeat in the Malvinas, the victory of human rights discourse was like a second defeat handed to the military. But in the longer term, the success of human rights discourse since 1985 sacrificed historical accuracy.

How so? At the narrative level, *Nunca más* established the figure of the *desaparecido* as innocent victim of state terror. This strategy "forgot" the political dimension of the leftist insurgency that the military dictatorship had been trying to root out. This forgetting was absolutely necessary at the time for two reasons. First, it was needed to foil the arguments made by the generals' defense, which was based on the notion that the coup and the repression were caused by the armed terrorism of the radical left, the *montoneros*, and the ERP (*Ejército Revolucionario del Pueblo*). Second, and more important, it was necessary to allow all of Argentine society, including the bystanders and beneficiaries of the dictatorship itself, to gather around a new national consensus: the clear separation of perpetrators and victims, the guilty and the innocent. This new consensus built on the recognition that generals such as Videla and Massera were not just old-style Latin American dictators but had become part of the infamous twentieth-century history of "administered massacres" (Hannah Arendt). This link of the dirty war to other bureaucratically organized killing fields of the twentieth century explains the strong presence of Holocaust discourse within the Argentinean debate, about which I have written in another context.[13] I would argue that without this acknowledgment, the Trial of the Juntas that led to jail terms for the generals would not have been possible.

Of course, the commission report had explicitly condemned all armed violence, that of the state as much as that of the left guerrillas. But by making all 30,000 *desaparecidos* into passive victims, it erased the political history of the conflict together with the political affiliations of individuals. The figure of the *desaparacido* became an *idée reçue*, a cliché of social memory that in the end may turn into memory's own form of forgetting.

In the early years after the dictatorship, it is interesting to note, Argentines did not want to hear from survivors of the camps what actually had gotten them into political trouble. The protests of the mothers of the Plaza de Mayo during the dictatorship had asserted the rights of family and kinship against the discourse of the state, thus creating a kind of "Antigone space," as Jean Franco has suggestively called it.[14] In order to assert their claims politically, they had to deny that some of their children had been armed guerrillas. But any distinction between leftist violence and nonviolent leftist politics fell victim to the official equation of all left politics with subversion and terrorism.[15] As a result in Argentina, the purified figure of the innocent nonpolitical victim became ever more powerful. Politics and history were reduced to the language of family and emotions, clearly visible in Luis Puenzo's powerful film *The Official Story*, which, not surprisingly, became an international success.

But the drive to achieve a new national consensus in the transition to democracy did have its downside. The push for "reconciliation" and compromise with the representatives of the military regime still at large was not long in coming. President Alfonsin had already argued that the top military should be put on trial together with the surviving leadership of the *montoneros*. This was the juridical version of the theory of *los dos demonios*. Soon after the generals had gone to jail, retroactive laws and amnesties under Presidents Alfonsin and Menem in the late 1980s and early 1990s attempted to absolve both the military and Argentinean society from their responsibility for the state terror by preventing any further trials and exculpating any lower charges (for example, the so-called managers and assistant managers of the camps) who were said to simply have been following orders. It was a blatant case of *oubli commandé*, only a few years after the dictatorship had come to an end. But neither the 1986 "full stop law" that became known as the *punto final* for initiating new prosecutions nor the 1987 law of *obediencia debida* (or Law of Due Obedience), nor even Menem's general amnesty of 1990 granted to the members of the various juntas tried in 1985 was able to stop the mothers and the human rights organizations from seeking justice through the courts. On the contrary, as official silence descended to cover the crimes of the past, the call for justice and the demand to remember the disappeared intensified in the public realm. The mothers of the Plaza de Mayo kept marching and shifted tactics toward legal prosecutions that were not covered by the amnesty and full stop laws, especially the kidnapping of babies born in the detention camps and placed in military families after their mothers were killed. By the mid-1990s, several high-level members of the system of repression cracked and went public with confessions. Furthermore, all through the 1990s, writers and artists have taken up the topic of memory and rights violations. The juridical focus on the dictatorship has been supplemented by an intense cultural focus leading to much-discussed memorial projects in Buenos Aires, La Plata, Tucumán, and other parts of the country. Time and again, there are new revelations, especially regarding the sites of terror themselves. Most recently, it was the digging up of the basement of the Club atlético in Buenos Aires, used by the police as a detention and torture center in the midst of a working-class neighborhood. The building was destroyed in the 1980s to make way for a highway overpass, but its remnants have now become a grassroots memorial, and it is being considered for a potential museum site, similar to Berlin's Topography of Terror, the residues of the former Gestapo headquarters.

With the memories of the dictatorship's crimes strong, new voices have emerged that argue for a recuperation of the forgotten political dimension of the fate of the *desaparecidos*. Some want to acknowledge the idealistic fight of many of the young victims for a just world, thus emphasizing agency rather than only passive victimhood without, however, justifying the terrorism of the armed urban guerrilla. Others, however, go further. They want to recuperate a politics of memory in relation to the militants' political identity, and they do so under the figure of impunity.[16] The alleged impunity of the dictatorship, achieved according to this account by the amnesty of 1990, is paralleled with the impunity of the neoliberal economic order that in recent years has not only destroyed the Argentinean middle class but also produced unemployment and poverty on a scale that is now threatening the very fabric of the country. In this account, the dictatorship is seen as nothing but the necessary first step to bring neoliberalism to power and to subject Argentina (and Latin America) to the new imperial rule of globalization. The militants of the 1960s and early 1970s are now being remembered by some as the heroes fighting against the root of all oppression—the continuity of economic domination and dispossession by the North. Although this recuperated memory of left militancy reductively short-circuits the relationship between the military and the subsequent civilian state, it has the merit of breaking with the fiction of the total innocence of victimhood and the familialization of the problem of the *desaparecidos*. Clearly, Argentina has reached a new stage of discussion in which a past public forgetting is replaced by a new configuration of memory and forgetting. This new account should allow for a historically more correct assessment of the period that led up to the military dictatorship. The gains of human rights politics, embodied in the figure of the *desaparecido* and the moral condemnation of the military regime, are strong enough to withstand the temptation of a falsely heroic leftist memory narrative that anyway strikes me more as a symptom of current despair than as a historically tenable account. The real terrain of struggle for Argentinean society today, after all, is not so much in memory politics as in the attempt to find a political solution to the collapse of the Argentinean economy and the bankruptcy of its political class, the roots of which lie not only in the dictatorship but also in the corruption and deluded politics that came with the transition to democracy itself. At an experiential level, however, one can understand why analogies are being drawn between the years of the dictatorship and the current social collapse. In the 1970s, thousands of Argentineans were driven into exile. Many have since returned, only to face another, now economically generated exodus of similar proportions. Argentina finds itself in the midst of a new stage of remembering and forgetting whose future outcome is anything but clear.

III

If *Nunca más* and the 1985 trial of the generals established a victory for human rights in Argentina on the basis of a certain public forgetting, an analogous case could be made for postwar Germany where the recognition of the basic criminality of the Nazi regime hinged on the strength of public Holocaust memory and the acceptance of war guilt. Of course, the story told time and again is that Germans repressed the Holocaust for decades until the American television series *Holocaust* of 1979 opened the floodgates of memory projects and led to a relatively successful working through of the past with all kinds of oral history projects, public monuments, and official memorializations. This simple story pitting repression against memory is questionable since debates about perpetrators and victims, guilt and responsibility, have occupied historians and the public in Germany for decades—from Karl Jaspers's 1946 lectures on the question of guilt and the Nuremberg trials, through the Eichmann and Auschwitz trials of the 1960s, all the way to Daniel Goldhagen's controversial *Hitler's Willing Executioners* and the historians' debate about structural causes versus personal responsibility for Auschwitz.[17] Scholars have shown that memory of the Nazi crimes against humanity was already publicly articulated in the 1950s at the government level, in the churches, and in the culture at large. From this basic recognition of the Holocaust as a crime against humanity, however, it was a long and difficult road to the point when the Holocaust and the Third Reich were seen no longer as a criminal aberration of German national history but rather as integral parts of that history and thus of German identity for generations to come. That is not the same as arguing that Auschwitz was the logical endpoint of German history or, in the transnational version of the argument, of enlightened modernity per se. Recent books by Gesine Schwan and by Daniel Levy and Nathan Sznaider have documented this German struggle for memory and for a civil sense of responsibility through the decades.[18] But even this new account stays with the story of *bad* repression versus *good* memory politics, even though the rise of Holocaust memory in Germany has been shifted backward into the 1950s. My point is that the binary structure of the discourse is itself reductive because it fails to acknowledge a dimension of public forgetting that was central to the victory of the memorians over those who wanted to forget. As in the Argentinean case, something had to be forgotten in the public political debate for Holocaust memory politics to be "successful" in the first place.

This, then, is my second example of an ethics and politics of public forgetting: not, to be sure, the German desire to "forget" the Holocaust, which in its move from evasive acknowledgment all the way to denial remains a permanent fixture on the political right, but rather the German experience of the strategic bombings of its major cities, first by the Royal Air Force and later by the Americans, in World War II. Of course, any such comparison of the German and the Argentinean case will have to acknowledge one fundamental difference: public visibility and documentation. The very nature of "disappearance" left few if any traces in urban space, whereas we all know the images of Germany's bombed-out cities. Obstacles to the very possibility of public forgetting, therefore, would seem to be stronger in the German case. And sure enough, in one sense the experience and the after-effects of the bombings were never forgotten—neither by the generation who lived through the firestorms nor by the first postwar generation who grew up playing cowboys and Indians in the ruins. But in the public memory debate in Germany, the air war against German cities has never played a major role. It was "publicly forgotten" for several decades, and, as I will argue, for good reason.

Then the topic emerged forcefully, though only briefly, in the debate on W. G. Sebald's book-length essay *Luftkrieg und Literatur* in 1999.[19] And it was catapulted into the center of public attention in the fall of 2002 with the publication of historian Jörg Friedrich's best-seller *Der Brand: Deutschland im Bombenkrieg 1940–1945*.[20] In both cases, an earlier forgetting was challenged, though in significantly different ways and at significantly different moments. But taken together, these two books and their public effects may well have altered German memorial culture in irreversible ways.

Sebald had become known in the early 1990s as a writer of memory narratives in a new mode. *Die Ausgewanderten*, a collection of four stories about German Jewish emigrants, quickly became an international success, and his 2001 novel *Austerlitz* received one of the most prestigious literary prizes in the United States.[21] Sebald's essay about the air war, published in English in 2003 as *The Natural History of Destruction*, is interesting for our discussion of forgetting since it implicitly questions the relationship between public memory of the Holocaust and public forgetting of the bombings. Of course, the Holocaust stands dead center in many contemporary trauma studies, and it is the historical event that has shaped Sebald's literary and ethical imagination. But if there ever was a trauma for the Germans during World War II, it surely was not the Holocaust but rather the experience of the bombings: close to 600,000 civilians dead, a million tons of bombs from the Royal Air Force alone raining down on 131 German cities, 3.5 million apartments destroyed, and 7.5 million people homeless at the end of the war (and that was before another 11 million refugees came pouring in from the East).[22]

Sebald starts from the paradox that this traumatic experience does not seem to have left a *Schmerzensspur*, a trace of pain, in the collective consciousness of the Germans and that it never played an important role in debates about the inner constitution of the Federal Republic.[23] He attributes this fact to an extremely efficient and successful collective psychic repression. He argues that postwar Germans (and he seems to have only the Federal Republic of Germany in mind) are bound together by the secret of the hundreds of thousands of corpses in the basement of the new state, as it were, a kind of family secret that fed the stream of psychic energy making the economic miracle possible in the 1950s. Forgetting, in other words, appears as yet another German repression, repression hypothesis number 2, as it were: after the repression of the Holocaust, in which Germans figured as perpetrators, comes the repression of the bombings, in which German civilians figured as victims.

Sebald himself is less concerned with the collective psyche of his compatriots or with the politics of his own intervention than with the literary dimension of this second German repression. He accuses postwar German writers of having failed to represent the destruction of German cities, lamenting the absence of "the great war and post-war epos."[24] At least literature, he seems to suggest, should have known better than to go along with this forgetting of an experience that must have left permanent traces in the consciousness of millions of people. But Sebald's complaint is not directed only at the forgetting of the empirical facts. Postwar literature is pronounced guilty of having participated in the tacit national consensus not to address what Sebald calls "the true state of material and moral annihilation" of the whole country.[25] True enough, the *Trümmerliteratur* of the late 1940s and 1950s, this often sentimental and self-indulgent "literature of ruins" written mostly by war veterans returning from the front or from POW camps, focused on life in the ruins after the war rather than on the experience of the bombings themselves or, for that matter, on the *univers concentrationnaire*.[26] And even later, literary texts dealing with the bombings came more often from abroad (Céline, Vonnegut, Pynchon) than from within. Of course, there were several German writers who dealt quite effectively with the bombings themselves (Böll, Nossack, Ledig, Fichte, Kluge), and Sebald does acknowledge some of their work. But it is also true that this literature never achieved the kind of public recognition that the literature of the Holocaust eventually and despite much initial resistance came to enjoy in Germany or abroad: texts by Rolf Hochhuth, Peter Weiss, Paul Celan, Jean Améry, and others.

Of course, it would be easy to argue against this new repression hypothesis on both historical and theoretical grounds. One doesn't even need the Foucauldean armature to make the point that the scarcity of literary texts about the bombings, which is certainly one factor in the ostensible absence of this experience from public debate, can be explained differently. One could point out for instance that many postwar writers themselves did not experience the bombings because they served at the front. Understandably, they focused their work on life after the war, but many of those writings, contrary to what Sebald suggests, were quite effective in attacking the moral bankruptcy of the country. This is certainly true for Borchert, Böll, and Koeppen. As to those writers of the Gruppe 47 who refused to deal with the Holocaust and who rejected the returning émigré and Jewish writers, Sebald's repression thesis does have a certain force. How could they have addressed German victimization by bombing without talking about the Holocaust? Clearly, the two events were linked in people's minds at that time. But Sebald's unconditional reproach against a whole generation is over the top. It leaves one to wonder what is literarily at stake for him in his repression claim.[27]

However questionable the value of Sebald's repression hypothesis may be as a sweeping argument about postwar German literature and mentalities, it is the public reception of Sebald's book that becomes interesting for my argument about a politics of public forgetting. Many reviews attacked *Luftkrieg und Literatur* as if it were part of the right-wing discourse indulging the Germans as victims of the allies and as if Sebald aimed at relativizing or even denying the role of Germans as perpetrators. This was a Pavlovian reaction to be expected from critics who simply recycle the left-liberal convictions of yesteryear, ignoring how the temporality of German forgetting and memory itself has changed in recent decades. The attack on Sebald reproduced an earlier political taboo on the *Luftkrieg* that had first emerged in the 1950s and gathered strength in the generational conflicts of the 1960s. In those times, speaking about the air war publicly or even privately in the family was inescapably tied to the discourse of German victimization (Germans as victims of the Nazis first, then of the allied bombings, and finally of the allied occupation). More often than not, talk of the air war meant relativizing the crimes of the Holocaust. And then the suffering of the air war was invariably linked to the stories of expulsion from the East that played an important role in right-wing West German politics at least until the late 1960s and that has recently reemerged after the publication of Günter Grass's novel *Im Krebsgang*.[28] One might even ask to what extent it was this "revanchist" politics of the influential expellee organizations (*Bund der Vertriebenen*) that blocked recognition of air-war suffering by the younger generation. By not recognizing the Oder-Neisse border with Poland as final, the Bonn government practiced a politics of illusion that made it impossible to separate the experience of real loss and suffering from its political instrumentalization. The right spoke of Dresden and the expulsion, the left of Auschwitz. Both sides displayed resistance to the other memory, and this reciprocal resistance fed the generational conflict that was to erupt fully only in the 1960s with the rise of the New Left and the protest generation. But it is important to remember, contrary to what Sebald suggests, that it was ubiquitous talk about the bombings and about the expulsion, familiar to anyone who grew up in West Germany in the 1950s, that produced the taboo on discussing the air war in the first place. In this political debate, the arguments of the left were politically legitimate. The notion of German victimhood, tied to a long-standing nationalist discourse, was fundamentally reactionary, and it had to be fought for the country to arrive at a new consensus regarding the German past. The price paid for this victory was the forgetting of the *Luftkrieg*, the forgetting of a traumatic national experience.

With the publication of Jörg Friedrich's hugely successful *Der Brand* (The Fire, The Burning) in the fall of 2002, the debate reached a new stage, pointing to an altered memoryscape in Germany. Within a few months, several hundred thousand copies were sold. The book was reviewed everywhere, and its publication was followed by a flood of documentary television programs, talk shows, special issues of *Der Spiegel* (*Als das Feuer vom Himmel fiel*), *GEO* (*Verbrechen gegen die Deutschen?*), and other mass-circulation magazines. Friedrich, a freelance historian known for his critical work on the Nazi war machine and on postwar trials, kept appearing on television, sometimes several times a night on different channels, and at the high point of this media frenzy it seemed you couldn't get through an evening of television without seeing bombs falling on German cities, firestorms raging, and survivors describing their harrowing experiences. Sebald's 1999 book *Luftkrieg und Literatur*, which first broke through the public silence about the air war and clearly serves as a hidden reference for Friedrich, now appears only as a prelude to this new wave of public memorial discourse in which the experience of an older vanishing generation of Germans is being transmitted to their children and grandchildren. As with Sebald, some critics have mobilized the old taboos against Friedrich's powerful narrative of the bombings but clearly not with much success and perhaps not even with much conviction.[29] Memory of the *Luftkrieg* is no longer a public taboo, nor should it be. But it does raise thorny historical issues, and it remains to be seen to what public purposes it will be put in the long run.

Clearly, some of Friedrich's narrative strategies are susceptible to criticism. He was taken to task for his emphatic tone, his ambiguity about whether the bombings were war crimes, and the occasional use of language reserved for the Holocaust (air shelters as crematoria, bomber crews as *Einsatzgruppen*, the very title of the book *Der Brand* approximating a German translation of Holocaust). But overall, there is wide agreement that this is not a revisionist book about Germans *as* victims, kind of a Goldhagen in reverse, as much as it is a book about German victims whose experiences needed to be acknowledged and absorbed into the national narrative about the war and postwar years.

Even such a differentiation, however, goes only so far. It does not fully explain the fascination the book evoked. Its enormous resonance in Germany makes sense only in light of the fact that it appeared midpoint between New York's 9/11 and the bombing of Baghdad. Of course, the book itself mentions neither, and from interviews we know that Friedrich actually supported the Iraq war, just as he never leaves much doubt that at least at the beginning of the air war, the allies were justified in fighting the Nazi war machine with everything they had. But the public reception of historical scholarship is a tricky business. Clearly, the book was timely in terms of German memory debates. The looming Iraq war, however, provided a broader context, and it intensified the reception. The book fueled the German peace movement precisely with its strategies to discuss the air war in terms of a contemporary antiwar and antibombing sensibility, thus expanding the present backward and offering the growing opposition to the Iraq war a decontextualized and experiential take on German history that made Baghdad look like Dresden, the firestorms of the 1940s like the "shock and awe" campaign of the allies.

Friedrich does not give us new facts about history. Most of what he tells is known from the work of British and American historians and, I would want to add, from the literary writings of authors such as Hans Erich Nossack, Alexander Kluge, and Hubert Fichte. The book's power rather lies in the force of its narration, which distinguishes it from a more distanced and contextual historiography. The lack of emphasis on political context has indeed been one of the major criticisms. In its focus on the experience of the bombings and the firestorms, its mix of obsessively detailed anatomical description of horror with an emphatic reconstruction of the subjective experience of suffering, Friedrich takes the reader directly to the place of destruction, making Germans into voyeurs of unimaginable horrors visited on the very sites they now inhabit. As the borders between past and present become fluid, it is as if one shared the experience itself. Certainly it becomes imaginable in ways not found in earlier historiographical work on the allies' strategic air command and its campaign. The reader is caught in an imaginary in which the firestorms of Hamburg and Dresden are immediately present, ready to be linked to other sets of images soon to explode on television screens once the bombing of Baghdad began. The near simultaneity on German television screens of bombing runs on Hamburg or Cologne with image sequences of the fireballs from Baghdad did the rest. The experientially focused proximity of Friedrich's kind of writing of history, combined with the visually generated false sense of simultaneity, generates a visceral memory that no longer allows for sober comparison and evaluation. Instead, we get a newly mediated form of experiencing other times and spaces in which the imagined past is projected onto the screen of the present. This historiography of proximity and immediacy is very different from Sebald's approach, which combines melancholy coldness with distance from the historical subjects of his books. The effect of Friedrich's book—intended or not—is to close the gap between past and present by collapsing fundamental political differences: America and England bomb, and civilians suffer—a facile and fallacious historical analogy between the German past and the Iraqi present, all the more questionable since the peace movement simultaneously covered the nature of Saddam's brutal regime with gracious silence or with references to the fact that Saddam was the fault of the Americans in the first place. The simplistic slogan "no war for oil" drowned out any argument that might question the desirability of total peace when facing a murderous dictator. This was, after all, a German lesson completely forgotten or angrily rejected in the debate. It is as if deep down some Germans have still not forgiven the Americans for liberating them.

I am not arguing here in favor of maintaining the taboo on the bombing war against German cities and civilians. Today, in the presence of a well-established Holocaust memory discourse in Germany, I see no justification for the continued unwillingness to discuss the experience of the bombings, their legitimacy, or their military usefulness. But I do argue against the facile and self-serving ways in which German suffering during the air war is amalgamated to an otherwise legitimate political critique of the Bush government's new doctrine of preemptive war and "democratization" by force. There is always and inevitably too much forgetting embedded in such facile historical analogies.

Whatever the merits of Friedrich's book are apart from the political context of its reception, I do recognize that the notion of Germans as victims or simply German victims will meet with vociferous resistance among the victims of the Nazis and among the nations that fought the Nazi dictatorship at great sacrifice. Seen from the outside, the bombings will still be judged by many to have been legitimate punishment of Nazi Germany. Understandable as it may be, this is of course a retrospective rationale, and it should not keep us from questioning the strategy of bombing wars today. To do so would be to sidestep the fundamental moral and political issue of such bombings and their inevitable civilian casualties. Clearly, the threshold for the acceptance of civilian bombings has been significantly raised since World War II. If Friedrich's dramatic account can help us focus on this issue in an international context, more power to it. But for that to happen, it must be uncoupled from German *Befindlichkeiten* and from the discourse of German victimhood. It is one thing to raise the issue inside Germany but quite another to raise it in an international context. Perspective really does matter.

IV

Both the former taboo against publicly discussing the *Luftkrieg* and the current mobilization of air-war memories have an explicit political dimension. Yet they are fundamentally different. The embrace of the *Leideform* (form of suffering), as Friedrich calls it, of the bombing war by the German peace movement today operates primarily on an experiential level and practices its own politics of forgetting politics. The current remembering of the air war unifies the nation, East and West Germans, old and young, intellectuals and the *Stammtisch*, and conservatives, liberals, and leftists in a somewhat spooky unanimity of the government and the people united against America. The taboo on the air war at an earlier time, on the other hand, was the expression of a genuine democratic struggle within West Germany, the struggle to recognize the crimes of the Third Reich without making up a balance sheet of sufferings. Forgetting then had a beneficial and purging influence on the national consciousness. Remembering the air war today by comparison seems rather self-indulgent.

As in Argentina, public forgetting in Germany at that earlier time was in the service of a memory politics that was ultimately able to forge a new national consensus accepting responsibility for the crimes of a previous regime. The irony in this quick dance of memory and forgetting is of course that when certain memories, even the "right" ones, are codified into national consensus and become clichés, as both Holocaust memory in Germany and memory of the *desaparacidos* in Argentina have become, a new threat to memory emerges. Repression inevitably generates discourse, as we have learned from Foucault. An omnipresent, even excessive public memory discourse and its mass marketing may generate another form of forgetting, an oblivion of exhaustion different from Ricoeur's *mémoire manipulé* as a *ne pas vouloir savoir*. The threat of exhaustion now affects both Holocaust memory and the memories of the air war. This is when the intense focus on memories of the past may block our imagination of the future and create a new blindness in the present. At that stage, we may want to bracket the future of memory in order to remember the future.

NOTES

1. Umberto Eco, "An *Ars oblivionalis?* Forget It," *PMLA* 103 (1988): 254–61.
2. Harald Weinrich, *Lethe: Kunst und Kritik des Vergessens* (Munich: C. H. Beck, 1997).
3. Frances A. Yates, *The Art of Memory* (London: Pimlico, 1966).
4. Paul Ricoeur, *La Mémoire, l'histoire, l'oubli* (Paris: Éditions du Seuil, 2000), 543.
5. Charles S. Maier, "A Surfeit of Memory: Reflections on History, Melancholy, and Denial," *History and Memory* 5 (1992): 136–51.
6. Friedrich Nietzsche, *On the Advantage and Disadvantage of History for Life*, trans. and intro. Peter Preuss (Indianapolis: Hackett, 1980), 8.
7. For a good critique of the binary, see Tzvetan Todorov, *Les Abus de la Mémoire* (Paris: Arléa, 1995).
8. Martin Heidegger, *Sein und Zeit* (Tübingen: Max Niemeyer Verlag, 1963), 339 and 345.
9. Jan Assmann, "Collective Memory and Cultural Identity," *New German Critique* 65 (spring/summer 1995): 125–34. Compare Andreas Huyssen, *Twilight Memories: Marking Time in a Culture of Amnesia* (New York: Routledge, 1995), and *Present Pasts: Urban Palimpsests and the Politics of Memory* (Stanford, Calif.: Stanford University Press, 2003).
10. On such misreadings of Adorno, compare Michael Rothberg, "After Adorno: Culture in the Wake of Catastrophe," *New German Critique* 72 (fall 1997): 45–81, also in Michael Rothberg, *Traumatic Realism: The Demands of Holocaust Representation* (Minneapolis: University of Minnesota Press, 2000), 25–58.
11. For the politically most incisive analysis of the development of memory discourse in Argentina, see Hugo Vezzetti, *Pasado y presente: Guerra, dictadura y sociedad en la Argentina* (Buenos Aires: Siglo veintiuno editores Argentina, 2002). My argument about the changes in Argentinean memory culture owe a lot to Vezzetti's book. See also Elizabeth Jelin, *Los trabajos de la memoria* (Madrid: Siglo veintiuno de españa editores, 2002). A lively debate on memory and its politics is also conducted in the journal *Puentes*, published in Buenos Aires.
12. *Nunca más: Informe de la Comisión Nacional sobre la Desaparición de Personas* (Buenos Aires: Eudeba, 1984).
13. See Andreas Huyssen, "Memory Sites in an Expanded Field: The Memory Park in Buenos Aires," in *Present Pasts*, 94–109.
14. Jean Franco, *Critical Passions: Selected Essays* (Durham, N.C.: Duke University Press, 1999), 50.
15. This pattern recalls the German situation in the mid-1970s, when Red Army faction terrorism was short-circuited with the political leftism of the so-called sympathizers

and the Frankfurt School was attacked as having mentored the terrorists. But of course there was no military coup.

16. I owe this argument to Vezzetti, *Pasado y presente.*

17. Karl Jaspers, *The Question of German Guilt* (Westport, Conn.: Greenwood Press, 1978); Daniel Goldhagen, *Hitler's Willing Executioners: Ordinary Germans and the Holocaust* (New York: Vintage Books, 1997).

18. Gesine Schwan, *Politics and Guilt: The Destructive Power of Silence* (Lincoln: University of Nebraska Press, 2001); Daniel Levy and Nathan Sznaider, *Erinnerung im Globalen Zeitalter: Der Holocaust* (Frankfurt am Main: Suhrkamp, 2001).

19. W. G. Sebald, *Luftkrieg und Literatur* (Munich: Hanser, 1999), translated by Anthea Bell (with two additional essays not contained in the German original) as *The Natural History of Destruction* (Toronto: Alfred A. Knopf Canada, 2003).

20. Jörg Friedrich, *Der Brand: Deutschland im Bombenkrieg 1940–1945* (Munich: Propyläen, 2002).

21. W. G. Sebald, *The Emigrants,* trans. Michael Hulse (New York: New Directions, 1996), and *Austerlitz,* trans. Anthea Bell (New York: Random House, 2001).

22. These are the statistics Sebald cites; see *Luftkrieg*, 11.

23. Sebald, *Luftkrieg*, 12.

24. Sebald, *Luftkrieg*, 6.

25. Sebald, *Luftkrieg*, 18.

26. The active reluctance of members of the famous Gruppe 47 (Richter, Andersch, Grass, et al.) to deal with the Holocaust and with the returning Jewish exiles has recently been elaborated in sad detail by Stephan Braese in *Die andere Erinnerung: Jüdische Autoren in der westdeutschen Nachkriegsliteratur* (Berlin: Philo, 2001). See also the indictment of German anti-Semitism after the Shoah in Klaus Briegleb, *Missachtung und Tabu. Eine Streitschrift zur Frage: "Wie antisemitisch war die Gruppe 47"* (Berlin: Philo, 2003).

27. On the literary aspects of Sebald's essay, compare Andreas Huyssen, "Rewritings and New Beginnings: W. G. Sebald and the Literature of the Air War," in *Present Pasts*, 138–57.

28. Günter Grass, *Im Krebsgang* (Göttingen: Steidl Verlag, 2002), translated as *Crabwalk.*

29. For a collection of some of the major responses to Friedrich in Germany and England, see Lothar Kettenacker, ed., *Ein Volk von Opfern? Die neue Debatte um den Bombenkrieg 1940–45* (Berlin: Rowohlt, 2003).

IV

GLOBALIZING VISIONS:
SCIENCE, TECHNOLOGY, AESTHETICS

10

Globalizing Critical Theory of Science

Eduardo Mendieta

Dates on a calendar are less significant for understanding an age, and the challenges humanity faces during those times, than the contradictions that determine the tasks that humanity itself can become conscious of and accomplish during those very times. Thus, it is less significant that we live in a new century and a new millennium than that we live in an age in which the utopian promise of the elimination of social problems by technological means has been thoroughly discredited, just as two centripetal but related processes have overtaken the very idea of science. On the one hand, we have the proliferation of scientific paradigms, spewed forth by the diversification of scientific practices. The idea of science has succumbed to the very empirical counterevidence that there are many sciences, or forms and practices of science, all equally "scientific" albeit all nonreducible to a common denominator. The project of a unified theory of science, which at the turn of the century was married to the project of putative tolerance and critique of political authoritarianism, has given way under the pressures of new historical forces and tragedies, to the disunity of science. The unity of science was evidence that there was a logical and rational ground on which we could hoist the Archimedean pivot that would allow us to dislodge the autistic historical units that posited themselves as immune to either criticism or contamination from the impurities of race or reason tainted by race.

This project has been turned on its head. It is the dream of a unified science, a science grounded on a purity of reason, that has been unmasked as being allied to the totalitarian temptation, not just of destined historical peoples but also of abstract "Western" men, to impose its particular universality on global humanity. Now, democracy, liberalism, and cultural heterogeneity are

187

defended and preserved by defending and demonstrating the very locality, contingency, and nonteleology of science and scientific progress.[1] Yet, and on the other hand, at this very moment in which the lingua franca of science studies and the philosophy of science is one of "disunity," there is an expanding and colonizing homogenization by technoscientific mediation of all social relations. This, in turn, has been exacerbated by the globalization of both finance and technological capitalism. The World Trade Organization as well as the General Agreement on Tariffs and Trade have accelerated not just the rate of accumulation of capital in fewer hands, thus also deepening global inequity, but also the imposition of a technoscientific regime.

With global economic and financial integration comes technological integration, although as this latter takes hold and is implemented, it inaugurates new levels of economic and financial integration. New levels of legal colonization match these forms of global integration. Under the cover of economic and trade agreements are smuggled and implemented new forms of global legality in the form of intellectual property rights. In a caricatured but not off-the-mark way, transnationals integrate financial markets that make their accumulation of capital safer and also more expansive and extensive. This integration demands technological expediency, proficiency, and efficiency, in other words, standardization and integration. Simultaneously, these transnationals are empowered to have legal recourse against the local consumers and producers, gerrymandered within the boundaries of nations. This legal empowerment, however, is neither symmetrical nor transparent.

The information revolution, thus, is not to be easily separated from the computer revolution, which in turn is not to be dissociated from the financial revolution of the 1970s and 1980s. Against this background, then, we ought to realize that science is not the disinterested discovery of some naked reality and that technology is not the unbiased and unmediated application of some pristine truth. Rather, science is produced by technology, and technology is enabled by the science it in turn produces. For this reason, in the age of global capital, we ought to speak of technoscience, that is, the technological mediation of science, and not just in the innocent sense that science is produced in the laboratory but in the more thorough sense that science is literally produced by the technological equipment that is industrially and materially produced to test, measure, and track the theories science produces. Technoscience, thus, also carries a trademark and copyright and more often than not the flag of a particular military-industrial complex. These are the stories not just of Microsoft, Intel, Coca-Cola, and Nike but also Monsanto, MDA, Celera, and Proctor & Gamble.

Just as a nuanced relationship to science, this side of technophilia and that side of Luddism, has began to seep into popular consciousness and science itself has grown skeptical of its own powers of rationality, at this very moment the world is integrated by the technoscientific might of global finance capitalism. It is at this very moment, when critical theory's power to think the local historically and epistemologically requires that we transform the critique of political economy into a geopolitical economy of the production of knowledge(s), of which technoscience is but an instance. This transformation will have to take up questions about what remains alive and contradiction-bound in classical historical materialism vis-à-vis almost 150 years of transformation.

It would be logical to begin an assessment of the Frankfurt School's potential in light of the present challenge vis-à-vis what I called already the technoscientific might of global capitalism by revisiting the debate between Marcuse and Habermas. Yet the tensions between both are less a disagreement and more a difference in focus and stress. This tension, which can be traced to Karl Marx's work and which was exploited in one direction by Engels, is maintained and transformed in the work not just of Marcuse but also of Horkheimer and Adorno. In this chapter, however, I will focus only on Adorno and Horkheimer, as Marcuse's work has received a lot of attention from commentators and critics. In Habermas, we have an attempt, initially couched in terms of anthropologically grounded knowledge interests, to overcome the aporetic tension between science and reification that collapses science and technology into pure ideology. More recently, Habermas has renewed this attempt to circumvent this tension by means of the linguistification of the foundations of critical social theory that, in the final analysis, retreats behind the critical insights of not just Marx but also the first generation of the Frankfurt School. After reconstructing the various debates among the various members of the Frankfurt School, I hope to have dispelled and clarified many misrepresentations. I hope that the first two sections of this chapter will put to rest many myths that have hindered the fruitful engagement with the work of both generations of Frankfurt School critical theorists. In the final section, I turn to elucidating what I take to be the challenges that must be taken up if Frankfurt School critical theory is to be transformed into a geopolitical critique of the political economy of knowledge(s).

SCIENCE AS REIFICATION

The Frankfurt School's contribution to a critical theory of science has to be understood in terms of its confrontation with a double betrayal. On the one hand, we have historical materialism's adulation for the scientific method. Science and technology are praised and in fact are to be emulated. This praise and emulation resulted in a temptation to turn Marx's method of historical analysis into a scientific method. On the other hand, we have the development of dialectical materialism that thought of the critique of political economy along the lines of a natural science and thus sought to treat society as a natural entity. Dialectical materialism was the positivism of Marxism, namely, reified social consciousness. Both betrayals became evident when the revolution failed to materialize, the proletariat betrayed itself, and dialectical materialism became a carte blanche for genocide and brutal modernization and the worst forms of epistemological violence. As the proletarian revolution failed to take place in accordance with the time line dictated by party intellectuals and professional revolutionaries, rethinking the teleology of history became imperative. Similarly, the use of technology for the devastating effects that were made evident in the carnage of two world wars, and the convergence of science with the industrial and technological imperatives of the ruling classes' interests, made science if not suspect at the very least not as benign and neutral as Marx and Engels suggested with their unalloyed praise. It is against this background that the Frankfurt School's work in the philosophy of technology, in particular, must be understood.

The Frankfurt School sought to rescue the critical spirit of historical materialism, that is, Marxism, by re-Hegelianizing its philosophical core. This meant, however, the rephilosophizing of Marxism, and this in turn meant the rehistoricization of the Marxian categories of social analysis. Rehistoricizing historical materialism meant viewing Marxism itself as the expression of a certain historical constellation of forces. In this way, then, the Frankfurt School sought to dereify and defetishize Marxism's idolatry of science, and furthermore, in this way it also sought to unmask dialectical materialism as a perversion of Marxism's fundamental historical character. Still, already in the shibboleths used, namely, re-Hegelianizing, rephilosophizing, and rehistoricizing, we have alluded to the side on which the Frankfurt School falls with respect to the primacy of the subject over the object, of history over nature, of critique over ideology, of reason over history.

It has become standard to take Theodor W. Adorno's critique of scientism and positivism as being representative of the whole school's positions. Yet a closer analysis will reveal differences that while not profound nonetheless are revelatory. In this case, we will begin with Max Horkheimer and in particular with an early text from 1935, "On the Problem of Truth."[2] This text begins with the mapping of two dominant but opposing positions on truth. On the one side, we have the idea that truth is historically circumscribed and relative. Cognition has "never more than limited validity."[3] This type of subjectivism results in a historical relativism. On the other side, we have a renewal of philosophical dogmatism that seeks to reinterpret the philosophical tradition's notion of truth, ontologically conceived, into an epistemological qua phenomenology notion. Truth becomes a matter of intuiting essences. For Horkheimer, Kant's work is exemplary of this position. Yet in both, Horkheimer discerned a common thread, a common form of relativism and subjectivism. In Kant's aftermath, everything that can be legitimately known is directly related to what is perceived, namely, to what are appearances. Here he quotes Husserl: "In the last analysis, all being is relative (as opposed to the false ideal of an absolute Being and its absolute truth), and is nevertheless *relative in some customary sense to the transcendental subjectivity*. But this subjectivity alone is 'in and for itself.'"[4] Yet in this subterranean relativism and subjectivism of both opposing positions are exhibited the fundamental characteristic of the bourgeois mind, exemplified in the work of Kant: "Analysis carried through to the end and skeptical distrust of all theory on the one hand and readiness to believe naively in detached fixed principles on the other, these are characteristics of the bourgeois mind."[5] Against this reigning skepticism and dogmatism, Horkheimer affirms the power of subjectivity and the unfinished character of truth. Yet both are linked. Truth is made in history, not discovered. But it is made partly because of deliberate action. As he wrote, "The correction and further definition of the truth is not taken care of by history, so that all the cognizant subject has to do is passively observe, conscious that even his particular truth, which contains the others negated in it, is not the whole. Rather, the truth is advanced because the human beings who possess it stand by it unbendingly, apply it and carry it through, act according to it, and bring it to power against the resistance of reactionary, narrow, one-sided points of view. The process of cognition includes real historical will and action just as much as it does learning from experience and intellectual comprehension. The latter cannot progress without the former."[6]

Truth does not come of its own accord; again it is not discovered, it is made. In this way, the dialectic breaks through the impasse between dogmatism and skepticism. Yet the dialectic gives no license either to blind optimism or naive realism. Truth can be missed, and there is no reality that is either unknowable or known a priori. The dialectic, in Horkheimer's view, is suspended between reserved hopefulness and optimism of the will, so long as this is informed by reason. As Horkheimer puts it eloquently, "According to pragmatism, the verification of ideas and their truth merge. According to materialism, verification forms the evidence that ideas and objective reality correspond, itself a historical occurrence that can be obstructed and interrupted. This viewpoint has no place for basically closed and unknowable truth or for the subsistence of idea not requiring any reality, but this does not mean that the concept of a conviction which, because of a given constellation of the world is cut off from verification and success, is a priori true."[7] In this view, truth is less than either an epistemic object and also less than an ontological status.

Truth has to do with history and in particular with historical justice. As he put it in an essay from 1932, "The test of the truth of a judgment is something different from the test of its importance for human life."[8] It would be utopian, Horkheimer notes at the end of his essay "On the Problem of Truth" to expect people to live under the sobering truth while they wait for the conditions of untruth to be removed. Indeed, it would be utopian, but we cannot expect less and cannot promise more in light of the way history can and will disappoint. Yet we cannot stand and wait. Truth is a made by removing the causes of untruth.[9] The causes of untruth, furthermore, can come in the way of the development of science itself. Science can be put in jeopardy by the distorting effects of ideology. This was a view that dominated Horkheimer's thinking at least until the later 1930s, and that was partially eclipsed by the darkness of the Shoah. Yet it would be entirely inaccurate to think that all science or science as such is merely or solely the performance of instrumental rationality. In the early 1930s, as Horkheimer reflected on the economic crash of 1929 and its relationship to science, he noted that science's ability to contribute to the improvement of the living conditions of the proletariat or, rather, its disproportionate application had to do less with the nature of science itself and more with those social conditions and ideologies that made it insufficient and misguided. In the face of the societal challenges of providing for the needs of people, science appears poorly outfitted. "The root of this deficiency, however, is not science itself but in the social conditions which hinder its development and are at loggerheads with the rational elements immanent in science."[10]

There is a rational core to science, one that is misappropriated and distorted by the social context of the production as well as practical application of science. But the sources of the crises that hobble science remain beyond the purview of science itself. Here we must take recourse to the dialectic and the historical will to change the historical situation for the production and appropriation of technology: "The historical process has imposed limitations on science as a productive force, and these show in the various sectors of science, in their content and form, in their subject matter and method. Furthermore, science as a means of production has not been properly applied. Understanding of the crisis of science depends on a correct theory of the present social situation; for science as a social function reflects at present the contradictions of society."[11] This same tendency to see science, technology, and even truth under the microscope of the dialectics, which neither reject nor affirms without dehistoricizing and pointing to the historical surplus of every moment of the actualization of reason, is affirmed toward the end of his life. In one of the last aphorisms in his *Notizen und Dämmerung*, he notes, "Today, Critical Theory must deal at least as much with what is justifiably called progress, i.e., technical progress, and with its effect on man and society. Critical Theory denounces the dissolution of spirit and soul, the victory of rationality, without simply negating it. It recognizes that injustice is identical with barbarism, but that justice is inseparable from that technological process which causes mankind's development into a sophisticated animal species that degrades spirit to the level it had attained in its childhood. Imagination, longing, love, artistic expression are becoming moments of infantilism."[12] The critique of instrumental reason is neither a refusal of reason nor an embrace of mysticism or negative theology. It is an attempt to preserve science from its own positivistic temptation and to rescue it from its dehumanizing and irrational applications. Again, we are beyond simplistic Luddism or naive positivistic endorsement of the intrinsic benignity of science.

Adorno would have put these thoughts of Horkheimer in different sentences, most of them colored with the gray of dusk and tuned to a death march, although the spirit of the letter would have been very much in line. Like Horkheimer, Adorno sought to rescue the philosopheme of truth from its detractors, be they phenomenologists, positivists, or metaphysicians. Just as for Marx, Prometheus was the most divine of gods in the calendar of human hope, for Adorno, truth is one of the most noble of metaphysical ideas in the book of philosophy. Like Prometheus, truth cannot be dispensed with, nor can it be grasped. Only in the perpetual sacrifice, death, and resurrection is Prometheus true to his gift of justice to humanity. Truth is the promise of wholeness and insight that can be obtained only at the price of refusing the promise of truth. As he put in *Negative Dialectics*, "The idea of truth is supreme among the metaphysical ideas, and this is where it takes us. It is why one who believes in God cannot believe in God, why the possibility represented by the divine name is maintained, rather, by him who does not believe. Once upon a time the image ban extended to pronouncing the name; now the ban itself has been in that form come to evoke suspicions of superstition. The ban has been exacerbated: the mere thought of hope is a transgression against it, and act of working against it."[13] Truth is preserved and made by those who refused to be bewitched by its promise of finality. Truth remains outstanding, a promise, and even if it is inchoate and incipient, it is nevertheless always still to be realized.

Like Horkheimer, Adorno links up the question of truth to the question of justice, a nondamaged life, and a nonmisspent life. Thus, for Adorno, "Without hope, the idea of truth would be scarcely even thinkable, and it is the cardinal untruth, having recognized existence to be bad, to present it as truth simply because it has been recognized."[14] Truth is a promise, but only if there is time for and possibility of hoping. Hope opens up this time and possibility. But to hope is also to transgress the ban against the fetishism of the godly and metaphysical. Yet in this transgressive act of hoping, truth as still outstanding is reaffirmed. For Adorno, however, the ban against icons is not so much about a vertical relationship to some reality as such, to things as they really are, but about the horizontal relationship between humans. Truth has to do with how we stand in relationship to other humans, for science is a relationship to nature but one that is always mediated by the tools, machines, and equipment that embody our interests. To refuse to name god is to refuse to escape my responsibility and duties before the other. To refuse truth ultimacy and to refuse to enshrine it on a metaphysical pedestal is to affirm the incompleteness of truth. It is to preserve truth from an inverted world, to save truth for what is still forthcoming.

It would be a failure to pass over in silence the severe criticisms that both Horkheimer and Adorno level against science, especially after World War II and prior to their return to Germany. In *Dialectic of Enlightenment*, Horkheimer and Adorno transform Edward Gibbon's narrative of decay and Martin Heidegger's *Verfallsgeschichte* into an ontoepistemological narrative. The enlightenment promise of liberation by means of reason is now unmasked as the ceaseless and unmitigated subjection of humans to a dehumanizing violence. Autonomy and scientific progress are rendered naked as forms of metaphysical torture. To gain its selfhood, the condition of possibility of moral and epistemological autonomy, humans must exercise a superlative domination over themselves. Domination for the quest of selfhood invariably, nay intrinsically, results in the "destruction of the subject in whose service it is undertaken; for the substance which is dominated, suppressed, and dissolved by virtue of self-preservation is none other than that very life as functions of which the achievement of self-preservation find their sole definition and determination: it is, in fact, what is to be preserved."[15] Selfhood and autonomy, then, are predicated on a remorseless and uncircumventable sacrifice. In this way, "the history of civilization is the history of the introversion of sacrifice."[16] With the normalization of sacrifice come the paroxysms of the autonomous subject to escape this self-obliterating violence. The autonomous subject submits to ritualized and normalized violence, for the sake of rationality, that is, survival and socialization. With blind fury, the subject rejects this exacting renunciation and does so by rejecting the sacrifice and the rationality in whose name it is enacted.

The domination of nature is coterminous with the domination of man. To dominate nature, humans must be rendered docile and calculable. There is complicity between selfhood, autonomy, and the domination over nature. It is this complicity that is betrayed in the cycle of irrationalism and atavistic explosions against the demands of civilization. The denial that is at the root of civilization, "the nucleus of all civilizing rationality, is the germ cell of a proliferating mythic irrationality: with the denial of nature in man not merely the *telos* of the outward control of nature but the *telos* of man's own life is distorted and befogged."[17] Something analogous takes place with science. Science that submits nature to the tyranny of concepts and tortures it with its laboratory techniques is rooted in a sublimation of the mimetic compulsion to repetition. "Science is repetition, refined into observed regularity, and preserved in stereotypes. The mathematical formula is regression handled consciously, just as the magic ritual used to be; it is the most sublimated form of mimicry. Technology no longer completes the approximation to death for the sake of survival by physical imitation of external nature, as was the case with magic, but by the automation of the mental process, by converting them into blind cycles."[18] The means for survival, the tools of humanization, and the social engineering for the sake of the good and well-ordered society turn into ends in themselves. Renunciation, denial, subjection to tools and regimes, and blind cycles of suppression and introjection of authority become ends unto themselves. Reason, autonomy, truth, and technology turn into their opposites: irrationality, heteronomy, untruth, and new forms of mysticism and alchemy—enlightenment reverts to mythology, a mythology that presages only disaster and decline. Here a long passage from *Negative Dialectics* must be cited:

> Universal history must be construed and denied. After the catastrophes that have happened, and in view of the catastrophes to come, it would be cynical to say that a plan for a better world is manifested in history and unites it. Not to be denied for that reason, however, is the unity that cements the discontinuous, chaotically splintered moments and phases of history—the unity of the control of nature, progressing to rule over men, and finally to that over men's inner nature. No universal history leads from savagery to humanitarianism, but there is one leading from the slingshot to the megaton bomb. It ends in the total menace which organized mankind poses to organized men, in the epitome of discontinuity. It is the horror that verifies Hegel and stands him on his head. If he transfigured the totality of historic suffering into the positivity of the self-realizing absolute, the One and All that keeps rolling on to this day—with occasional breathing spells—would teleologically be the absolute of suffering. . . . The world spirit, a worthy object of definition, would have to be defined as permanent catastrophe.[19]

In the face of the unmitigated disaster that universal history has turned and in the face of the weakness of the concept to arrest this storm, Adorno affirms the power of dialectical thinking that seeks to use the concept against the concept and to use the "strength of the subject against constitutive subjectivity."[20] Again, like Horkheimer, Adorno does not reject science in toto. To use the concept against the concept also entails seeking to salvage science from its ideological distortion and arrest under bourgeois society.

In a text from the late 1960s, Adorno returns to the dialectical view of science that he as much as Horkheimer as well as Marcuse had begun with when they had launched the Frankfurt School's version of critical theory. "The more science is rigified in the shell which Max Weber prophesied for the world, the more what is ostracized as pre-scientific become the refuge of knowledge. The contradiction in the relationship of the spirit to science corresponds to the latter's own contradiction. Science postulates a coherent immanent connection and is a moment of the society which denies it coherence. If it escapes this antinomy, be it by canceling its truth content through a sociology of knowledge relativization, or by failing to recognize its entanglements in the *faits sociaux*, and sets itself up as something absolute and self-sufficient, then it contents itself with illusions which impair science in what it might achieve. Both moments are certainly disparate but not indifferent to one another. *Only insight into science's inherent societal mediation contributes to the objectivity of science, since it is no mere vehicle of social relations and interests.*"[21] If science is not just a mere "vehicle of social relations and interests," what else is it? Is science at the service of truth? Is science at the service of something else than the ideologically sugarcoated interests of one class that suppresses the interests of a larger group of humanity? Something else lingers here, and it is not simply the reduction of science to mere functional and instrumental rationality. As truth is unthinkable without hope, science is unthinkable without truth. Yet truth is always suspended, still to come, as Derrida would put it. This truth is suspended in the waiting for the justice that will unmake and dismantle the conditions of untruth. "The idea of scientific truth cannot be split off from that of a true society. Only such a society would be free from contradictions and lack of contradiction. In a resigned manner, scientism commits such an idea to the mere forms of knowledge alone."[22] The true society, however, is not a teleological given but a regulative idea that is approximated by way of the negative, a negative that is historically indexed by the suffering that has been inflicted and that cannot be reconciled, or *aufgehoben*, in either a theodicy of universal history, or an Arcadian technological paradise.

SCIENCE AS SPECIES LEARNING

Jürgen Habermas's contributions to the Frankfurt School critical theory have been acrimoniously debated and contested. To some, Habermas has dissolved the critical edge of critical theory. To others, Habermas has reconstructed and revitalized the tradition by bringing it in dialogue with contemporary developments in the social sciences and philosophy. Yet if we recognize that the Frankfurt School's own relationship to Marxist theory was one of both appropriation and transformation, then Habermas's work preserves this tradition faithfully and with gusto. Before I proceed to discuss the two texts that help us locate Habermas's views on technology and science, it is important to underscore that for Habermas a theory of society must operate on three distinct levels: the metatheoretical, methodological, and empirical levels.[23] At the metatheoretical level, a theory of society turns into a theory of rationality and the differentiation of modes of rationality. At a methodological level, this theory of society must raise the issue of how its object domain is to be accessed from the perspective of understanding goal-oriented actions of social agents and the conditions under which those acts are evaluated to be either successful or to have failed. At an empirical level, the theory seeks to elucidate and offer warrant for the idea that the transformation of society, sometimes called modernization, can be understood in terms of both societal and cultural rationalization.

For this reason, Habermas's critical theory of society is a metatheory of rationality that conceives rationality from the standpoint of communicative action, which at the methodological level differentiates types of rationality that allow agents to evaluate the validity of their goal-oriented actions in accordance with object realms and types of action, and that, at the empirical level, argues that European modernity reflects precisely these forms of rationality in their rationalized social structures and cultural traditions. Only if a theory is able to meet these criteria can it offer itself as a viable theory of society. And only if it can secure these tasks can it secure its own normative foundations. Securing these foundations is fundamental for a critical theory of society[24] lest it get caught up in eviscerating and aporetic renunciations of the element that allows it to critique in the first place: reason itself.[25] The second major aspect of Habermas's reconstruction of the foundations of historical materialism and critical theory is the performance of a paradigm shift from the philosophy of consciousness to the linguistically mediated human action. This paradigm shift entails relocating the locus of reason from the autarkic subject engaged in a monologue in which ideas mirror the world to communities of communication in which agents are socialized into language competencies that enable, nay force, agents to take normative positions vis-à-vis the objective, subjective, and social worlds. Instead of mental representation, which imprisons the subject in a camera obscura of the mind, agents now are engaged in communicative interactions that place the subject in the role of always having to give and redeem reasons, that give primacy to the social world, that is the intersubjective world. In this way, then, Habermas's reconstruction of critical theory turns the critique of reason into an analysis of the way in which communicative interactions have different normative criteria according to the object realm to which they are aimed. By freeing the subject from its mental prison to the sociality of language, Habermas frees reason from the reifying hold of instrumental reason to communicative rationality that is differentiated, differentiating, and self-legitimating.

Habermas's interest in reconstructing the foundations of critical theory become explicit in the essay in which he also clarified his own views on technology, and this was done in the essay "Technology and Science as 'Ideology'" written in 1968 on the occasion of Marcuse's seventieth birthday.[26] In this essay, Habermas proceeds to critique Marcuse's romantic ideal of a New Technology and a New Science. For Habermas, such views "will not stand up to critical scrutiny."[27] Habermas offers two major reasons. On the one hand, postulating the possibility of an alternative to existing technology, one that would relate to nature not as object but as an "Other" subject, entails conflating the purposive-rational action with symbolic interaction. On the other hand, the possibility of another form of technology that may be related to nature differently puts in question the very coherence of science and technology, inasmuch as now they appear as projections of "an individual epoch, a specific class, or a surpassable situation."[28] Insofar as technology and science are achieved through language and work, they are the result of a phylogenetic learning process that cannot be replaced, for language and work are projects of the human species as a whole. Thus, if we are not to lose this evolutionary gain, this phylogenetic learning of the species that cannot be undercut by ontogenetic transformations of individual societies in given specific historical periods, Habermas proposes, we must differentiate between work and interaction. To work, or purposive-instrumental action, corresponds instrumental, rational choice, or a combination of both. This type of instrumental action is guided by technical rules and empirical knowledge. In contrast to interaction and more precisely communicative action or symbolic interaction corresponds the intersubjectivity of mutual recognition. This type of communicative interaction is governed by consensual norms.[29] These two types of interaction allow us to distinguish between different social systems and subsystems. This allows Habermas to make the distinction between the institutional framework of society, or what he also refers to as "the sociocultural life-world," and the "subsystem of *purposive-rational* action that is 'embedded' in it."[30]

These methodological and analytical distinctions allow Habermas to reformulate Marcuse's critique of capitalist society not in terms of ideology critique but in terms of pathological rationalization, distorted communication, and the colonization by purposive-rational action into the realm of symbolic interaction. In this way, therefore, Habermas is able to critique "technocratic consciousness" that conquers the lifeworld of symbolic or communicative interaction by evicting ethics from its constitution and regulation. The ideological nucleus of technocratic consciousness is *"the elimination of the distinction between the practical and the technical."*[31] Curiously, it would follow from Habermas's analysis that both first-generation Frankfurt School critical theory and positivism converge in this assimilation of the practical into the technical, the ethical into the instrumental.

The disaggregating of purposive from consensual action allowed Habermas also to elucidate the ways in which social progress can take place in such a way that not all forms of rationalization turn into an unmitigated disaster in which we are not able to differentiate advances from regressions. In fact, we now may view social subsystems as repositories of the learning acquired through the testing and implementing of purposive-rational action. "Purposive-rational action represents the form of *active* adaptation, which distinguishes the collective *self*-preservation of societal subjects from the preservation of the species characteristic of other animals. We know how to bring the relevant conditions of life under control, that is, we know how to adapt the environment to our needs culturally rather than adapting ourselves to external nature."[32] In other words, and here Habermas takes recourse to Arnold Gehlen's philosophical anthropology, if we "see the inner logic of technical development as the step-by-step disconnection of the behavioral system of purposive-rational action from the human organism and its transferal to machines, then the technocratic intention could be understood as the last stage of his development. . . . According to this idea the institutional framework of society . . . would now, in a fundamental reversal, be absorbed by the subsystems of purposive-rational action, which were embedded in it."[33] To put it curtly and succinctly, technology and science, which allow us to objectify and instrumentalize nature, absorb and preserve the human species' evolutionary adaptation, but now as a sociocultural achievement and not as a genomic adaptation. In this way, Habermas essentializes both science and technology, succumbing to the positivist temptation of a "naive instrumentalism" that conceives science as a neutral and always advancing species project.[34] Preserving and properly recognizing that rationalization at the institutional level, that is the lifeworld, can "only occur in the medium of symbolic interaction itself, that is, through *removing restrictions to communication,*"[35] has been won at the price of removing scientific-technical progress from the type of critique that makes critical theory critical. In short, and as Stanley Aronowitz put it, "the hegemony of technocratic consciousness may not be overcome— it must be taken for granted."[36]

Between 1968 and 2003, Habermas pursued relentlessly his project of a theory of communicative rationality. After the Marcuse essay of 1968, Habermas returned to the problems of rationality, but now from a philosophical-anthropologically grounded theory of knowledge interests, in *Knowledge and Human Interests* of 1968. There, the idea that science and technology are evolutionary gains reappears.[37] This is pursued in *The Theory of Communicative Action*, which, while shedding the language of philosophical anthropology, nonetheless retains a naturalistic understanding of science and technology and critical thought itself.[38] Yet as Andrew Feenberg and Steven Vogel have noted with consternation and surprise, references to either nature or technology are conspicuous in their absence.[39] After a long detour through "practical philosophy," Habermas announces in his introduction to his recent collection of essays *Wahrheit und Rechtfertigung* a return to those questions he had not dealt with since *Knowledge and Human Interest*, that is, questions that pertain to "theoretical philosophy."[40] In this introduction, titled "Realism after the Linguistic-Pragmatic Shift," Habermas has returned to the question of the status of technology and science vis-à-vis the theory of rationality, albeit a thoroughly linguistified rationality. Yet this linguistically elucidated reason must distinguish between how subjects cope with the objective world while they come to an understanding about that world with other subjects. We look at the objective world while we come to an understanding with others in the social world. "The practical as well as the semantic reference to objects confront us with 'the' world, while the truth claim that we raise with our statements about objects are confronted with the disagreement [*Widerspruch*] 'of others.' The vertical look toward the objective world entwines itself with the horizontal relation among members of an intersubjectively shared lifeworld."[41] These vertical and horizontal looks that look at the objective and social worlds, respectively, give rise to a bifurcated architecture that pairs up a methodological dualism that distinguishes between understanding and observation. For Habermas, understanding and observing echo another important distinction, namely, that between transcendental and empirical knowledge.[42]

Yet one of the fundamental aspects of the linguistic-pragmatic turn is precisely the detranscendentalization of all knowledge and rationality claims. How, then, is Habermas to reconcile the detranscendentalizing agenda of the linguistic-pragmatic turn, which the theory of communicative action embraced, and the reference to species-based learning experience? In Habermas's view, only with a postempiricist and postrepresentational type of realism, coupled with a "weak" naturalism, can the postlinguistic theory of knowledge circumvent the aporias bequeathed to us by the project of detranscendentalization.[43] By "weak" naturalism, Habermas means the view that sees "our" processes of learning as continuing "evolutionary processes of learning."[44] Habermas's type of naturalism, however, harkens us back to Marx's idea already quoted about the naturalization of humanity and the humanization of nature. For the idea of learning as natural processes does not preclude the idea of learning as a self-reflection of the species. As he writes, "For the conception of natural evolution as an analogue of learning process secures itself for the naturally emerged structures, which our learning process made possible, a cognitive content. This in turn explains why the universality and necessity of 'our' perspective on the objective world cannot be derogated because of their contingent context of genesis."[45] Be that as it may, Habermas reinscribes what Feenberg called "naive instrumentalism" in his renewed theoretical efforts, pursued in terms of a postempiricist, postrepresentational, postpositivist[46] realism and a weak naturalism.

TOWARD A GEOPOLITICAL CRITIQUE OF THE POLITICAL ECONOMY OF KNOWLEDGE(S)

If the Frankfurt School critical theory tradition is to have any viability in the global, postcolonial, and both postorientalist and postoccidentalist horizon that opened up after decolonization, the end of the Cold War, and the rise of neoliberal, American-driven globalism, then future critical theorists will have to come to terms with the aporias rendered explicit in the reconstructions presented here. However, instead of restating what was already explicated, I would like to bring to a provisionary closure this chapter by enumerating a series of desiderata and tasks.

First, and foremost if critical theory is to have any voice in the near future, by opening itself to a planetary and/or global agenda, then it must localize itself both spatially and temporally. It is quite evident that not just the object but also the form of the Frankfurt School's critical theorization emerged from western Europe during the first three quarters of the twentieth century. Frankfurt school already registers for us a spatial marker. But as our analysis of Horkheimer, Adorno, Marcuse, and Habermas has shown, their works have also been indelibly and irreversibly marked by the particular historical traumas that German society has undergone over the century. This does not make the Frankfurt School's critical theory less interesting but rather precisely more relevant as a critique of the pathologies of modernization and allow us to pursue Habermas's own theoretical insights into the methodological and empirical desiderata that a critical theory of society must fulfill. The context of the genesis of the critical theory should not lead us to underappreciate or dismiss their relevance and theoretical perspicuity. This applies mutatis mutandis to other critical projects that may have pursued the same goals, taking recourse to other critical languages, in other spatial and temporal contexts.

Second, and moving closer to the critical theory of science, if we accept that what has made the Frankfurt School's critical theory of science distinctive is the way it conceives science and science's view of nature as socially and thus historically constituted categories, then we have to raise both historiological and historiographical issues about the philosophy of science. By historiological, I mean the logic according to which we formalize and organize the very history of science, a logic that can by no means be simply developmental or even synchronic. In order to clarify what I mean, I would like to make reference to a recent essay by Peter Galison titled "Material Culture, Theoretical Culture, and Delocalization."[47] In this essay, Galison distinguishes among, first, the conditions of theoricity, or what a theory must exhibit and possess in order to count as reasonable and tenable before it can be submitted to experimentation or what counts as theory of science; second, the conditions of experimentality, which have to do with what would count as corroboration or refutation of a theory and what terms any kind of laboratory argumentation must use to proceed (in other words, what counts as an experiment and what the conditions are for experiments to count as the tests of theories); and, finally, the conditions of instrumentality, which have to do with the material constraints of the production of laboratory equipment for the testing of theories. In Galison's view, a positivist periodization of scientific progress would be characterized by the continuity of observation but a discontinuity in theories, although these would be seen as building on the preceding ones. In contrast and keeping in mind the differentiation of conditions of theoricity, experimentality, and instrumentality, we would have a far more fragmented and disaggregated periodization of science, technology, and scientific objects. Galison calls this disaggregated and noncontinuous periodization "intercalated periodization." This type of periodization makes evident a historical nonsynchronicity among the theories that may be formulated under a given epistemological regime, the technological media for the embodiment of observation and perception, and the possible conceptual and categorical schemata used to make sense of those observations and theories. In this way, then, neither naive instrumentalism, nor nonrepresentational realism, nor especially weak naturalism "stand up to critical scrutiny."

On the other hand, by historiography, I mean the less theoretically exacting although far more scholarly demanding writing of the history of scientific practices and technological regimes. What unequivocally links Habermas with Adorno and Horkheimer is the absence of even an awareness of the global history of science. Marcuse intimates in places that Third World societies may have different sciences from which westerners could learn.[48] Yet even in Marcuse's case, even superficial familiarity with the history of technology is absent. Two things will become quite evident once we begin to pay attention to these global histories of technology and science. First, from an internal perspective, there have been competing technologies whose acceptance or abandonment have been determined by extratechnological and extrascientific factors.

A classic example is the implementation of alternating current through the industry of electricity and the suppression of Thomas Edison's direct current. The acceptance of George Westinghouse's transformer over Edison's system was determined by socioeconomic and political requirements rather than by scientific ones.[49] Analogously but now as if from without, or cross-culturally, technologies as well as certain scientific paradigms and ideas either have been easily pirated and assimilated or have been resisted precisely because they belong to other cultures, although a more detached analysis would have revealed their superiority. Two cases are illustrative. One was the use of crop rotation to augment crop output, and the other was the English copying of metallurgic technique that allowed English industrialization to take off in the nineteenth century.[50] Indeed, not only is the incorporation and development of certain technologies dictated by intercultural conflicts and interactions, but technological paradigms themselves are affected by culture. As Feenberg has pointed out, if the computer had been invented in Japan or China first, it is unlikely that the keyboard would have become the primary device for input.[51] Indeed, this example illustrates Marcuse's prescient idea of another technology and another science without even making reference to whether we treat nature as another subject.

Third, fields of inquiry, that is, disciplines and methods of investigation, as well as their objects of investigation, are directly linked to the social and technical division of scientific labor. In this way, the sociality of both "nature" and "technology" is elucidated to go deeper than the very material and technical application. The very "objects" of science are socially and historically constituted.[52] There is no example that illustrates this better than the "gene." In Evelyn Fox Keller's words, the gene has a Janus face: "it is part physicist's atom and part Platonic soul—at one and the same time a fundamental building block and an animating force."[53] This nifty theoretical creation became the impetus for "mobilizing resources, for identifying particular research agendas, for focusing our scientific energies and attention in particular directions."[54] Yet the genomic revolution that the "invention" of DNA by Crick and Watson launched would not have been possible without some basic technical equipment that itself would not have been possible without certain corporate interests but especially the military-industrial complex's financial backing.[55] In his 1844 *Philosophical and Economic Manuscripts*, Marx talked about nature as a theoretical abstraction of universal social consciousness. Similarly, the gene is an abstraction, a theoretical construct that has allowed certain technologies to be developed and imposed. As Lewontin has noted, the gene is both bad biology and bad biochemistry.[56] The concept of the gene is so thoroughly ideological that it hinders us from seeing its ideological effects, of which genetic determinism is only one.[57] Thus, today, the survival of the fittest, genetic determinism, like "penis envy," is the opium of the people.[58]

Fourth, and to close, without having to appeal to either a romantic philosophy of nature, with roots in Judeo-Christian mysticism or a form of naive naturalism, we can acknowledge that the history of nature is the history of human society and that the history of human society is entwined with its relationship to that "human-built" environment. When we look at the plains of the Midwest, the Latin American mountains planted with coffee and plantain trees, the valleys of California, the plains on the coasts of the Mediterranean, and so on, we see a nature that is human landscape. A "green history" or an "environmental" history of the planet cannot but be also a history of human society and its ethical, political, and economic aims.[59] We have been seeding and reseeding the planet, creating both gardens of affluence and vast expanses of desert. Yet since the middle of the twentieth century, the pace at which the planet has been turned into a huge greenhouse has accelerated because of the so-called green revolution.[60] The green revolution was the name given to the project of the industrialization and biotechnological enhancement of agriculture. The promise was that world hunger would be eradicated. Yet this green revolution has been green in only one sense: the accumulation of green money in the hands of fewer and fewer agro-businesses. The green revolution has turned into the corporatization and monopolization of world agriculture.[61] In 1995, of the 1,500 seed companies in the world, 24 held more than 50 percent of the combined market share. Of those, 8 were transnational corporations.[62] In 1996, this consolidation of the global agro-business has only increased. In 1996, in fact, Monsanto acquired Agracetus (a small biotech company that has patented all future genetically modified versions of cotton and soybeans), Calgene (the designer of "FlavrSavr," the genetically modified tomato that has delayed rotting), Asgrow seed company, 40 percent of DeKalb, and the Holden Foundation Seeds (which supplies one-third of all corn seed planted in the United States).[63] Since then, Monsanto has also bought Delta and Pine Land, granting Monsanto control of 85 percent of the U.S. cottonseed. In 1998, Monsanto also acquired Unilever's European wheat-breeding subsidiaries. Monsanto has also bought India's largest seed company, MAHYCO. In a similar move, Monsanto bought from Cargill its operations in Central America, Europe, Asia, and Africa.[64] At the same time that monopolization has increased, the control of patents for genetically modified crops and seeds has similarly been monopolized. In 1997, there were 2,000 patents for genetically modified seeds pending, most of them submitted by U.S.-based agro-biotech multinationals. Slowly but surely, the plentiful planet, cultivated over the history of human evolution into a rich garden of biodiversity, is being turned by Monsanto and DuPont into a weed planet,[65] a monocrop greenhouse, a genetically eroded and depleted biosphere.[66] Any future critical theory of science will have to begin with this state of affairs: growing global inequity, exacerbating water scarcity, unequal consumption of global resources, and unprecedented levels of the monopolization of the industries and sciences that feed and clothe humans. More than ever, science and technology manifest themselves as socially mediated practices, now dominated by tyrannical geopolitics of the production of knowledge.

NOTES

1. See Peter Galison's introduction to Peter Galison and David Stump, eds., *The Disunity of Science: Boundaries, Contexts, and Power* (Stanford, Calif.: Stanford University Press, 1996), especially 32–33.

2. Max Horkheimer, "On the Problem of Truth," in *The Essential Frankfurt School Reader*, ed. Andrew Arato and Eike Gebhardt (New York: Urizen Books, 1978), 407–43.

3. Horkheimer, "On the Problem of Truth," 407.

4. Horkheimer, "On the Problem of Truth," 409. Here Horkheimer is quoting Edmund Husserl, "Formale und transzendentale Logik," in *Jahrbuch für Philosophie und phänomenologische Forschung*, vol. 10 (Halle, 1929), 241.

5. Horkheimer, "On the Problem of Truth," 410.

6. Horkheimer, "On the Problem of Truth," 422.

7. Horkheimer, "On the Problem of Truth," 429.

8. Max Horkheimer, "Notes on Science and the Crisis," in *Critical Theory and Society: A Reader*, ed. Stephen Eric Bronner and Douglass MacKay Kellner (New York: Routledge, 1989), 52–57, quote at 52.

9. Horkheimer, "On the Problem of Truth," 443.

10. Horkheimer, "Notes on Science and the Crisis," 54.

11. Horkheimer, "Notes on Science and the Crisis," 57.

12. Max Horkheimer, *Dawn and Decline: Notes 1926–1931 and 1950–1969* (New York: Seabury Press, 1978), 238–39. This quotation comes from the aphorism titled "Antinomies of Critical Theory."

13. Theodor W. Adorno, *Negative Dialectics* (New York: Continuum, 1983), 401–2.

14. Theodor W. Adorno, *Minima Moralia* (London: Verso, 1974), 98.

15. Max Horkheimer and Theodor W. Adorno, *Dialectics of Enlightenment* (New York: Continuum, 1982), 54–55.

16. Horkheimer and Adorno, *Dialectics of Enlightenment*, 55.

17. Horkheimer and Adorno, *Dialectics of Enlightenment*, 54.

18. Horkheimer and Adorno, *Dialectics of Enlightenment*, 181.

19. Adorno, *Negative Dialectics*, 320.

20. Adorno, *Negative Dialectics*, xx.

21. Theodor W. Adorno, "Introduction," in Theodor W. Adorno et al., *The Positivism Dispute in German Sociology* (New York: Harper Torchbooks, 1976), 19 (emphasis added).

22. Adorno, "Introduction," 27.

23. Steven Vogel's *Against Nature: The Concept of Nature in Critical Theory* (Albany: State University of New York Press, 1996), contains one of the most expansive and insightful discussions of both the idea of nature and technology in Habermas's work; see in particular chapters 5 and 6.

24. See Jürgen Habermas, *The Theory of Communicative Action, Vol. 1. Reason and the Rationalization of Society* (Boston: Beacon Press, 1984), 6–7.

25. See the section "The Critique of Instrumental Reason" in volume 1 of Habermas, *The Theory of Communicative Action*, 366–86.

26. Jürgen Habermas, "Technology and Science as 'Ideology,'" in *Toward a Rational Society: Student Protest, Science, and Politics* (Boston: Beacon Press, 1970), 81–122.

27. Habermas, "Technology and Science as 'Ideology,'" 88.

28. Habermas, "Technology and Science as 'Ideology,'" 88.

29. Habermas, "Technology and Science as 'Ideology,'" 92–93. See the table on page 93 that nicely maps the differences between work and symbolic interaction.

30. Habermas, "Technology and Science as 'Ideology,'" 94.

31. Habermas, "Technology and Science as 'Ideology,'" 113.

32. Habermas, "Technology and Science as 'Ideology,'" 115.

33. Habermas, "Technology and Science as 'Ideology,'" 106.

34. Andrew Feenberg, *Questioning Technology* (New York: Routledge, 1999), 152.

35. Feenberg, *Questioning Technology*, 118.

36. Stanley Aronowitz, *Science as Power: Discourse and Ideology in Modern Society* (Minneapolis: University of Minnesota Press, 1988), 162.

37. Jürgen Habermas, *Knowledge and Human Interests* (Boston: Beacon Press, 1971), especially the appendix, 301–17. Thomas McCarthy has analyzed thoroughly this text and shows its lingering metaphysical tendencies. See Thomas McCarthy, *The Critical Theory of Jürgen Habermas* (Cambridge, Mass.: MIT Press, 1978), especially chapter 2.

38. See Michael Theunissen, "Society and History: A Critique of Critical Theory," in *Habermas: A Critical Reader*, ed. Peter Dews (Malden, Mass.: Blackwell, 1999), 241–72. See also Karl-Otto Apel, "Normatively Grounding 'Critical Theory' through Recourse to the Lifeworld? A Transcendental-Pragmatic Attempt to Think with Habermas against Habermas," *Philosophical Interventions in the Unfinished Project of the Enlightenment*, ed. Axel Honneth, Thomas McCarthy, Claus Offe, and Albrecht Wellmer (Cambridge, Mass.: MIT Press, 1992), 125–70.

39. Feenberg, *Questioning Technology*, 157; Vogel, *Against Nature*, 150–51.

40. Jürgen Habermas, *Wahrheit und Rechtfertigung: Philosophische Aufsätze* (Frankfurt am Main: Suhrkamp Verlag, 1999), 7.

41. Habermas, *Wahrheit und Rechtfertigung*, 25.

42. Habermas, *Wahrheit und Rechtfertigung*, 25.

43. Habermas, *Wahrheit und Rechtfertigung*, 32.

44. Habermas, *Wahrheit und Rechtfertigung*, 37. Habermas contrasts weak to "strong" naturalism. This latter form of naturalism aims to substitute the conceptual analysis of practices in the lifeworld with an analysis of cerebral functions by the natural sciences. Thus, epistemology would be naturalized into neurochemistry, and this in turn would become neuromolecular evolutionary biology. See Habermas, *Wahrheit und Rechtfertigung*, 38.

45. Habermas, *Wahrheit und Rechtfertigung*, 39. Here Habermas cites approvingly a particularly telling passage from a manuscript by Peter Dews, although, as he notes, the juxtapositions in it are rather unusual: "It is the combination of anti-idealism with anti-scientism *and* a propensity toward naturalism which makes for the distinctiveness of Habermas's work. It marks him out as belonging to a sub-tradition which ultimately derives from the work of Hegel's left-wing followers during the 1830s and 40s." Habermas, *Wahrheit und Rechtfertigung*, 39 n. 41.

46. For a discussion of postpositivist realism, see Paula Moya and Michael R. Hames-Garcia, eds., *Reclaiming Identity: Realist Theory and the Predicament of Postmodernism* (Berkeley: University of California Press, 2000), especially the essays by Linda Martín Alcoff and Paula Moya.

47. Peter Galison, "Material Culture, Theoretical Culture, and Delocalization," in *Schools of Thought: Twenty-Five Years of Interpretive Social Science*, ed. Joan W. Scott and Debra Keates (Princeton, N.J.: Princeton University Press, 2001), 179–206.

48. William Leiss, *The Domination of Nature* (Boston: Beacon Press, 1972), 211.

49. See Aronowitz, *Science as Power*, 81.

50. See Susantha Goonatilake, *Toward a Global Science*, 53–55.

51. See Andrew Feenberg, "Technology in a Global World," in *Science and Other Cultures: Issues in Philosophies of Science and Technology*, ed. Robert Figueroa and Sandra Harding (New York: Routledge, 2003), 237–51, and the discussion of computers, keyboards, and faxes at 242.

52. See Aronowitz, *Science as Power*, 320.

53. Evelyn Fox Keller, *Refiguring Life: Metaphors of Twentieth-Century Biology* (New York: Columbia University Press, 1995), 9–10.

54. Keller, *Refiguring Life*, 21.

55. This is a complicated history, but a rich insight can be gained from N. Katherine Hayles, *How We Became Posthuman: Virtual Bodies in Cybernetics, Literature, and Informatics* (Chicago: University of Chicago Press, 1999). See also Richard Lewontin, "Science and Simplicity," *New York Review of Books* 50, no. 7 (May 1, 2003): 39–42. See also the discussion on the biotech revolution in Freeman J. Dyson, *The Sun, the Genome, and the Internet* (New York: Oxford University Press, 1999).

56. See Richard C. Lewontin, *The Triple Helix: Gene, Organism, and Environment* (Cambridge, Mass.: Harvard University Press, 2000), and Richard Lewontin, *It Ain't Necessarily So: The Dream of the Human Genome and Other Illusions*, 2nd ed. (New York: New York Review of Books, 2000); see also Barry Commoner, "Unraveling the DNA Myth: The Spurious Foundation of Genetic Engineering," *Harper's Magazine* 304, no. 1821 (February 2002): 39–47.

57. See Ruth Hubbard and Elijah Wald, *Exploding the Gene Myth* (Boston: Beacon Press, 1993).

58. Lewontin, *It Ain't Necessarily So*, 61.

59. J. R. McNeill, *Something New under the Sun: An Environmental History of the Twentieth-Century World* (New York: Norton, 2000).

60. See Vandana Shiva, *The Violence of the Green Revolution* (London: Zed Books, 1991).

61. Biotechnology has made this trend only more acute. See Hope Shand, "Gene Giants: Understanding the 'Life Industry,'" in *Redesigning Life? The World Wide Challenge to Genetic Engineering*, ed. Brian Tokar (London: Zed Books, 2001), 222–37.

62. Kristin Dawkins, *Gene Wars: The Politics of Biotechnology* (New York: Seven Stories Press, 1997), 25.

63. Dawkins, *Gene Wars*, 26.

64. Vandana Shiva, *Stolen Harvest The Hijacking of the Global Food Supply* (Cambridge, Mass.: South End Press, 1999), 81.

65. David Quammen, "Planet of Weeds: Tallying the Loss of Earth's Animals and Plants," *Harper's Magazine* 297, no. 1781 (October 1998): 57–70. As of 2001, DuPont and Monsanto controlled 73 percent of the U.S. seed corn market, while 40 percent of U.S. vegetable seeds come from one provider, and the top five agricultural providers control 75 percent of the global seed market. See Shand, "Gene Giants," 231.

66. David Shenk, "Biocapitalism: What Price the Genetic Revolution?," *Harper's Magazine* 295, no. 1771 (December 1997): 37–45. See also Marc Lappé and Britt Bailey, *Against the Grain: Biotechnology and the Corporate Takeover of Your Food* (Monroe, Maine: Common Courage Press, 1998), especially 1–18.

11

In the Stocking-Steps of Walter Benjamin: Critical Theory, Television, and the Global Imagination

F. Scott Scribner

In his work *The Information Bomb*, Paul Virilio speaks of two prime aspects of globalization both of which are embodied in the paradigm of television. The first is a ubiquitous telesurveillance, while the second is a temporal compression that is the effect of the translation of an expansive geographic space into a temporal register. Virilio, of course, will recognize the political implications of this transition as one "from a real space of geopolitics" to a chronopolitics, "the 'real time' of the transmission of images and sounds."[1] Those who are familiar with the work of both Paul Virilio and the Frankfurt School should not be surprised to hear an echo of Walter Benjamin's understanding of the relation between the truth of historical transiency and our metaphysical speculations about it, as a "stocking turned inside out," in Virilio's own account of globalization in terms of the relation between geophysics and metaphysics.[2] Virilio explains that "geostrategy is turning the globe inside out like a glove. . . . The global is the interior of a finite world."[3]

While Virilio is not forthcoming in what he means by the phrase "the global is the interior of the finite world," his discussions of globalization in terms of television and the compression of time would certainly lead one to take this phrase to mean that the global is marked by the conquest of the interior space of time and that the central means of its capture is television. In fact, theorists of television, such as Richard Dienst, have made similar observations. Dienst writes, "Televisual images do not represent things so much as they take up time, and to work through this time is the most pervasive way that subjects suffer through, participate in, and perhaps even glimpse, the global unification of contemporary capitalism."[4] In other words, global capitalism takes place through the conquest of inner sense, through a monopolization of "the time of the imagination."[5] Like Benjamin's stocking turned inside out or, in Virilio's case, a glove, television would seem to stand as the paradigm of a global imagination whose conquest of space through speed has externalized inner sense and in doing so marks time and its limit condition in eternity: it is the nexus between the historical transiency of geophysics and the eternity of metaphysics.

IMAGINATION AND THE TIME OF INNER SENSE

For Virilio, it is the technology of speed, as a chronopolitics, that marks globalization as a glove (or stocking) turned inside out in which the "interior finite world" of imaginative time consciousness is the very product of the global. In fact, this transition from a geopolitics to a chronopolitics would seem to mirror Kant's own account of the imagination in the *Critique of Pure Reason* as one in which outer sense is taken as space and translated into time through the generative presentation of temporal succession. But for Virilio, this temporal succession will be radically transformed through the technology of speed. By recapitulating the Kantian translation of the outer sense of space to the inner sense of time, through a synthesis of apprehension that itself produces time, globalization would seem to represent an ever-expanding technology of the imagination. In fact, the Kantian account of inner sense as the translation of space into time, as a function of the imagination, is taken over directly by technologies of speed—with the sole exception that inner sense is now externalized. Inner sense has gone global. Yet if Kant had defined the nature of inner sense as time, its externalization was presciently articulated by the Frankfurt School—both in Benjamin's account of a material imagination and in Adorno's description of its appropriation by mechanisms of control.

Through his interpretation of Kant, Martin Heidegger has made clear that the transcendental imagination is itself primordial time.[6] The transcendental synthesis of imagination produces time. The central role of the imagination in Kant is representing "in intuition an object that is not itself present."[7] It is worth emphasizing that here the very discussion of time appears on the model of space.[8] The imagination is essential for the representation of both space and time because it must represent both past and future times—times not present—through the analogy of space. Kant asks us to consider drawing a line in thought in which one must hold the antecedent markings as well as anticipate the future ones if one is to grasp this object.

The reproductive capacity of the imagination to hold that which is not present in thought gives unity to the whole and thus makes spatial and ultimately temporal synthesis possible. Through this temporal synthesis, the manifold is presented as a single time to a single consciousness. One issue that plagues such a discussion is the relation between this transcendental synthesis of the imagination and the transcendental unity of apperception or, in other words, the relation between inner sense and apperception. Even a cursory outlining of such a distinction stands as essential groundwork for later analyses of the impact of the temporality of industrial society and electronic media on a self-conscious subject.

There is no necessary unity between the unity of consciousness and the unity of time.[9] While the exact relation between apperception and inner sense is a point of contention within Kant scholarship, some basic distinctions can nevertheless be made.[10] Inner sense gives unity to the manifold in order to offer representation to a single consciousness. Inner sense offers an account of the "subjective unity of consciousness," but it cannot explain knowledge of the self. As Henry E. Allison highlights, "Inner sense has no manifold of its own, there are no sensible representations (intuitions) by means of which the self can represent itself as object."[11] Apperception, by contrast, is a nonempirical substratum that does not exist as an (empirical) object of inner sense.

The unity of experience takes place in the register of the temporal ordering called inner sense. When in his most famous analysis of apperception Kant notes that "it must be *possible* for the I think to accompany all of my representations,"[12] he is asserting that any experience must *be able* to be grasped self-reflexively but need not be.[13] The only necessity is that an accompanying "I think" be possible. One need not perform a reflexive act to think anything. In fact, Kant even allows for "unconscious representations."[14]

While the notion of a transcendental self has been a philosophical quandary at least since the time of Descartes, Berkeley, and Hume, the study of the impact of industrial modernity on the human sensorium by the Frankfurt School and others suggests that the unity of time or, rather, its fragmentation does indeed have impact on the unity of consciousness. The diverse rhythms of machine time establishes an exteriorized inner sense whose distinctness can no longer be theorized as merely contingent or benign. At the point of sensory overload, the temporal rush might be such that the "I think" can, in fact, no longer accompany representations, as Kant had insisted.

THE CRITIQUE OF THE IMAGINATION AND ITS MATERIALIZATION

To the extent that that temporality called the imagination, which gives unity to representations, need not be tied to apperception itself, inner sense has come to be externalized and the inner life eviscerated. Indeed, Virilio's reference to a glove turned inside out not only reiterates Benjamin's stocking metaphor, but if anyone is to make sense of the interior world as the global, one would also have to have recourse to Benjamin's own account of an externalization of the imagination. While any detailed analysis of such a development is beyond the scope of this chapter, I will nevertheless highlight three significant moments in Benjamin's project.

First, with the rise of mechanical reproduction and the concomitant waning of an autonomous creative imagination, the aura is said to decline. Auratic value is replaced with an "exhibition value": interior life is eviscerated.[15] Second, Benjamin reads the contemporary desire "to bring things closer," through photographic close-ups and so on, as itself a response to this inversion, to the exteriorization of interior time consciousness, visible in mechanical reproduction. The decline of "pathos at distance" is, of course, tied to the need to bring things closer and to recapture the loss of inner life. Finally, an account of an externalized imagination is made concrete in Benjamin's analysis of the dreamscapes of both the Salon and the Parisian Arcades. In the "Material for the Exposé of 1935," he likens the Parisian streets themselves to a "vascular network of the imagination."[16]

In fact, Adorno (and Horkheimer) will assert quite emphatically that there is "no scope left for the imagination."[17] To a great or lesser degree, for much of the Frankfurt School, the imagination has been usurped by means of its mechanized rival, reproductive media, and driven by the demands of consumer culture. As Adorno explains, "Any achievement of the imagination, any expectation that the imagination might of its own accord gather together the discrete elements of the real into its truth, is repudiated as an improper presumption. *Imagination is replaced by a mechanically relentless control mechanism.*"[18] Adorno's central point is that the autonomous power of image production that gathered together discrete elements into a presented whole, through the schematism of time, is now taken over by mechanical means. The transformation of the autonomy and spontaneity of the transcendental imagination must begin with the colonization of time. In this sense, to the extent Nam Juin Paik's assertion that the fundamental concept of television is time, such a claim would seem to reiterate in a mechanical register what Heidegger would say of the imagination, thereby suggesting that television stands as the paragon of a mechanized imagination.

THE TIME OF TELEVISION

If, as Heidegger noted, the power of image production called the transcendental imagination (*Ein-bildungs-kraft*) was fundamentally the work of time, then to the extent that television's own capacity for image production is tied to its role as the preeminent machine of time, I will argue that television stands as the fundamental model of the global imagination—perhaps even the very liminal medium of a stocking turned inside out. It is necessary to foreground the discussion of television as a time machine and its exchange of free images for free time through an analysis of the temporality of attention and distraction.

At least since Kant, the "epistemological dilemma of modernity" has been to bring unity and stability to the diffuse and fragmented fields of experience.[19] Part of the entire Enlightenment project of autonomy and the willful self-direction implied in such a concept requires a self-reflective attention or unity that hopes to find its ground in some anterior, transcendental, cognitive unity. With Schopenhauer's translation of Kantian apperception into the notion of the will, in which the cognitive unity was no longer a universal law but a mere constellation of forces often beyond the subject's control, philosophic grounds gave way to more psychological explanations for contingent capacities of association and synthesis.[20]

The scale of attention and distraction, like work and free time, must be thought of as a dependent relation, a continuous scale of gradation in which, at the extreme, one becomes the other. It is with the highest demands of attention that distraction ensues.

This critique of distraction, of course, was essential to the Frankfurt School's own analysis of subjectivity within modernity. One thinks of Simmel's "Metropolis and Mental Life," Benjamin's "Motifs on Baudelaire," and Kracauer's "Cult of Distraction." A central tenet of their foregoing analysis is not that distraction ruptures attention but rather that it is the excessive demands on attention by industrial modernity that requires distraction.

The cadences of industrial modernity that offer a unifying or focusing experience largely eclipse the previous unifying power(s) of inner sense. The irony, of course, is that the competing elements within capitalism that exhibit the selfsame desire to appropriate an attentive subjectivity in its full presence ultimately undermine their own goal by thoroughly overloading the human sensorium: the subject at peak attentiveness collapses into distraction. In this respect, the self-effacing structure of human subjectivity seems to stand as its own limit-condition, as that precarious limit or intersection between networks of information and rationalized exchange.[21] Adorno, of course, had outlined a "developing domination of needs," as "advertising, information, and command," in which the temporality of the circulation of goods would structure consciousness (albeit a false one) and political life.[22] Virilio will suggest that the construction of our mental environment and social life by logotypes, brand names, and so on is not the effect of reproductive media alone but "the logical outcome of a systematic message intensification."[23] If the external-ization of inner sense through the rhythm of machines produces not merely products but mental life itself, such that the form of time is inseparable from the structuring of attention, then how do we conceive of the temporality of its failure in distraction? Could one even map the dependent binary of attention and distraction onto the dual aspects of time and eternity, of Benjamin's stocking turned inside out?

Benjamin quotes Freud to explain that, for an organism, "protection against stimulus is an almost more important function then the reception of stim-uli."[24] Thought as a principle of "white noise," one wonders whether the speed of technology could ever be articulated as a form of the death drive in which stimulus, at infinite intensity, comes full circle and achieves a home-ostasis on par with its total absence.

NOWTIME

The "experience" undergone by individuals is impoverished in the age of in-formation. Like any form of production, electronic media eviscerate human experience and establish only machine time.[25] Like the experience of Ben-jamin's gambler, capitalist production offers the homogeneous repetition of a time emptied of the real content of concrete experience.[26] Here the homoge-neous experience of time is occasionally ruptured by shock experiences, but even these stand as mere jolts that cannot sufficiently realize real historical experience.

While the shock experiences that are the effect of reproductive media's as-sault on the senses do interrupt inner sense and thus must be read as a certain form of temporal interruption, Benjamin's notion of Nowtime (*Jetzeit*) forms a more fundamental temporal interruption. Benjamin's concept of Nowtime radicalizes the dialectical structure of the present as both a moment of exten-sive duration and an ultimate source or point of instantaneity. By exploding the antithesis inherent in the instant as both the temporal mark of "now" and infinity, as the expansive "abridgment" of the "entire history of humanity," Benjamin delimits Nowtime as the ultimate interruption, situated at the seem-ingly incommensurable registers of time and eternity.[27]

What does it mean for Benjamin to say that "truth is loaded to the bursting point with time"?[28] If time becomes finite only through space, then with Vir-ilio's suggestion that at peak speeds space is eradicated and time reaches an absolute deterritorialization, we have before us the very limit between time and eternity. The question before us is whether eternity, as the end of time itself, is achievable at infinite speed—the speed of light become stasis. While Benjamin's notion of Nowtime offers a messianic interruption that seems categorically distinct from the shock of industrial modernity, he does also offer the suggestion, much like the surrealists, that such interruption is not distinct from but in fact is dependent on technology. Perhaps revelation is somehow contingent on our technical access to it. For instance, in the essay "One Way Street," Benjamin expresses the hope that technology will provide a new cadence, transforming the rhythm of interior time "from which the sick will draw strength."[29]

THE TIME OF TELEVISION

If it was once the temporality of the reproductive imagination that gave rise to images, this productive relation between time and images is now one of clear commodified exchange in which free images are exchanged for free time.[30] Adorno aligns the boredom of free time with the atrophy of the transcendental imagination.[31] In the boredom of free time, the spontaneity of the imagination is functionalized and therefore foreclosed at the outset. The distractive structure of boredom, in its obverse codependency with attention, stands as an afterimage of work.[32] When Sartre in the *Critique of Dialectical Reason* explains that "it was the machine in her that was dreaming of love," his point is that subjectivity, in its subjection to machine time, can only play—that is, dream—in the images made possible by the cadence of the machine.[33]

Television stands most directly as that machine that trades on images and time. Watching television, like any form of attention, is work. What is traded is free images for the attention of one's free time. Here there are two orders of time: the first is the temporal flow of the images that is used as bait to capture the second order of time, the attention of human free time.[34] In fact, Dienst argues against what he sees as the crude account of advertising, which maintains that television stands as an economic transaction between a determinate corporation and specific local individual viewers, establishing a direct connection between perception and consumption.[35] Rather, he suggests that the time an advertiser buys is not a group of specific individual's attention but instead a more generalized "socialized time." He explains,

> By generating a realm of collective shared time, and by setting standards for the valorization of this time, television advances capitalism's temporal rule: everyone is free to spend time in his own way only because, on another level, that time is gathered elsewhere, no longer figured in the individual.[36]

Time is gathered elsewhere because the paradigm of television dictates the terms of the trade—whether surfing the Internet or at gas station monitors—as images are traded for the expenditure of time. It is the value of time per se that is determined at the outset by the rules of global economic exchange. In Dienst's words, "television, by delimiting and monopolizing the time of the imagination, allows us to offer up our social lives as free contributions to capitalist power."[37] While the transcendental imagination had generated its own images through the synthesis of time, the imagination is now externalized insofar as the production of images is established by a temporality that is received from without. Like an addict, images are traded for the attention of free time, out of an utter lack, in a misguided spontaneity, that is simultaneously the cause and effect of an atrophied imagination.

The temporality of the image that is exchanged for free time certainly seems to fulfill Virilio's second thesis of globalization in which a transcendental imagination is tied to space, to a geophysics, become wholly temporal in its translation into time. His additional remark, which forms the first part of his definition of globalization, delimits the ubiquity and persistence of television as "telesurveillance" and stands as the flip side of the translation of Benjamin's metaphor of the stocking turned inside out.

As the very limit of the compression of space become time, at infinite speed, eternity is approached. Through the technology of speed, geophysics becomes metaphysics. As Marx would highlight, "the tendency of capital is circulation without circulation time."[38] Geophysics defines a temporality still dependent on the referent of space; the transition to metaphysics, however, is one of pure time: time at infinite speed become eternity.

Our receptive relation to televisual images can be understood in terms of relative and absolute speed, time and eternity. As we suggested, the terms of the form of a televisual visibility are constituted at the outset. And the glare of this visibility is most often persistent and ubiquitous. In the free time of boredom, we seek free images. Its combination of temporality and temporal exchange between free time and free images, however, is part and parcel of its inescapable persistence—a profane presence not unlike Emmanuel Levinas's notion of the "*Il y a*" (there-is).[39]

The diacritical structure of our perceptive relation to televisual images offers, on the one hand, the subjective, if not solipsistic, excitement of recognition and commodified interpellation and, on the other hand, an assured reiteration of a failed adequation that jars subjectivity and binds it to this failure, as desire, as an urge to wrench oneself from his or her own finite spatial coordinates into the pure time of this profane "there-is." This is admittedly a profane version of an eternity achievable by the technology of absolute speed or, in short, time.

Dienst maintains that there are two dominant aspects or directions to televisual time—automatic time and still time—which "constitute the intensive and extensive limits of the apparatus itself."[40] Still time is constituted in a series of rapid-fire instants or displacements, much like the "cut" in film. It's the specific temporality of this switch that "structures seeing."[41] By contrast, automatic time signals the ambient presence of "scanning," an image left running, a televisual presence, or, in Virilio's words, the telesurveillance I described previously in terms of an electronic presence (*Il y a*).

In the same way, however, that the temporality of attention that structures seeing leads to its disintegration in distraction, the peak of speed, in the eradication of space, would seem to reach its own internal limit and become its other—eternity. This same dynamic is played out in the realm of television.

At the extreme, the rapidity of switches in still time would generate images that could not in principle be received and "could not, strictly speaking, be discernible."[42] Here, still time, at the extreme, is received as automatic time. And automatic time provides a "loose" ambient environment of the image, a seemingly inescapable background sensorium of white noise in which the "logic of subjective visibility" is usurped by a "machinic visibility."[43] Here, through the externalization of inner sense, the temporality of the once transcendental imagination is structured by the temporality of an externalized imaging or, in short, the time of television.

In conclusion, it would seem as if the time of television, as a new paradigm of the imagination, is embroiled in the impasse between television as a form of ideology and those who would invoke its normative potentiality, as a technology with revolutionary potential. After all, for Adorno, with television, "reality has become its own ideology."[44] On the other hand, figures such as the video artist Nam Juin Paik affirm television's redemptive potential. For instance, Paik's remark that he left Zen for video because Zen was too boring implicitly suggests a latent possibility within this machine of time for overcoming its own internal limits—as Benjamin and the surrealists had suggested—by catalyzing a Nowtime in and through technologies of speed. Regrettably, the question of whether television clearly embodies a revolutionary potential or stands as a mere ideology is an extremely interwoven issue that cannot be easily resolved, particularly in the context of this chapter. In fact, in television's current incarnation, it is unlikely such a distinction could ever be sorted out.

Nevertheless, what has been made clear is that television, as the preeminent machine of time, would certainly seem to model a global imagination whose exchange of images for free time has externalized the inner sense of the transcendental imagination. Television would additionally seem to stand as a surrogate "glove" or "stocking" to the extent that its technology of speed both marks time and, at its peak, irrupts in its own undoing. And while I am not suggesting that such a surrogate is the legitimate heir to the Nowtime of the dialectical image—it is surely not—the tension between such accounts makes real the importance of Benjamin's thought—as well as Adorno's—for rethinking globalization in terms of a global imagination.

NOTES

1. Paul Virilio, *The Information Bomb*, trans. Chris Turner (New York: Verso, 2000), 13.

2. See Walter Benjamin's notes for the *Trauerspiel* study, 1:918, cited in Susan Buck-Morss, *The Dialectics of Seeing* (Cambridge, Mass.: MIT Press, 1989), 21.

3. Virilio, *The Information Bomb*, 10.

4. Richard Dienst, *Still Life in Real Time: Theory after Television* (Durham, N.C.: Duke University Press, 1994), 64.

5. Dienst, *Still Life in Real Time*, 62.

6. "If the transcendental imagination as the pure formative faculty in itself forms time . . . then the thesis . . . that transcendental imagination *is* primordial time, can no longer be avoided." Martin Heidegger, *Kant and the Problem of Metaphysics* (Bloomington: Indiana University Press, 1962), 193.

7. Immanuel Kant, *Critique of Pure Reason*, trans. Norman Kemp Smith (New York: St. Martin's Press, 1965), B151. Emphasis added.

8. Recourse to an analogy of space is testament to the poverty of our vocabulary of speaking of inner sense.

9. As Henry Allision emphasizes, "There is no purely conceptual constraint on the possibility of uniting under a concept in a judgment the representation of objects located in different time-frames." Henry E. Allison, *Kant's Transcendental Idealism* (New Haven, Conn.: Yale University Press, 1983), 162.

10. Allison, *Kant's Transcendental Idealism*, 259–62.

11. Allison, *Kant's Transcendental Idealism*, 262.

12. Kant, *Critique of Pure Reason*, B131–32.

13. Allison, *Kant's Transcendental Idealism*, 137.

14. Allison, *Kant's Transcendental Idealism*, 137.

15. Frisby emphasis this point. David Frisby, *Fragments of Modernity* (Cambridge, Mass.: MIT Press, 1986), 258.

16. Walter Benjamin, *The Arcades Project*, trans. Howard Eiland and Kevin McLaughlin (Boston: Belknap/Harvard University Press, 1999), 901.

17. T. W. Adorno and Max Horkheimer, *The Dialectic of Enlightenment* (New York: Continuum, 1972).

18. "Any achievement of the imagination, any expectation that the imagination might of its own accord gather together the discrete elements of the real into its truth,

is repudiated as an improper presumption. *Imagination is replaced by a mechanically relentless control mechanism* which determines whether the latest imago to be distributed really represents an exact, reliable reflection of the relevant item of reality. The only element of aesthetic semblance here is the empty abstract semblance of a difference between culture as such and practice as such, the division of labor as it were between different departments of production." T. W. Adorno, *The Culture Industry*, ed. J. M. Bernstein (New York: Routledge, 1991), 64. Emphasis added.

19. Jonathan Crary, *Suspensions of Perception: Attention, Spectacle, and Modern Culture* (Cambridge, Mass.: MIT Press, 1999), 14.

20. Crary, *Suspensions of Perception*, 15.

21. Jonathan Crary, *Techniques of the Observer* (Boston: MIT Press, 1990), 2.

22. Habermas develops Adorno's account in terms of four levels of progressive rationalization: 1) the application of social science techniques to social problems, 2) rationalized decision theory, 3) value as successful self-assertion, and 4) cybernetic, self-maintained steering systems.

23. Paul Virilio, *The Vision Machine*, trans. Julie Rose (Bloomington: Indiana University Press/BFI, 1996).

24. Walter Benjamin, *Illuminations*, ed. Hannah Arendt, trans. Harry Zohn (New York: Schocken Books, 1968), 161.

25. Benjamin, *Illuminations*, 175.

26. This, of course, is the distinction between *Erfahrung* and *Erlebnis*.

27. Benjamin, *Illuminations*, 263.

28. Cited in Peter Osborne's "Small-Scale Victories, Large-Scale Defeats: Walter Benjamin's Politics of Time," in *Destruction and Experience*, ed. Andrew Benjamin and Peter Osborne (Manchester: Clinamen Press, 2000), 83.

29. "In technology, as *physis* is being organized through which mankind's contact with the cosmos takes a new and different form from that which it had with families. One need only recall the velocities by virtue of which mankind is now preparing to embark on incalculable journeys into the interior of time to encounter there rhythms from which the sick shall draw strength." Walter Benjamin, *Reflections*, ed. Hannah Arendt, trans. Harry Zohn (New York: Schocken Books, 1968), 94.

30. Dienst speaks of the exchange relation between free images and free time in *Still Life in Real Time*, 61–62.

31. T. W. Adorno, *The Culture Industry*, ed. J. M. Bernstein (New York: Routledge, 1991), 193.

32. Adorno and Horkheimer, *The Dialectic of Enlightenment*, 137.

33. Cited by Dienst, *Still Life in Real Time*, 47.

34. Dienst, *Still Life in Real Time*, 60.

35. Dienst, *Still Life in Real Time*, 61.

36. Dienst, *Still Life in Real Time*, 61–62.

37. Dienst, *Still Life in Real Time*, 61–62.

38. Cited by Dienst, *Still Life in Real Time*, 46.

39. See, for instance, Emmanuel Levinas, *Totality and Infinity*, trans. Alphonso Lingis (Pittsburgh: Duquesne University Press, 1969).

40. Dienst, *Still Life in Real Time*, 159–60.
41. Dienst, *Still Life in Real Time*, 161.
42. Dienst, *Still Life in Real Time*, 162.
43. Dienst, *Still Life in Real Time*, 163.
44. Adorno, *The Culture Industry*, 63.

12

Adorno; or, The End of Aesthetics

Carsten Strathausen

As a philosophical discipline, aesthetics today is in decline. Inaugurated by Baumgarten in 1750 as the "science of sensory knowledge," the history of aesthetics blossomed with Kant and Burke and reached its first ambivalent pinnacle with a philosopher who has made quite a comeback recently, namely, Hegel. That is hardly surprising, for it was Hegel who in his lectures on aesthetics (published in 1835) first gave rise to the popular notion of the "end of art" in circulation today.[1] The traditional interpretation of Hegel's dictum is well known: since art is essentially oriented toward philosophical thought and pure ideas rather than material substance, it becomes superfluous once its ideal content—with the help of Hegel's own philosophy—can be thought abstractly and no longer needs to be (ad)dressed in a sensuous form. Hence, Hegel can proudly proclaim that "art is and remains for us . . . a thing of the past."[2]

Contrary to this common understanding of Hegel's *Aesthetics*, recent critics insist on its underlying ambivalence vis-à-vis the "end of art." Since the proclaimed dissolution or surpassing of art into philosophy requires the rebirth of the former within the realm of the latter, as Hegel himself repeatedly emphasizes in his writings, the frontier separating the two realms becomes porous and unstable. Instead of overcoming art once and for all, Hegel's thought requires it to oscillate continuously between its necessary demise and its equally necessary restitution. This hybrid status of art as that which persists only through the process of its own dissolution renders the "end of art" logically impossible.[3]

Without trying to settle accounts as to the "correct" reading of Hegel's *Aesthetics*, it is fairly obvious that the "end of art" can be read either in a strictly referential or in a discursive manner. Focusing on the manifest content of Hegel's idea, the referential reading has been advocated by Arthur C. Danto, who maintains that contemporary art is indeed a posthistorical art or "art after the end of art."[4] Danto identifies two major periods in the history of art: the Vasari episode (dating roughly from 1300 or the invention of monocular perspective to 1880 or the arrival of modernism) and the Greenberg episode (ranging from 1880 or postimpressionism roughly to 1960 or the arrival of pop). Both periods referred to art in strictly normative terms and readily dismissed all those forms of representation that did not adhere to certain aesthetic principles (such as mimesis and the conquest of visual appearance for Vasari and the material conditions of the artistic medium for Greenberg) as nonart and thus outside the "pale of history," as Hegel had phrased it.

Ours, by contrast, is a time of nonnormative art or aesthetics and thus similar to "art produced before art" (Hans Belting), that is, before the year 1300. For given the lack of stylistic unity among contemporary artworks, Danto concludes that any attempt to conceive of a universally binding, grand narrative or theory about the essence of art must necessary fail. Thus, the end of art precipitates and heralds the end of aesthetics: "Though art may continue to exist in what I have termed a post-historical fashion, its existence carries no historical significance whatever," Danto declares. "Artmaking is its own end in both sense of the term: the end of art is the end of art. There is no further place to go" because "art has exhausted its conceptual mission."[5] Some differences notwithstanding, Danto's definitive story about the end of art reinforces an earlier observation by Peter Bürger, who already claimed in 1974 that "no movement in the arts today can legitimately claim to be historically more advanced *as art* than any other."[6] In contrast to Danto, Bürger, however, privileges the historical avant-garde as the time period in which all aesthetic forms and materials became readily available to the artist, thus inaugurating the severe crisis of the "institution of art" still lingering today. Hence, although Bürger and Danto agree on the final result as to the "end of art," they differ with regard to the model of historical periodization they advance, thus leading the discussion full circle back to Hegel and his claim that art had already come to an end with the demise of the classical period in the mid-nineteenth century—a view that neither Danto nor Bürger is willing to support.

Given this interminable debate as to the actual beginning of the "end of art," critics have recently shifted focus from a referential to a discursive (or rhetorical) analysis of the historical vicissitudes of Hegel's dictum. Instead of adding yet another twist to the story herself, Eva Geulen, for example, suggests examining the already existing stories with regard to the rhetorical means and formal structures that enable them to circulate precisely as *stories*. The goal, then, becomes a concise analysis of the different narrative guises of this particular philosophical statement, a kind of "prolegomena to the phenomenology about the end of art as rumor."[7] Geulen's deconstructive intervention into the history of philosophical discourse deliberately blurs the lines between philosophy and literature: it examines the former strictly according to the implicit characteristics of the latter when, in fact, the original project of aesthetics had stipulated precisely the reverse, namely, the subordination of art and sensory experience to the rules of philosophy.

Unlike Jürgen Habermas, I welcome this dissolution of disciplinary boundaries as a productive way of reexamining philosophical questions on the level of discourse—Geulen's excellent readings of texts from Hegel to Heidegger are a case in point. Yet one must also acknowledge that aesthetics is not simply a matter of discourse either, for it should function as a bridge (at least since Kant) that connects theory and practice rather than separating them even further. Geulen's shift from reference to rhetoric, however, requires her to remain silent about both the present status (and quality) of art as well as its possible contribution to a critique of the current socioeconomic development known as globalization. Of course, that silence is a problem only for those who, like myself, continue to believe in the power of art and aesthetics to enable such a critique—a doctrine that, to paraphrase Adorno, is nowhere written down and hence open to contestation.[8] If one holds fast to this belief, however, then the exclusively rhetorical (or deconstructive) analysis of aesthetic discourse cannot suffice, for it remains severed from the empirical, sensuous realm aesthetics originally sought to render intelligible.

Adorno's goal in *Aesthetic Theory* was precisely to renegotiate this dilemma. He wanted to come to terms with that which refuses to be spelled out and which he named nonetheless, in a deliberate act of dialectical self-contradiction, as the "non-identical" or the "truth content" of the work of art. Needless to say, Adorno failed, for his was a project conceived in terms of failure from the very beginning. It was a grandiose failure, to be sure, a deliberate failure, certainly—but a failure just the same. Indeed, the history of Western aesthetics both culminated in and was eclipsed by Adorno's *Aesthetic Theory*. Published posthumously in 1970, this brilliant fragment is a swan song not only for Adorno's own philosophy but for aesthetics in general.

This chapter proceeds from this premise and thus shares Danto's basic arguments concerning the "end of art." Unlike many recent scholars aiming to demonstrate "the ways in which Adorno's thought can be remobilized for a variety of critical projects that matter now,"[9] I regard the Adorno renaissance of the past decade as irrefutable evidence that Adorno finally has become what he never wanted to be—an academic "classic."[10] As such, Adorno's failure is beyond reproach but also beyond repair, unless one is willing to question some of his basic assumptions, as I will demonstrate in the next section of this chapter. To be sure, my goal is not to endorse Peter Sloterdijk's radical claim that "critical theory is dead"[11] but to argue for a new and updated understanding of aesthetics in the context of postmodernism and today's globalized culture. Hence, I shall discuss in detail what I consider the most important aspects of Adorno's *Aesthetic Theory* to be discarded or salvaged for this project. The second section of this chapter discusses a variety of deliberate attempts to resurrect aesthetics today and finally advocates the study of new media and communication networks as the most promising revival of "aesthetics" in the age of globalization.

I

It is impossible to discuss the end of art without at one and the same time discussing the end of aesthetics. Particularly for the later Adorno, art and philosophy are inextricably intertwined. True artworks silently call for their critical reflection in thought so that they may become what they already appear to be: truthful representations of the whole. Adorno's position vis-à-vis the end of art is essentially ambivalent, and the same necessarily applies to his understanding of aesthetics as well. Although Adorno explicitly acknowledges the inevitable "end of art" (for example, in his radical verdict on "Poetry after Auschwitz" or in his essay on Beckett's *Endgame*), he also recognizes this process of disintegration as the essential characteristic of modern art as such. The latter thus survives precisely through its own negation: "Art itself seeks refuge in its own negation," Adorno claimed, for "it wants to survive by means of its death."[12] And again: "This demise is the goal of every work of art in that it seeks to bring death to all others. That all art aims to end art is another way of saying the same thing" (4:84). The same, of course, holds true for aesthetics and philosophy in general: both "stay alive because the moment of [their] realization has been missed" (6:15). The entire *Negative Dialectics* can thus be read as its own epitaph or an extended footnote to a closed chapter in human history that must remain open for as long as the eulogy lasts, and critics have rightly pointed to these topoi of anachronicity and "survival through death" as central to Adorno's philosophizing.[13]

This intimacy with death is one of the main reasons why the Adornian variant of critical theory, contrary to Sloterdijk's pronouncement, cannot possibly die, for it thrives on the immanence of its own death. Adorno's thought moves too agilely between the insterstices opened up by the many aporias and death scenarios he evokes. He is the master of the Benjaminian "dialectics at a standstill," which he performs in almost every sentence and with such velocity that his language attains a mesmerizing, if not hypnotic, quality. It is by means of these continuous dialectical twists that Adorno's aesthetics can proclaim the death of art as the genuine expression of its being alive or celebrate the absence of meaning as meaningful in and of itself. The same dialectics also allows him to assert the paradoxical "double character of art" as both "*fait sociale* and autonomous" and thus to collapse the two poles without, however, eradicating the contradictory tension between them, meaning that the socially most isolated and seemingly indifferent artworks now emerge as the most critical and politicized ones: "If any function can be ascribed to art at all," Adorno exclaims, "it is the function to have no function" (7:322).

Such dialectical wizardry comes at a price, however. Adorno's aesthetics can remain true to itself only by self-critically recognizing and endlessly revisiting—dialectically, of course—its own inherent contradictions. Hence, Adorno's insights always contain a rhetorical and performative aspect: they cannot and must not be proclaimed as static truths lest they succumb to the same process of reification they so vehemently oppose. Eva Geulen refers to this process as Adorno's "parodic practice" or "excess" that requires critics actively to engage rather than to summarize his ideas: "Art and post-aesthetic art after the end of art are Adorno's texts—some of Adorno's texts, sometimes—because they not only temporalize and delay the end of art, they parody it."[14] Art survives its own death in the form of aesthetic theory parodying as art. Given this performative and autoreferential quality of Adorno's text, the latter not only outlines but actually partakes of the characteristics of autonomous art and thereby renders itself aesthetic.[15] Moreover, like any other "authentic" artwork, *Aesthetic Theory* requires a critical exegesis in order to speak truthfully about itself qua art, and this, in turn, guarantees its own survival *in* and *as* discourse. Despite Adorno's exhortation to the contrary, *Aesthetic Theory* is art in the guise of philosophy—a claim that has been advanced again and again over the past thirty years.[16]

Indeed, the problem with Adorno's rhetoric is not the much maligned *Gehirnakrobatik* evident in his texts, which is, after all, the shared characteristic of all great thinkers. The real problem is the mechanistic simplicity of the rhetorical device that sustains this complexity—negative dialectics. Left unchecked, the latter develops a totalizing tendency and creates a vortex that swallows up everything within its reach. Adorno's (negative) dialectics always wins because failure makes it stronger, much like art always survives by staging its own death. Eva Geulen puts it most succinctly: "dialectics' self-immunization against failure through failure has become problematic today. Its more subtle failure is dialectics'—even and precisely negative dialectics'—failure to ever fail."[17] Lyotard goes even further than that. For him, Adorno's dialectics is of a theological nature, and he must act "as the devil" to sustain its colonizing power through negativity: "The diabolical figure is not just dialectical, it is expressly the failure of dialectics in dialectics, the negative in the heart of negativity, the suspended moment or momentaneous suspension."[18] One might conclude that Adorno relates to Hegel the way Mephistopheles relates to the Lord in Goethe's play: both must perform the art of (self-) contradiction in order to serve the public good and avoid the slovenly affirmation of the status quo.

Of course, Adorno himself knew that all along and therefore repeatedly endorsed "the necessity to think dialectically and undialectically at the same time" (4:173). This is precisely what Fredric Jameson has tried to do. Jameson rejects the charge that Adorno aestheticizes theory as "outrageous" but soon thereafter concedes the dominance of the aesthetic in Adorno only to the degree to which it can immediately be transcribed into "history" and the "substantive" socioeconomic forces that underlie it: "If everything in Adorno leads into the aesthetic," he maintains, then "everything in Adorno's aesthetics leads out again in the direction of history. . . . In that case, it may by no means be so reassuring in the long run to have successfully demonstrated that Adorno's philosophy is 'merely' aesthetic."[19] Jameson's defense, however, not only implicitly accepts the charge of aestheticization as having been "successfully demonstrated" after all but also falls prey to a circular logic. In a fairly typical gesture, Jameson evokes "history" as the *passe-partout* supposed to open the door from Adorno's autoreferential texts to the extradiegetic outside when, in fact, his reference to "history" merely explains *why* Adorno must embrace self-referentiality and aesthetic autonomy as the only means to immunize his texts against the colonizing power of capitalism. To paraphrase Jameson, then, one might say that if everything in Adorno's aesthetic leads out in the direction of history, then everything in history leads Adorno back into the aesthetics again and so on—a never-ending circuitry powered by the totalizing machinery of negative dialectics.

Jameson, I imagine, would disagree, particularly since his overall goal is to use Adorno as a means to historicize or "Marxize" postmodernist theory for the twenty-first century. Hence, he strongly privileges a production-oriented approach toward cultural development and aligns Adorno with the Engels–Lenin–Althusser notion of the socioeconomic as the determining factor in the "last instance." The question of whether this does justice to Adorno's philosophy as a whole seems less interesting to me than the theoretical consequences that ensue from this approach. Most important, Jameson must hold on to some notion of social "totality" that can neither be replaced nor rendered obsolete by the postmodern hypostatization of openness, fragmentation, and multiplicity. For Adorno's concept of dialectics as well as his social utopianism hinges on the irreducible, material reality signified by the "concept of totality": "The critical instrument of contradiction is inseparable from a conception of totality," Jameson contends, because of our "*objective experience of social reality* and the way in which one isolated cause or issue, one specific form of injustice, cannot be fulfilled or corrected without eventually drawing the entire web of interrelated social levels together *into a totality* which then demands the invention of a politics of social transformation."[20] In other words, Jameson embraces the persistence of the dialectic and Adorno's aestheticization of theory only up to the point at which these devices encounter the objective reality of the social whole. There, dialectics and the art of presentation must stop because this ontological level is constituted by the lived experience of real people and remains unaffected by (theoretical or philosophical) questions of presentation (or *Darstellung*).

Confronted with the choice of reading Adorno "more" dialectically or "less" dialectically, Jameson opts for the latter and plants himself firmly on the traditional soil of Marxist "reality": the economic forces at work throughout human history, analyzed with the help of dialectics as the basic principle of Marxist "science." What I find problematic in Jameson is not his pragmatic use of dialectics but his insistence on the abstract notion of totality according to which the social whole can be studied scientifically or objectively by the Marxist science-philosopher. This belief strikes me as epistemologically naive at best. And yet, in spite of the tough criticism leveled against Jameson,[21] I believe his attempt to "think dialectically and undialectically at the same time" is nonetheless an important step in the right direction precisely because of Jameson's somewhat utilitarian effort to break away from the perpetuum mobile of dialectical thought. The fallacy of some of his critics, on the other hand, is their continued loyalty to Adorno's homeopathic method: they treat the disease as the remedy and paradoxically prescribe more dialectics to solve the very problems it causes.

The major achievement of Jameson is precisely his effort to break away from that model, leading only deeper and deeper into the spiraling abyss of negativity and thus away from actual, lived experience. For there is a real world beyond Adorno's texts, and to address it effectively requires more than the parodic exercise of rhetorical skills. One should therefore welcome Jameson's attempt to read Adorno's dialectics as "a handbook and an operating manual," as he himself puts it, since the end of both dialectics and aesthetics is not to create a "superior" dialectics but to reveal the contradictions of lived reality and to guide leftist political action.[22] This effort may be less sophisticated than Adorno's, it may "get him wrong" and may even succumb to "common sense," as Hullot-Kentor and others have argued, but it is nonetheless in dire need today.[23]

For what is the alternative to Jameson's practice-oriented approach toward Adorno's aesthetics? Is it indeed the meticulous excavation of his latent theory and rhetorical use of language, as some critics maintain?[24] What do we gain if we regard the self-aestheticizing tendencies of Adorno's texts as a form of parodic practice meant to disrupt the instrumental logic of capitalism, as Adorno himself used the concept in his "Effort to Understand Endgame"? Does not all this simply lead us back to a mystical notion of the "true language of art" and toward discourse as a corrective if not substitute for existing reality? And what kind of (poetic, philosophical, parodic) language should we use today in light of the fact that the high-modernist distinction between cultural and economic production has finally and irrevocably collapsed? If postmodernity is indeed characterized by "the becoming cultural of the economic and the becoming economic of the cultural," as Jameson reminds us,[25] then art cannot possibly keep alive Adorno's dream of "a world in which things would be different" (11:40). For in the Western world of constant (superficial) change, nothing ever changes fundamentally, giving rise to a process that, in Jameson's words, "discredit(s) the utopian imagination itself."[26] More precisely, global capitalism has captured our imagination and succeeded in reabsorbing it into its own logic. Once securely confined within the parameters of the capitalist system, the imagination is allowed to roam freely among gigantic shopping malls and the endless rows of consumer products. And while the West celebrates the current status quo as the "end of history," the lingering idea of real social change in many parts of the Third World does not undermine capitalism but embraces it: people everywhere dream of food, shelter, and a home-video entertainment set, which is to say that the dream of utopia is still alive worldwide, but this utopia, unlike Adorno's, carries a concrete name and a specific location — Western capitalism, the place where utopia already appears to have been realized. Aesthetic theory today needs to come to terms with the prophetic language global capitalism uses every day (in local advertisement slogans as well as in official speeches given by leaders of the International Monetary Fund and the Word Bank) instead of conjuring the silent language of renunciation allegedly inherent in "true" works of art.

By contrast, Adorno's *Aesthetic Theory* confines art and aesthetics to a "windowless monad" (*fensterlose Monade*) severed from the realm outside, and Adorno's ethical commitment is to fortify these borders in an effort to protect the void from being assimilated by the capitalist forces of production. Today, however, we need to move beyond this language of negative utopianism, which has lulled itself to sleep in the darkness of the black hole where it sought refuge. Following Adorno, critics all too often remain locked in some kind of mournful negativity that is forced to withdraw from rather than productively engage with the world it critiques, leading to a regressive and limiting rather than empowering investigation of the role of art in contemporary society.[27] In other words, Adorno's self-grinding method of dialectical reflection has become counterproductive today. This is not to say that we should give up critical thought; it means only that such reflection must pursue a purpose outside itself. And this is exactly where the problem lies: in global capitalism, it has become difficult even to imagine an alternative to the system in which we live because there simply remains no "outside"—a genuinely Adornian insight, to be sure, but one that cannot be answered anymore with the totalizing denunciation of the whole "as the untrue" or by pointing to the negative power of modernist art or by using *Aesthetic Theory* as the parodic substitute of art after the end of art. Today's "culture industry," and postmodernism in general, has already parodied parody to the *n*th degree yet still gets *Dumb and Dumber* every day. Adorno's parody has become the "parody of nothing" (Lyotard), and even the most vapid Hollywood movie today slyly advertises and exploits its own stupidity as a kind of self-parody, thereby dialectically immunizing itself against criticism. In other words, capitalism has not only instrumentalized historical genres and their aesthetic materials (including modernism and the traditional realm of high art) but, more important, has also appropriated the very dialectical means by which *Aesthetic Theory* had sought to resist this process of instrumentalization.

Adorno placed too high hopes and too heavy a burden on art and aesthetics alike, and it is clear today that they could not possibly live up to his demands outside of or beyond the closed universe of his own texts. It should also be clear that this autoreferentiality was not a serious problem during Adorno's lifetime. The student revolt in the 1960s and the various protest movements all over the world provided enough of a counterweight to let his *Aesthetic Theory* appear as a viable alternative. Given the blind activism Adorno encountered among his students, it was pertinent for him to advocate "thinking as a doing" and "theory as a means of practice" (10/2:761), and he was right to warn against mere spontaneous action as a substitute for thinking through its consequences. But times have changed, and although Adorno did not need "to be afraid of the ivory tower" (20/1:403), leftist intellectuals today certainly should be, given the enormous power and ideological appeal capitalism enjoys worldwide. In the twenty-first century, it is simply unreasonable to endorse Adorno's antipragmatism and to reject "theory in the service of practice" as a form of "instrumental rationality" that perpetuates the system (10/2:798). The opposite is true today: anybody who, like Adorno, still believes that the "false, once recognized and determined" would already be "the index of what is right and better" (10/2:793) simply has not paid attention over the past thirty years. For we know what is wrong with capitalism, but we are far less sure about how to fix it. While I am certainly not simply advocating for artists and intellectuals to take to the streets, I do maintain that aesthetic theory can no longer afford to regard the realm of practice as its genuine opposite.

Thus, any renewal of a leftist aesthetics must abandon rather than embrace the "persistence of the dialectic" in order to move beyond the Marxist legacy of thinking totality as a binary structured whole. Unlike Jameson, I believe that the dialectical mode of thinking has become epistemologically doubtful and historically obsolete with the rise of postmodern global capitalism. Today, Adorno's effort to think dialectics against itself no longer leads to a "superior dialectics" (Britta Scholze) but moves away from dialectics altogether toward a "pragmatist aesthetics" (Richard Shusterman) whose goal is to "reconceive art so as to enhance its role and appreciation" toward an improved experience of life (rather than theory).[28] As I have argued in this chapter, Adorno's *Aesthetic Theory* did not get to this point but instead remained stuck in the repetitive performance (or parody) of its own theory as a rhetorical substitute for the kind of genuine practice it was unable to inaugurate. By contrast, aesthetic theory becomes pragmatic the moment it no longer tries to define the truth or essence of art but instead serves the purpose of enhancing "our immediate experience which invigorates and vitalizes us, thus aiding our achievement of whatever further ends we pursue."[29] Without reference to and further incorporation of this pragmatic dimension, the project of aesthetics is doomed to become increasingly futile and to disappear not only in practical but also in theoretical terms.

In fact, this effacement of aesthetics is already well under way today. After Adorno's death, the second- and third-generation Frankfurt School moved away from aesthetics toward sociology and political philosophy. References to art, not to mention interpretations of particular works, are entirely absent from Jürgen Habermas's notion of communicative action or his more recent examination of legal discourse in Western democracies. Similarly, Axel Honneth emphasizes the sociopsychological effects of our increased demand and need for ethical criteria of social justice but has little to say about the role of art or media in this context. The same is true of American feminism inspired by Habermas (for example, Seyla Benhabib, Nancy Fraser). Of course, the historical development of the Frankfurt School is somewhat more complicated, and there have been attempts to reconcile Adorno's aesthetics with the current state of critical theory, as I will demonstrate later.[30] But one cannot fail to notice a general trend away from aesthetics even among leftist critics unaffiliated with the Frankfurt School, such as Alain Badiou, Judith Butler, Ernesto Laclau and Chantal Mouffe, Michael Hardt and Antonio Negri, and so on, all of whom disregard art and aesthetics in favor of ethical and political discourse in their effort to resist global capitalism.

Hence, Adorno's was not only one of the most accomplished aesthetic philosophies of the twentieth century but also a dead end. Once art is said to survive through its own death, aesthetic theory is condemned forever to re-

peat this rhetorical play of death and resurrection. To follow Adorno to the letter leads only "Back to Adorno,"[31] for there is no constructive way out of his
Aesthetic Theory that would not violate its intricate rhetorical structure or, yet
again, fall prey to its negative dialectics. In the words of Norbert Bolz, "The
categorical imperative of the media-age demands: communicate in such a
way as to enable others to connect. Yet hardly anybody was able to connect
to Adorno's extraordinary art of reflection."[32] Like all modernist artworks,
Aesthetic Theory creates an autonomous universe of its own. In order to escape its inherent negativity, that universe needs to be exploded and the various particles evaluated afresh according to their practical *usefulness*—I use
this term deliberately—for renewing the leftist aesthetic project. For the end
of aesthetics is not Adornian philosophy but the critical analysis of contemporary culture in the effort to improve the quality of life experiences.

II

In the following, I shall discuss different answers to this challenge, all of
which try to situate Adorno within the contemporary scene of globalization
and postmodern culture. Apart from the Marxist (Jameson and Eagelton) and
the rhetorical or deconstructive approach (Geulen) discussed previously, I
recognize three more versions: the first is to emphasize the ethical dimension
of art and aesthetics (Elaine Scarry, Wolfgang Welsch), the second is to reconcile Adorno's aesthetics with the postmodern emphasis on contingency
(David Roberts, Peter Uwe Hohendahl) and Habermas's concept of communicative rationality (Albrecht Wellmer), and the last effort consists in replac-
ing traditional aesthetics with media aesthetics (Norbert Bolz).

1. Elaine Scarry's book *On Beauty and Being Just* is symptomatic of the
widespread conservative tendency to return to an idealist understanding of art.[33]
According to Scarry, the experience of beauty can avoid the pitfalls of postmodern relativism and identity politics provided that "one is willing to labor,
struggle, wrestle with the world to locate enduring sources of conviction—to
locate what is true." Beauty "ignites the desire for truth," for it "creates, without itself fulfilling, the aspiration for enduring certitude." Moreover, beauty is
a "call" for ethical fairness and social justice, and it occasions a process of "un-
selfing" and "nonself-interestedness" within the individual beholder.[34] Unfortunately, Scarry provides little evidence for these contentions besides her own
personal experiences. She deliberately bypasses most of the recent critical approaches in the humanities (such as deconstruction, feminism, postcolonialism,
and so on) that have struggled to reveal the inherent ambivalence and historical
abuse of notions such as "justice" and "truth" in a variety of different contexts.

Instead, she simply defends the ethical dimension of beauty against a group of anonymous critics whom she mysteriously labels the "opponents of beauty." In doing so, however, she neither engages "them" directly nor provides a single example—much less an analysis—of the actual encounter between art and ethics in light of today's socioeconomic and political situation (that is, globalization, the rise of neoliberal politics, and "the end of history"). Short of such an analysis, however, Scarry's claims about the truth content of art ring hollow and anachronistic at best. Her book fully justifies Jameson's skepticism vis-à-vis the recent "return to the aesthetic," which, in his eyes, is "singularly ill equipped to deal with the aesthetic dimension of postmodernity" as well as modernism: "All beauty today," Jameson rightly concludes, "is meretricious and the appeal to it by contemporary pseudo-aestheticism is an ideological maneuver and not a creative resource."[35] Any attempt to salvage aesthetics today must confront and move through Adorno's *Aesthetic Theory*.

This is the expressed goal of Wolfgang Welsch, who reads Adorno in the context of postmodernist theories of the past two decades and Lyotard in particular. In his numerous articles on contemporary aesthetics, Wolfgang Welsch emphasizes the ubiquity of what he calls the "superficial beautification" of our public sphere that serves as a global economic strategy for increasing customer satisfaction (that is, strip malls, shopping centers, corporate architecture, and so on).[36] Welsch opposes this process of simple aestheticization with a different and more profound one he calls "aesthetic thinking." According to his view, the history of philosophy from Kant and Nietzsche to today's postmodernism has increasingly unveiled reality as an aesthetic construction whose nature depends on the biological and sociocultural limitations of our own perceptual apparatus. Our aesthetic goal must be to develop a "culture of the blind spot" that recognizes its own inherent limitations and appreciates the fact that perception always includes nonperception just as insight is necessarily tied to blindness.[37] This knowledge, Welsch argues, helps us recognize a "postmodern aesthetics of resistance" within contemporary art. Art and contemporary culture literally improves "our health" by inoculating us against the simplistic hope for an easy reconciliation of differences in a totalizing (and totalitarian) aesthetic state: "The shell of aesthetics may become identified with design, but its . . . core aims toward justice."[38]

Welsch's concept of aesthetic justice is more astute and complex than Scarry's. Its major problem, however, resides in Welsch's limited understanding of the irreducible "blind spot" inherent in human perception. Welsch argues correctly that "one sees visible objects, not seeing itself or visibility as such."[39] Yet he fails to draw the necessary conclusion from this observation, namely, that an act of perception can never see its constitutive blind spot. It sees only what it sees and not what enables it to see. Welsch's notion of an "aestheticized thinking" implicitly relies on a central aspect of Niklas Luhmann's systems theory while, at the same time, eschewing the epistemological consequences of that theory. The latter include the structural impossibility of achieving the very kind of critical and self-reflective perception Welsch attributes to his version of "aesthetic thinking" simply because it takes a second act of observation to discover the blind spot of the first. This, however, reproduces another blind spot that in turn can be discovered only in a third act of observation and so on. This irreducible time lag between first- and second-order observation thwarts all efforts both to see something and, at the same time, to see the means by which we see what we see: "In a somewhat Wittgensteinian formulation," Luhmann argues, "one could say that a system can see only what it can see. It cannot see what it cannot. Moreover, it cannot see that it cannot see this."[40] It follows that Welsch's ideal of self-transparent vision remains a myth—even if he defines this self-transparency not in metaphysical terms as a form of complete self-presence but in the postmodern sense as a form of perception that "knows" about its constitutive limitations.

In other words, I take issue with this lingering idealist notion that art carries within itself some inherently critical or emancipatory potential that inevitably leads to justice. In my view, art does *not* miraculously instill within those who experience it a kind of aesthetic transformation that equips them with the ability better to handle difference and heterogeneity, as Scarry, Welsch, and others continue to argue. This is not to deny that art may serve as a tool to practice whatever a given society understands to be ethical behavior. My point is simply that art does not automatically gravitate toward ethics as part of its intrinsic nature. Art is no more suited for the ethical education of mankind than any other form of human practice such as politics or religion. It follows that aesthetics can play a role in the hegemonic struggle of the academic left only to the extent to which critics are willing to abandon the concept of a "truthful" art and its allegedly inherent and thus somehow "objective" ethical imperative, which, for all practical purposes, has become neutralized by twentieth-century politics and economics alike. Contrary to Adorno, art and aesthetics do *not* provide an autonomous vantage point from which to mount and sustain a serious critique of the way things are, and one must be extremely suspicious of an unreformed Marxist theory that claims to rediscover or reinvent such a dialectical model of criticism based on the inside/outside dichotomy.

Instead, we must abandon the concept of totality as well as Jameson's privileging of the economic over and against culture, of basis over and against superstructure. Not only does the superstructure follow its own logic of autonomous development, as Habermas has convincingly argued for more than two decades,[41] but the "whole" itself is of a rhizomatic nature and cannot be conceptualized abstractly without violating its historical specificity. Structurally unstable and forever changing, the "whole" (understood in either a Hegelian/Marxist or a Deleuzian sense) remains a metaphysical concept and should simply drop out of the equation altogether. Contrary to his own belief, even Adorno's aesthetics did not require the concept of "totality" or a theory of general history, as Peter Uwe Hohendahl rightly points out.[42] Aesthetics today is left with the analysis of particular artworks that, although shining light on a particular sociohistorical situation, do not suffice to elucidate or "explain" it in absolute terms.

2. The end of art and aesthetics is not the "determinate negation" of an "untrue" society but the exploration of alternative and innovative modes of experience. Unveiling the historical contingency of the way things are, art is "critical" simply by virtue of exploring difference as such. This emphasis on the contingency and "communicative potential" of art moves contemporary aesthetics into the direction of Habermas's philosophy of communicative action.[43] Since Habermas himself never developed an aesthetic theory along these lines, Albrecht Wellmer has articulated it for him. Wellmer, too, explicitly rejects what he calls the "dialectical negativism" prevalent in Adorno's thinking.[44] What is needed, he claims, is "a turn away from Adorno's meta-theoretical premises that serve to fixate real history a priori on negativity; it is a turn away from the connection between negativism and messianism that is constitutive of Adorno's philosophy."[45] Wellmer advocates a postmetaphysical aesthetics that, unlike Adorno's, relinquishes the utopian ideal of "total reconciliation" and embraces the "historically possible" one in its place: "Part of this historical possible reconciliation is a moment of disparity," Wellmer concludes. This, in turn, liberates Adorno's *Aesthetic Theory* from the "illusion and terror of some lasting objective and comprehensive meaning" and allows Wellmer to reconceptualize it in the "finite spirit of communicative reason."[46] In other words, Wellmer revisits Adorno's *Aesthetic Theory* only to have it dissolve within Habermas's notion of communicative action:

> Once we relocate Adorno's "non-identical" from the realm beyond language back into the horizon of an intersubjective linguistic practice, it will become clear when and in what sense the discrepancy between the universal and the particular could signify a "violation" or "appropriation" of the non-identical, and which specific disturbances, blockages, or limitations of communication could be expressed in these discrepancies. However, to the degree to which we are able to name this "injustice," . . . we have already implicitly named the linguistic resources inherent in speech that we can mobilize in order to help the particular to be heard.[47]

Although Wellmer thus clearly states what Adorno can learn from Habermas, it is less clear in his account what, if anything, Habermas is supposed to learn from Adorno. For the most part, Wellmer's route is a one-way street, and we are left with a liberated, postmetaphysical version of *Aesthetic Theory* that, oddly enough, becomes subjected to the teleological universalism of communicative reason and the persuasive power of the better argument.

Only in one of his essays does Wellmer recognize this problem and point to a remainder in Adorno's philosophy that cannot be assimilated into Habermas's theory of intersubjective communication. He refers to Adorno's "contributions to a linguistic and rational theory that function as a necessary complement to" the communicative model. Located "beyond instrumental and communicative reason" alike, Adorno's implicit notion of rationality, Wellmer surmises, keeps open "the possibility to think reason without hoping for a final reconciliation."[48] In these cryptic passages, Wellmer explicitly contradicts Habermas by insisting that the constitutive rules of rational argumentation cannot themselves be founded on the communicative model they inaugurate. Instead, Adorno's philosophy keeps reminding us about the "non-communicative aspects that help constitute the communicable linguistic relations of meaning."[49] Of course, neither Adorno nor Wellmer can name these noncommunicable aspects of communication, which, unfortunately, brings the discussion full circle back to Adorno's messianism and his hope for the kind of unspeakable reconciliation Wellmer explicitly rejected in the first place. In other words, Wellmer's model of postmetaphysical aesthetics remains stuck between Adorno's metaphysical notion of "total reconciliation" and the allegedly secular notion of a "historically possible reconciliation" favored by Habermas.

The ultimate goal, however, must be to move beyond reconciliation altogether and to embrace antagonism as constitutive of a postmetaphysical art and society. Like Wellmer, I believe that we need to turn away from metaphysics toward that which is historically possible to achieve. But this can be done only pragmatically, via a hegemonic struggle for discursive power, and not by stubbornly insisting on the "better argument"—a persuasive rhetoric will do just fine for our purposes. Aesthetics becomes a tool in this hegemonic struggle of the left for political power—not more, not less. It mobilizes art as a means both to criticize particular social problems and to point toward a possible solution without mobilizing some grand narrative of history that explains why this solution not only is preferable to others but also constitutes the "right" one. On a more practical level, this means that aesthetics needs to enlarge its traditional terrain to include not only low or popular forms of entertainment, as Fredric Jameson and Andreas Huyssen already argued in the 1980s. Instead, in a broader and more general sense, we need to examine and

challenge the new technologies and digital media that underlie them because
they literally shape global capitalism today. Aesthetic theory today is media
theory, and its objects are no longer primarily individual works of art but the
channels of communication of society at large.

3. This move toward media theory is exemplified in the recent work of
Norbert Bolz, who renounces aesthetics and criticism altogether in favor of
what he calls "the rhetoric of cyberspace" and "world communication."[50]
The latter replaces the traditional debate about the function of art with that
about competing information resources. Intellectuals no longer ought to be
trained in the history of art but should "be recognized by their ability to
speak intelligently and in an differentiated and articulate manner about the
users of cell-phones, Nike shoes and activists of Greenpeace."[51] Aesthetic
criticism, Bolz argues, has become superfluous because it has lost both its
specific objects and its privilege of being critical. In cultural terms, this
means that design replaces art, superficiality replaces depth, and interconnected systems replace aesthetic autonomy: "Design forms life. . . . It is no
longer directed toward individual objects, but toward systems. Structures,
figures, patterns, networks—these are the key terms for a non-linear process
of design that corresponds to our modern condition of life."[52]

While I appreciate Bolz's shift toward the analysis of network systems as
crucial for any attempt to revive the project of aesthetics in the context of
global capitalism, I reject his binary logic that pits art and aesthetic criticism
against media theory rather than trying to combine the two. Bolz is certainly
correct in renouncing the scientific aspirations of classical and orthodox
Marxism, meaning that the notion of an observable social totality—whether
in its original (Marx/Engels), structural (Althusser), or postmodern (Jameson)
garb—can no longer be maintained. Likewise, Jameson's focus on the economic forces of production as the determining factor "in the last instance"
must be abandoned in favor of an antifoundationalist and pragmatic epistemology as outlined by Richard Rorty, Ernesto Laclau, and Chantal Mouffe,
for example. In particular, Laclau's and Mouffe's notion of hegemony has
provided a powerful model for a non–consensus-oriented form of political engagement that remains both committed yet undogmatic at the same time.[53]

On an aesthetic level, it follows that even a "true" work of art is not, as
Adorno claimed and Jameson reaffirms, a picture of the whole *in nuce*. Art
certainly partakes of the whole and relates to other elements therein, but it
does not adequately represent or even mirror social totality, nor does it allow
for an "autonomous" critique of that totality projected from inside a windowless monad. Once we acknowledge that these terms (for example, monad, totality, truth) are what Laclau and Mouffe call "empty universal signifiers," we
can also relieve art from the burden of Adorno's negative utopianism and use

it instead as a tool to help shape the (contingent and historical) meaning of these signifiers for pragmatic purposes. This is the point at which Bolz's neoliberal appreciation of market laws and autopoietic systems as well as his passionate rejection of the Habermasian paradigm or any kind of normative critique of society clearly overreacts against what he considers the arrogant pedantry of leftist intellectual discourse. Although I am sympathetic to some of his concerns, the solution is certainly not abstention from critique but its reconceptualization along the lines of social conflict instead of metaphysical reconciliation. Similarly, aesthetics can analyze and criticize the cultures of global capitalism (its art and architecture, its media and networks of communication) without being grounded in some absolute theory of knowledge or advocating another version of utopia.

The possibility for reviving a leftist aesthetics today hinges on critics' ability and willingness to make it matter within the contemporary world of technological and economic globalization. As argued in this chapter, Adorno's *Aesthetic Theory* has held this possibility hostage to the antipragmatic ideals of a self-absorbed modernist work of art from which there is no escape. Adorno's lasting legacy is thus partially responsible for maintaining the current theoretical vacuum that allows conservative critics to call for a return to beauty and neoliberals to proclaim the death of any critical enterprise whatsoever. Needless to say, this is not Adorno's fault but rather the fault of history, so to speak. Nonetheless, in trying to combat these trends, we must venture beyond the self-enclosed universe of Adorno's texts. The task ahead is to invent new concepts able to trace new connections between art and politics unbound by the epistemological constraints of representationalism. A leftist aesthetics must remain flexible and responsive to the technological changes that continue to define global capitalism—Deleuze's and Guattari's notion of "virtuality" will be of vital importance in this regard. If, on the other hand, there is still something to be learned from Adorno apart from his personal commitment to advocate a world in which things would be better—a commitment all intellectuals should try to emulate—it lies precisely in his aesthetic sensibility toward historical change and his willingness to engage it intellectually. Ironically, however, this is the very reason why being true to his legacy today requires not a return to Adorno but to move beyond him.

NOTES

1. Georg Wilhelm Friedrich Hegel, *Vorlesungen über die Ästhetik: Erster und Zweiter Teil* (Stuttgart: Reclam, 1971). Author's translation.

2. Hegel, *Vorlesungen über die Ästhetik*, 50.

3. See, for example, Jean-Luc Nancy, *The Muses*, trans. Peggy Kamuf (Stanford, Calif.: Stanford University Press, 1996); Werner Hamacher, "Das Ende der Kunst mit der Maske," *Sprachen der Ironie—Sprechen des Ernstes*, ed. Karl Heinz Bohrer (Frankfurt: Suhrkamp, 1999); Alexander Garcia Düttmann, *Kunstende: Drei ästhetische Studien* (Frankfurt: Suhrkamp, 2000); and Eva Geulen, *Das Ende der Kunst: Lesarten eines Gerüchts nach Hegel* (Frankfurt: Suhrkamp, 2002).

4. Arthur C. Danto, *After the End of Art: Contemporary Art and the Pale of History* (Princeton, N.J.: Princeton University Press, 1997).

5. Arthur C. Danto, *The Philosophical Disenfranchisement of Art* (New York: Columbia University Press, 1986), 209.

6. Peter Bürger, *Theory of the Avant-Garde*, trans. Michael Shaw (Minneapolis: University of Minnesota Press, 1984), 63.

7. Geulen, *Das Ende der Kunst*, 20.

8. "Kunst müsse es geben: das steht nirgends geschrieben," quoted in Düttmann, *Kunstende*, 6.

9. Gerhard Richter, "A Portrait of Non-Identity," *Monatshefte* 94, no. 1 (Special Issue on Rereading Adorno): 7.

10. Peter Uwe Hohendahl, *Prismatic Thought: Theodor W. Adorno* (Lincoln: University of Nebraska Press, 1995), 243.

11. Peter Sloterdijk, "Die Kritische Theorie ist tot," *Die Zeit* 37 (1999).

12. Theodor W. Adorno, *Ästhetische Theorie*, vol. 7 of *Gesammelte Schriften*, ed. Rolf Tiedemann (Suhrkamp: Frankfurt, 1974), 503. All future references to Adorno will be cited in the main body of the text and refer to this edition, beginning with the volume number followed by the page number.

13. See Eva Geulen, "Reconstructing Adorno's 'End of Art,'" *New German Critique* 81 (fall 2000): 153–68, and Düttmann, *Kunstende*, 14–128.

14. Geulen, "Reconstructing Adorno's 'End of Art,'" 164.

15. See Rüdiger Bubner, "Kann Theorie ästhetisch werden? Zum Hauptmotiv der Philosophie Adornos," in *Materialien zur Ästhetischen Theorie*, ed. B. Lindner and W. M. Lüdke (Frankfurt: Suhrkamp, 1979), 108–37.

16. Among the earliest scholars to critique Adorno's aesthetiziation of theory are Thomas Baumeister and Jens Kulenkampff, "Geschichtsphilosophie und philosophische Ästhetik: Zu Adorno's 'Ästhetischer Theorie,'" *Neue Hefte für Philosophie* 5 (1973): 74–98. More recently, the charge was repeated by Martin Asiain, *Theodor W. Adorno: Dialektik des Aporetischen* (Freiburg: Karl Alber, 1996), who refers to the "idiosyncratic circularity" (18) of Adorno's philosophy that "necessarily leads to the 'aestheticization of theory'" (39). For a complete list of references, see Britta Scholze, *Kunst als Kritik: Adornos Weg aus der Dialektik* (Würzburg: Köngishausen & Neumann, 2000), 290 n. 7.

17. Eva Geulen, "Mega-Melancholia. Adorno's *Minima Moralia*," in *Critical Theory: Current State and Future Prospects*, ed. Peter Uwe Hohendahl and Jaimey Fisher (New York: Berghahn, 2001), 50.

18. Jean-François Lyotard, "Adorno as the Devil," trans. Robert Hurley, *Telos* 19 (spring 1974): 136.

19. Fredric Jameson, *Late Marxism: Adorno, or The Persistence of the Dialectic* (London: Verso, 1990), 238, 239.

20. Jameson, *Late Marxism*, 232, 251 (emphasis added).

21. See Eva Geulen, "A Matter of Tradition," *Telos* 89 (fall 1991): 155–66. Whereas Geulen suggests that Jameson's dialectics is too superficial, Robert Hullot-Kentor maintains that Jameson's reasoning is "hardly dialectical" at all because it confuses "paradoxes and complexity" with dialectics: "Instead of dialectical research the book is the work of common sense" (171). Robert Hullot-Kentor, "Suggested Reading: Jameson on Adorno," *Telos* 89 (fall 1991): 167–77. Similarly, Peter Osborne, "A Marxism for the Postmodern? Jameson's Adorno," *New German Critique* 56 (spring–summer 1992): 171–92.

22. Jameson, *Late Marxism*, 50.

23. From a Marxist perspective, the real problem with Jameson is not his ontological bias toward material reality but his refusal to follow through to its logical conclusion and to proclaim a materialist aesthetics founded on the transhistorical notion of "human nature," as Terry Eagleton has done. See Terry Eagleton, *The Ideology of the Aesthetic* (Oxford: Blackwell, 1990), 408 ff.

24. Britta Scholze, *Kunst als Kritik*, 183–203; Eva Geulen, *Das Ende der Kunst*, 135–42.

25. Fredric Jameson, "Notes on Globalization as a Philosophical Issue," in *The Cultures of Globalization*, ed. Fredric Jameson and Masao Miyoshi (Durham, N.C.: Duke University Press, 1998), 60; see also Fredric Jameson, *The Cultural Turn: Selected Writings on the Postmodern, 1983–1998* (London: Verso, 1998), 73.

26. Jameson, *The Cultural Turn*, 60.

27. A good example of this tendency on the philosophical level is the collection of essays by Tom Huhn and Lambert Zuidervaart, *The Semblance of Subjectivity: Essays in Adorno's Aesthetic Theory* (Cambridge, Mass.: MIT Press, 1997), which, in Peter Hohendahl's words, "simply reassert the lasting significance of Adorno's philosophy" instead of demonstrating its relevance in the context of postmodernism and global capitalism. See Hohendahl, *Prismatic Thought*, 258 n. 30.

28. Richard Shusterman, *Pragmatist Aesthetics: Living Beauty, Rethinking Art*, 2nd ed. (Lanham, Md.: Rowman & Littlefield, 2000), xv.

29. Shusterman, *Pragmatist Aesthetics*, 9.

30. For an excellent discussion of the various positions, see Hohendahl, *Prismatic Thought*, 3–20, and Peter Uwe Hohendahl, "From the Eclipse of Reason to Communicative Rationality and Beyond," in Hohendahl and Fisher, *Critical Theory*, 3–28.

31. Robert Hullot-Kentor, "Back to Adorno," *Telos* 81 (fall 1989): 5–29.

32. Norbert Bolz, *Die Konformisten des Andersseins: Ende der Kritik* (Munich: Fink, 1999), 21.

33. Elaine Scarry, *On Beauty and Being Just* (Princeton, N.J.: Princeton University Press, 1999).

34. Scarry, 31, 52 f., 109, 113, 117.

35. Jameson, *The Cultural Turn*, 100, 135.

36. Wolfgang Welsch, *Grenzgänge der Ästhetik* (Stuttgart: Reclam, 1996).

37. Welsch, *Grenzgänge der Ästhetik,* 133; see also his book *Ästhetisches Denken* (Stuttgart: Reclam, 1990), 38.

38. Welsch, *Grenzgänge*, 134.

39. Welsch, *Ästhetisches Denken*, 33.

40. Niklas Luhmann, *Ecological Communication*, trans. John Bednarz (Chicago: University of Chicago Press, 1989), 23.

41. Jürgen Habermas, *Zur Rekonstruktion des Historischen Materialismus*, 6. Auflage (Frankfurt: Suhrkamp, 1995); my translation.

42. See Hohendahl, *Prismatic Thought*, 179.

43. David Roberts, *Art and Enlightenment: Aesthetic Theory after Adorno* (Lincoln: University of Nebraska Press, 1991), 229.

44. Albrecht Wellmer, *Endspiele* (Frankfurt: Suhrkamp, 1999), 229.

45. Wellmer, *Endspiele*, 228.

46. Wellmer, *Endspiele*, 201, 203, 185.

47. Albrecht Wellmer, *Zur Dialektik von Moderne und Postmoderne: Vernunftkritik nach Adorno* (Frankfurt: Suhrkamp, 1985), 88f.

48. Wellmer, *Endspiele*, 235.

49. Wellmer, *Endspiele*, 235.

50. Bolz, *Die Konformisten des Andersseins*, 186; see also Norbert Bolz, *Weltkommunikation* (Munich: Fink, 2001).

51. Bolz, *Weltkommunikation*, 43.

52. Bolz, *Weltkommunikation*, 135.

53. Ernesto Laclau and Chantal Mouffe, *Hegemony and Socialist Strategy: Towards a Radical Democratic Politics* (London: Verso, 1985).

13

Peripheral Glances: Adorno's *Aesthetic Theory* in Brazil

Silvia L. López

ELECTIVE AFFINITIES: AESTHETICS, GLOBALITY, AND CRITICAL THEORY

The idea of globalizing critical theory may present us cultural critics, in truly dialectical fashion, with both a redundancy and the possibility of an important rearticulation. Rhetorically, it draws attention to the fact that implicit in the idea is a commitment to a global understanding of cultural production, and insofar as the background of a critical-theoretical analysis always is, or at least attempts to be, an understanding and a theorization of culture under capitalism (which is by definition a global phenomenon), one can speak here of a redundancy. The way we engage critically with cultural materials produced in nonmetropolitan centers of the world may indeed require us to begin a discussion about the elective affinities of critical theory and peripheral cultures or, in other words, may require us to deal with the previously mentioned redundancy.

The particular case in point I will present in the pages that follow will be that of Brazilian literary critic Roberto Schwarz, whose writings on the import of the novel to Brazil present us today with one of the most exemplary Adornian contributions to the study of a literary phenomenon in the periphery of capitalism. The fact that Adorno did not work on peripheral cultures or make it his intention to theorize them is neither problematic nor ironic in the case in point. It is simply irrelevant. In other words, the critical-theoretical impetus of the Frankfurt School travels rather well because it attempts an understanding of culture within the global phenomenon of capitalism. What is at stake is a dialectical understanding of cultural phenomena, which by definition find their specific and particular expression in the historicity of their materials that is in a dialectic of the global and the local.

Before I turn to the case of Schwarz, allow me a brief excursus that may help explain why the particular affinities of the aesthetic writings of the Frankfurt School, particularly Adorno's *Aesthetic Theory*, together with cultural criticism in nonmetropolitan centers, have been structurally inaudible within our academic milieu. Much of the problem resides in a particular lack of understanding of the historical dynamics of cultural processes on the periphery of capitalism. And here, if Fredric Jameson offered us at one point Adorno as the representative of late Marxism and as thinker for our times, with him too lies the responsibility of the dissemination of unfortunate ideas and endless debates, such as those generated by his now infamous statement that "all third world texts are necessary allegorical."[1] Perhaps this position of Jameson's and the subsequent debates surrounding it need to be understood within the larger context of the institutionalization of the study of "third world literatures" in the United States, which says more about the status of the institution of literature in this part of the globe than about literary processes elsewhere in the world.[2]

There is no need here to rehearse the well-known debate between Fredric Jameson and Aijaz Ahmad for its own sake since that may seem like old history. However, it may be worth remembering and resituating it now when the discourses of both globalization and the bioconcept of "empire" seem to fold all cultural problematics into themselves. In other words, while the Jameson–Ahmad debate in itself is no longer at stake, the fundamental dynamic of that debate, its consequences, and the preoccupation with the global character of cultural analysis today require, if only for heuristic purposes, a brief discussion of it.

"THIRD WORLD LITERATURE," *WELTLITERATUR*, OR LITERATURE?[3]

In his polemic with Jameson, Ahmad points out that the term "third world" has no theoretical status whatsoever because the issues that fundamentally delimit the problem of literature—such as those of social and linguistic formations, political and ideological struggles within the field of literary production, periodization, cultural institutions, and so on—cannot be posed at such a level of generality. Not only has this category no epistemological status, but the attempt at formulating it is empirically ungrounded as well. In light of the merely empirical problems for such classification, Jameson's recourse to the experience of colonialism and imperialism as the basis for setting up this division between "first" and "third" world is just as problematic. His binary world is entangled in an essentialist politics whereby the diverse experience of colonialism necessarily leads to a nationalist response as the only alternative to the postmodern ideological formation of "first" world nations. The essential binary that runs through Jameson's proposition not only trivializes the problem of nationalism in the peripheral context but also explains nothing about the different experiences of colonialism and imperialism in different parts of the world. Jameson's general assumptions about nationalism lead him to believe in allegory as a main form of cultural expression in the "third world." As Ahmad pointedly notes, this can be sustained only if no inquiry is made into the way writers enter into commerce with the institutions of culture in their own contexts. The actual experience of nonmetropolitan intellectuals in highly contradictory societies may actually inhibit any kind of capacity for allegorization and exhibit a more profound experience of alienation and desolation than that of any of their postmodern counterparts in the Western metropolitan centers.

The presence of certain forms of writing in different cultural contexts does not depend on some essential quality of the experience of the writers. Rather, these forms vary in direct relation to their institutionalized traditions and conventions. Writers depending on the social and historical circumstances that define the institutional space from within which these writers choose forms, whether consciously or unconsciously.

It is clear that any attempt to theorize globally about literary production in terms of the "third world" is doomed to failure. However, Jameson's claim about the preoccupation with nationalism in the third world deserves important consideration because the history of its theorization provides a good example of how the logic of difference has been inscribed in world-historical terms. The discussions of nationalism in Jameson's text prove precisely how the "first"/"third" world classification justifies itself. In other words, the very conditions of possibility of such a dichotomy can be found in the historical treatment of the problem of nation formation and nationalism available to us since the Enlightenment.

Against Jameson's hypostatizing of "third world literatures" and in spite of the strategic claims that such a rubric may have in the politics of the American academy, the task of articulating a project of the study of national cultures under conditions of modernity is crucial to intellectuals in places such as Latin America. This kind of project would permit a negation of the logic of alterity that makes the cultural products of so-called lesser developed regions of the world necessarily this or that (allegorical readings of the nation, anticanonical, revolutionary, antirepresentational, emergent, and so on) and would confront the provincial understanding of modernity supporting these schemas of classification that are based on a spatialization of time in world-rhetorical terms. Between China and Africa, Latin America dances in and out with great unease in Jameson's text, an uneasiness that is symptomatic of precisely the historical differences with the Chinese and African examples that Jameson discusses, differences based in the national configurations in which Latin American literature has been produced. The national problem returns here with a vengeance to castigate the speculative dimension of the mode of production narrative in which Jameson is inscribed. The nation, as empty coeval form and as sociopolitical reality, remains the locus of the inscription of the institution of literature. While the political claim of comparatism makes itself evident in the urge to understand this "other" literature, in an effort to deprovincialize the metropolitan reader, the effect of allochronic distancing is unavoidable in a text that divides the world into three different ones. Perhaps the most significant consequence of this result of the spatialization of time is the production of a sovereign metropolitan reader in the unending quest of making justice, in political terms, to his or her reading of these literary objects, always from the vantage of point of his or her own construction of them.

This problem was at the core of the Jameson–Ahmad debate and continues to trouble current debates on the global understandings of literature. Perhaps the exception here is Franco Moretti's proposition of a comparative study of the form of the novel in the modern world through the systematic analysis of a phenomenal accumulation of studies from all over the world. Unfortunately, Moretti conceptualizes his project as one that seeks to elucidate a law of literary evolution (a law whose formulation Moretti attributes to Fredric Jameson).[4] In this mode, all novels outside Europe are the result of the encounter of particular social realities that when expressed in a Western form don't quite fit that reality and end up generating variations of the European form. This is an interesting thesis based on a notion of *Weltliteratur* that avoids the allochronic deficit of other positions, but the obvious question becomes, if one may be allowed to be so blunt: What else would the encounter of particular European forms with non-European realities yield? What else would all dialectical interactions between global forms and local realities yield? Moretti's conclusion ought to serve here as premise for the study of the actual mediations between form and social reality and not as conclusion of an evolutionary law.

The coevalness of modernity as experienced by the globalization of monopoly capitalism at the end of the nineteenth century poses the challenge of a differential theory of modernity that can account for the status of cultural production under conditions of modernity in the periphery of the industrialized world. It is only through these comparative and differential understandings that European cultural modernity can be shown to be the exception rather than the rule in the global context. As far as the political repercussions of such a stance, which is what seems to concern Jameson after all, they would prove to be far more radical than the ghettoization of diversity in the American university, where, through the visible marking of gender and race, a "different" form of knowledge is institutionalized. This "difference" and its current recognition through classifications such as "third world literature" (as just one example) reinscribe the racism of alterity politics. It is perhaps the fear of places and peoples all too contemporary and coeval, the disavowal of global capital relations, and the denial of the minority status of "first world" culture that prevent a different kind of politics in the institutionalization of new ways of understanding modern cultural developments on a global scale.

If we understand the importance of the critical-theoretical understanding of capital as global phenomenon and of the dialectics of globality and locality, then that a methodologically far more radical and more sophisticated dialectical apparatus, such as that of Adorno's *Aesthetic Theory*, finds wider purchase among critics in the periphery should come as no surprise. Inscribed within a Marxist tradition of worldwide aspirations, their search for explanations lies not with the problem of being "third world" critics or "postcolonial" or the "other" of a defined American vantage point but rather in the belief that their tradition, the same one as Adorno's, offers ways of reading the dialectics of cultural form and social reality.

FORM AS SOCIAL CIPHER: THE IMPORTING OF THE NOVEL TO BRAZIL[5]

The essays of Roberto Schwarz are difficult to decipher because of the astute way that this Brazilian critic has of situating himself with respect to his tradition. On one level, as the preeminent student of Antônio Cândido, Schwarz always offers an up-to-date and committed reading of Cândido's work and always defends his contribution as a precursor to the social study of form. On another level, to update and revitalize his teacher's contributions, Schwarz reconceptualizes Cândido's insights by drawing on the development of Marxist aesthetics of the last third of the century, especially as it is to be found in Adorno's *Aesthetic Theory*. Adorno's fundamental concepts enter Schwarz's critical work in an organic and natural way. As a critic on the left, Schwarz constructs strategies of writing that permit him to legitimize himself as a Brazilian who defends a sociohistorical approach to literature while at the same time offering a perspective on the social codification of literary form that permits him to outdistance the sterile debate between realism and modernism that the other great literary critic of

Brazil, Luiz Costa Lima, persists in reenacting. According to Schwarz, Costa Lima classifies literary production in the following way:

> On the one hand, the backward looking, mere imitation of historical reality, absence of formal anxiety, ideological redundancy, the illusion of an unbounded linguistic transparency; on the other hand, the forward looking, literary production of the new, the anti-mimetic rupture, awareness of the efficacy specific to language, the disconnecting of the antennae of reference.[6]

Instead of repeating the debate between Lukács and Adorno that took place in the 1930s, Schwarz ingeniously proceeds to dismantle Costa Lima's premises about realism and as a consequence enters into a serious exploration of Adorno's later elaborations on mimesis and literary forms. In reframing the debate and in offering us his careful analysis of the later fiction of Machado de Assis, Schwarz makes a unique contribution to our understanding of how the ciphering of the social referent works. The concept of mimetic impulse in Adorno and in Schwarz recasts the problem of the tracing of reality as something internal to the literary object. The mimetic impulse is not the reflection of reality that Lukács talked about but rather a rethinking of the dynamic of form that distinguishes the Marxist study of form from that of a simple literary formalism. Or, as Schwarz puts it so well, the problem with literary formalism, ironically, is to have underestimated literary form itself.

Although Schwarz had already made reference to the importance of the Frankfurt School for our times, especially in his intellectual and personal history titled "Um Seminário de Marx,"[7] the fundamental text in which Schwarz firmly posits his position on literary forms is the essay "Critical Adequation and National Originality." Some of the basic Adornian principles in this essay include the idea that the work in its specific historical time codifies reality and returns it to us articulated in a formal language that reveals the contradictions of its production. In contrast to the theory of realism as reflection, here society appears encapsulated in a formal apparatus of autonomous unfolding, whose logic escapes external comparison. A second concept elaborated by both Benjamin and Adorno, that of constellation, appears in the essay in order to explain why there cannot be only one way of tracing reality or, to refute Lukács, why there is no prescription for writing like Balzac: one must instead find the configurations or the constellations within the text that illuminate its historical moment. As Schwarz says,

> We can say that a good eye for an historical likeness *between unlike structures* is perhaps the key faculty of materialist criticism—a criticism for which literature is understood to work with materials and formations engendered (in the fi-

nal analysis) outside of its own literary domain—materials and formations that give to the literary its substance and that make possible its dynamism. Let us reiterate that the goal of this type of conception is not to reduce one structure to another, but to reflect historically on their mutually-formed constellation. Here we follow in the *stereoscopic* line of Walter Benjamin, with its particular acuity for noting, e.g., the importance of market mechanisms in the overall shape of Baudelaire's poetry.[8]

This idea of the ciphering of social truth in a momentary, unconscious, and kaleidoscopic way distances Schwarz from Lukács as well as from the geneticism of Goldmann and leaves Costa Lima out of the debate. It also declares mute the byzantine speculation revolving around the relationship between original and copy.

The great merit of Roberto Schwarz's work results from his having dedicated his life to studying the codification of the social life of Brazil under slavery in the fiction of Machado de Assis. How do we explain these novels that are not representative of what we understand by nineteenth-century realism but whose formal innovations are nevertheless directly related to the social reality of Brazil? It is here that Schwarz's exemplary way of making Adorno's premises on literary form and their historicity his own allows him to elaborate a convincing reading of how the narrative function of Machado de Assis's later novels traces rather than reflects the contradictions of the Brazilian dominant elite. In his meticulous study on the work of this author, Schwarz demonstrates how Machado de Assis's formal innovations operate on the level of a narrator whose volatile character, rather than being a narrative flaw, articulates the subject position of the Brazilian elites of the end of the nineteenth century. It is in this articulation of the narrator's point of view that, according to Schwarz, Machado de Assis achieves "a realism," not in the traditional sense of the term but in the sense of the unconscious tracing of social reality. The clash characterized by the importation of liberal European ideas received into a slave-based economic model produced this peripheral form of the realist novel, one that redefined both realism and novel in a specifically Brazilian way. What is best exemplified in these Brazilian novels is that the subjective is not reduced to the linguistic or communicative realm but is embedded in a configurational form of the novel, one that exceeds the description of what is said. The narrator functions in his relations to other characters and to the structure of the plot as a cipher of the social articulation of subjectivity. The volatility of the narrator is not modest in scope, for "it reaches to the world at large and to the artistic medium in depth."[9] Schwarz writes,

> The outstanding feature of this and other novels by Machado de Assis is the extraordinary volatility of the narrator, who will change his mind, his subject and his mode of speech at almost every sentence, and will not hold the same course

for longer than a short paragraph. There is an aspect of self-gratification to this changing disposition and to the rhetorical virtuosity that goes with it, a sort of kick to be derived from each one of these switches of level, which links up with the desire for recognition we just talked about. It will be decisive for my argument. And since this feature subordinates everything else in the book, we may call it the principle of its form.[10]

For Schwarz, the Brazilian character of Machado de Assis does not reside in the extraordinary thoroughness of the local observation that he well understood, nor is it canceled out by his universal discourse, which is an important level of the work, but it lies rather in the fact that these two dimensions are present in a simultaneous, complex, and negative way. It is this dissonant combination that relativizes them and gives them an intimate historical character. What Schwarz has elucidated for us is more than just workings of the novel form in nineteenth-century Brazil (which in his typical modesty is all he would aspire to claim); rather, he has provided us with a powerful literary illustration of what Adorno calls "exact imagination," which shows us, according to Shierry Weber Nicholsen, "that the primacy of the object is inseparable from reliance on genuine subjective experience, and that configuration is an activity of the subject as well as a feature of form."[11]

GLOBALIZATION: COMPLEX, MODERN, NATIONAL, AND NEGATIVE

Let me return to the apparent redundant idea of globalizing critical theory to point out that the work of Roberto Schwarz brings us to the question of how a culture, even in this period of globalization, is still embedded in a national experience that is modern, complex, and negative and that, whatever the effects of the process of globalization, mediates these experiences through an idiom that is linguistically, culturally, and nationally specific, as well as in dialogue with a defined and inherited tradition.

The enthusiasm that seems to have overtaken the humanities about the possibilities of a politics that is truly global is in contrast with the economic realities of globalization and its relationship to the nation-state.[12] The economic reality is that global corporations continue to rely heavily on domestic state structures that fall within the traditional bounds of individual governments, presiding over bordered territories, advancing domestic agendas, and regulating national economies. A cohesive nation-state regulating the free market seems to be essential for capitalist growth. Michael Mann[13] has most convincingly explained this. Allow me to quote him fully:

The theory of "breathless transnationalism" has been challenged in recent years. The international economy system seems to be emerging as dual: transnationalism is much more pronounced in finance than it is in trade and industry. . . . The national bases of production and trade seem undiminished. Ninety per cent of global production remains for domestic market. The shift from manufacturing toward services in the advanced economies is now reinforcing this localism. Though manufacturing imports from the "South" have increased, they still represent a tiny part of total manufactured goods. Furthermore, almost all the so called "multinational corporations" are still owned overwhelmingly by nationals in their home-base country, and their headquarters and research and development activities are still concentrated there. . . . International patterns are still dominated by geography and tradition: most trade and cross ownership occurs between neighbors and long-standing allies, like Britain and the U.S., Britain, the Netherlands, Denmark and Sweden remain the most internationalized economies, the U.S. remains quite national, Japan remains the most nationally insulated. Domestic savings and investment rates correlates about 75 per cent among OECD countries, indicating that foreign capital is not all that internationally mobile—though this correlation is now dropping slightly. And the differences in real interest rates between countries are about the same as they were a century ago. Indeed, it is doubtful whether in many respects capitalism is more transnational than it was before 1914, except for the special case of integration of the European Union. This is hardly an economic base on which to ground any grand generalizing theories of the end of the nation-state—or indeed of the emergence of a "postmodern" society.[14]

Yet the financial institutions of global capitalism differ from those of the early part of the twentieth century. Finance zooms across the world with a velocity gratifying the most breathless transnationalist. The point to stress here is that while, yes, this is a new configuration of financial institutions, the pressure on states is to conform to the working of capital while still retaining some semblance of control of their states. In this context, the discussions in humanities classrooms on the decline of the nation-state may be somewhat premature. Rather, the contemporary, complicated intersection of national states and financial capital announces the crisis of the neoliberal model that must confront increasing economic inequality, the incapacity of the state to consolidate itself and to act as promoter and supporter of institutions, its inefficiency in the control of corruption, and the impossibility of reconciling transnational interests with domestic rights, as we all have witnessed recently in the case of Argentina. The pressures on governments are not new. But what is new is the pressure that the collapse of a "recuperative modernization" (*nachholende Modernisierung*) has put on the national bourgeoisies, according to the German political economist Robert Kurz.[15]

The cultural forms, including literature, are inscribed in this highly complex interaction between global capitalism and local responses to the discourses of globalization, mediated through specific linguistic and national formations. It is perhaps in this context that—as the work of Roberto Schwarz has shown—a return to Adorno for an illumination of the functioning of aesthetic forms may be not as anachronistic as one could have thought but is rather quite timely if one is willing to pay attention to the impact peripheral glances may have on the critical-theoretical tradition of Adorno himself.

NOTES

1. Fredric Jameson, "Third World Literature in the Era of Multinational Capitalism," *Social Text* 15 (autumn 1986): 65–88.

2. I refer here not only to the debate carried out in the pages of *Social Text* in the years 1986–1987 between Jameson and Ahmad but also to the way in which this debate continues to construct our horizon of where to look for answers to questions of literary production outside the metropolis. His former pupils continue to cling to possible defenses of Jameson's position (see Imre Szeman's "Who Is Afraid of National Allegory? Jameson, Literary Criticism, Globalization," *South Atlantic Quarterly* 100, no. 3 [summer 2001]: 801–25), while more interesting propositions such as that of Franco Moretti on the study of world literature (see "Conjectures on World Literature," *New Left Review* 1 [January–February 2000]: 54–68), frame themselves unnecessarily vis-à-vis what Jameson may or may not have said on this topic. The responsibility for the parochialism of the debate, to be fair, lies not so much with Jameson as with the interpellative markers required by the audiences who read about it.

3. I have made this argument elsewhere. See "National Culture, Globalization, and Post-War El Salvador," *Comparative Literature Studies* 41, no. 1 (2004): 3–6.

4. Moretti, "Conjectures on World Literature."

5. A version of this section appeared in the introduction to *Critical Theory in Latin America* a special issue of *Cultural Critique* 49 (fall 2001).

6. Roberto Schwarz, "National Adequation and Critical Originality," in *Critical Theory in Latin America*, a special issue of *Cultural Critique* 49 (fall 2001): 24.

7. Recently translated as "A Seminar on Marx," *Hopscotch* 1, no. 1 (1999): 18–42.

8. Schwarz, "National Adequation and Critical Originality," 7.

9. Schwarz, "National Adequation and Critical Originality," 7.

10. Schwarz, "National Adequation and Critical Originality," 7.

11. Shierry Weber Nicholsen, *Exact Imagination, Late Work: On Adorno's Aesthetics* (Cambridge, Mass.: MIT Press, 1997), 5.

12. Lisa Lowe and David Lloyd, eds., *The Politics of Culture in the Shadow of Capital* (Durham, N.C.: Duke University Press, 1997).

13. Michael Mann, "As the Twentieth Century Ages," *New Left Review* 214 (1995): 104–24.

14. Mann, "As the Twentieth Century Ages," 107.

15. Robert Kurz, *Zur Kollaps der Modernisierung: Vom Zusammenbruch des Kasernensozialismus zur Krise der Weltökonomie* (Frankfurt am Main: Eichborn Verlag, 1991). See also his *Schwarzbuch Kapitalismus: Ein Abgesang auf die Marktwirtschaft* (Frankfurt am Main: Eichborn Verlag, 2000).

Index